Praise for *Lorca in Vermont*

"The story of Lorca's 1929 visit to Vermont to see his friend Philip Cummings is a key episode in the poet's biography that has never been told in full. Patricia Billingsley fleshes out the relationship between the two men with a keen eye for detail."—Jonathan Mayhew, author of *Lorca's Legacy: Essays in Interpretation*

"With details providing the look, sound, and feel of Lake Eden, Vermont, Billingsley weaves together the context and interactions of Lorca and Cummings's time together, ultimately showing how these intense experiences inspired some of the poems in *Poet in New York*. This fascinating and meticulously researched biography will leave people wanting to read more about Lorca's art and life."—Celia Stahr, author of *Frida in America: The Creative Awakening of a Great Artist*

"Over ten years in the making, Patricia Billingsley's *Lorca in Vermont* burrows deep into a brief and overlooked moment in Federico García Lorca's life, revealing long-hidden secrets as alluring and unforgettable as the Spaniard's beloved poetry. While steeped in the past, this is a book skillfully written for the present."—Aaron Shulman, author of *The Age of Disenchantments: The Epic Story of Spain's Most Notorious Literary Family and the Long Shadow of the Spanish Civil War*

"Though Federico García Lorca's work and life have been the subject of enough books and articles to fill a small library, little has been written about his brief but significant stay in Vermont and his relationship with Philip Cummings, his American lover. Until now, that is. Patricia Billingsley's thoroughly researched and beautifully written *Lorca in Vermont* fills that void. Billingsley writes powerfully about Lorca's ambivalence about his sexuality, his encounter with Cummings, and their subsequent stay in a cabin in Lake Eden, Vermont, which inspired Lorca to write a series of poems later collected in his masterpiece, *Poet in New York*. Billingsley's *Lorca in Vermont* is biographically revealing and narratively irresistible."—Pablo Medina, poet, novelist, and cotranslator of the Grove Press edition of *Poet in New York*

"The extensive and groundbreaking research that Billingsley has conducted into Lorca's relationship with Cummings and Vermont, and its subsequent importance in his poetry, provides a valuable contribution to Lorca scholarship."—Andrew Samuel Walsh, author of *Lorca in English: A History of Manipulation Through Translation*

"Patricia Billingsley's gripping, carefully reconstructed account of the intimacy that flared up between these two poets enriches our sense of the past and shows us an extended moment of tenderness in a long-suppressed episode that will fascinate poets and lovers while becoming required reading for any subsequent study of Lorca. Billingsley has mastered this material—not only the details of the affair but also the history of its suppression at the hands of academics and biographers. In this clear-eyed narrative, she allows us to savor a prolonged moment when these two promising poets were allowed to be themselves."—Daniel Bullen, author of *The Love Lives of the Artists: Five Stories of Creative Intimacy*

"Patricia Billingsley's secret history involving an unknown American and an icon of Spanish poetry represents an act of biography at its finest. The long-suppressed story of Federico García Lorca and an aspiring poet named Philip Cummings travels from Madrid to New York to, of all places, Vermont. *Lorca in Vermont* reveals passions and literary source material that will fascinate and surprise even seasoned readers of García Lorca's cherished works."—Steve Paul, author of *Literary Alchemist: The Writing Life of Evan S. Connell*

"When I was in college and learned about the poetry of García Lorca and even attended a college production of one of his plays, no one told me that he was gay. Even when I learned he was a foe of the fascist Franco and was murdered during the Spanish Civil War, no one told me that his reputation as 'queer' was part of the narrative. One of the goals of the gay liberation movement, early on, was to end the stifling 'closet'—the silence and invisibility and even the lies—and Billingsley's vital research continues that endeavor. The publishing world should welcome it."—Allen Young, author of *Left, Gay & Green: A Writer's Life*

"*Lorca in Vermont* is poised to take its distinguished place among recent biographies of same-sex literary couples whose lives had to be carefully guarded because of societal prejudice."—Carl Rollyson, author of *The Making of Sylvia Plath*

"Patricia Billingsley's book artfully explores a little-known aspect of Federico Garcia Lorca's life—the poet's relationship with Philip Cummings, a young North American. Her work provides a much-needed analysis of the relationship between Lorca's personal life and his poetry, especially during the formative time he spent in New York and New England. This is a welcome and intriguing contribution to the critical literature on Lorca as well as to the literary history of the LGBTQ community of the early 20th century."—Velma García-Gorena, editor and translator of *Gabriela Mistral's Letters to Doris Dana*

Lorca in Vermont

Lorca in Vermont

The Spanish Poet and His American Lover

Patricia A. Billingsley

High Road Books | Albuquerque

Printed in the United States of America

Library of Congress Cataloging-in-Publication Data
Names: Billingsley, Patrica A., 1952- author
Title: Lorca in Vermont : the Spanish poet and his American lover / Patricia A. Billingsley.

Identifiers: LCCN 2025036247 | ISBN 9780826369352 hardcover | ISBN 9780826369369 epub
Subjects: LCSH: García Lorca, Federico, 1898-1936—Criticism and interpretation | Cummings, Philip H., 1906-1991
Classification: LCC PQ6613.A763 Z57225 2026 | DDC 868.6209--dc23/eng/20250808
LC record available at https://lccn.loc.gov/2025036247

Founded in 1889, the University of New Mexico sits on the traditional homelands of the Pueblo of Sandia. The original peoples of New Mexico—Pueblo, Navajo, and Apache—since time immemorial have deep connections to the land and have made significant contributions to the broader community statewide. We honor the land itself and those who remain stewards of this land throughout the generations and also acknowledge our committed relationship to Indigenous peoples. We gratefully recognize our history.

Cover illustration: courtesy of Archivo Fundación Federico García Lorca, Centro Federico García Lorca, Granada.
Designed by Felicia Cedillos
Composed in Adobe Caslon Pro

(*right*) Figure 1. Federico García Lorca (1898–1936), age thirty-three, Madrid, 1931. From José Luis Cano, *García Lorca: Biografía Ilustrada* (Barcelona: Ediciones Destino, 1962), 73 (detail).
(*left*) Figure 2. Philip Cummings (1906–1991), age twenty-one, Winter Park, Florida, September 1928. Private collection.

To John,
who was with me every step of the way

The world was all before them, where to choose
Their place of rest, and Providence their guide:
They hand in hand, with wandering steps and slow,
Through Eden took their solitary way.

—John Milton, *Paradise Lost*

Contents

Prologue

On 12 July 1936, Spanish poet Federico García Lorca brought a packet of loosely organized papers to the office of José Bergamín, his editor in Madrid. Upon learning that Bergamín was away, Federico left the packet on his desk, along with a note promising to come back the next day.

But Federico never came back. He left Madrid the next evening for an impromptu visit with his family in Granada, perhaps unaware of the intense political turmoil that had begun to grip his home city. As the level of extremist violence in Granada continued to rise, Federico was arrested at the home of a family friend by Francoist sympathizers who hated his politics and his homosexuality. In the early hours of 18 August 1936, the thirty-eight-year-old poet was summarily executed in a ravine outside the city in one of the earliest atrocities of the Spanish Civil War.

The packet that Federico left behind for Bergamín was his long-awaited manuscript for what would eventually become *Poeta en Nueva York* (Poet in New York), a collection of thirty-five poems he had written during his ten-month stay in the United States and Cuba in 1929 and 1930. As the fighting in and around Madrid became increasingly hazardous for the city's inhabitants, Bergamín left Madrid, taking the manuscript with him, and went into exile in Mexico. There, he established a new publishing house, Editorial Séneca, which in 1940 released the first Spanish-language edition of *Poeta en Nueva York*. English translations of the work followed that same year, but the original manuscript was lost soon afterward, leaving a host of unanswered questions about its contents.[1]

Two of those questions are of particular interest: Why, in a collection ostensibly focused on New York City, were so many of the poems set in the countryside? And why did two of the section titles include references to Vermont in particular? Scholars and critics in the first decades after Federico's death set these questions aside in the apparent absence of any way to find the answers, while the few who understood Federico's connection to Vermont chose to stay quiet about what they knew.

Starting in the mid-1950s, a few details about the Vermont trip began to emerge, inspiring a new generation of scholars and biographers to try to learn more about Federico's visit and his friendship with Philip Cummings, the young Vermonter who had invited him there. These researchers sought Philip out and documented what they could, but they encountered a range of obstacles, including from Philip himself, that prevented them from discovering the whole truth about his relationship with Federico. They saw Philip just as he wanted to be seen: as a thoroughly heterosexual family man with fond memories of his long-ago platonic friendship with Federico. In the early 1970s, Philip finally revealed to one Lorca scholar that he and Federico had once had a sexual encounter, but he did not share the full story with anyone until almost the end of his life.

In the late 1990s, the manuscript that Federico had left for Bergamín in 1936 resurfaced, and in 2003 it was purchased at auction by the Fundación Federico García Lorca. When scholars at last had the opportunity to examine it, they discovered that what had appeared to be questionable editorial choices, or even outright mistakes, made by Bergamín in his Editorial Séneca edition of the work, had in fact reflected Federico's original intentions.[2] Among many other revelations, the manuscript confirmed the poet's Vermont-themed titles for two of the sections, as well as the full set of poems he had chosen for each section. Unfortunately, by that time it was widely assumed that there was nothing more to be learned about Federico's visit to Vermont or how it might have affected him, so the topic remained in the background—until now.

Though there are still significant gaps in our knowledge of what happened between Federico García Lorca and Philip Cummings before, during, and after their time together in Vermont, a broad array of new evidence has come to light in recent years. That evidence, combined with a close reexamination of previously known source materials, has made it possible to bridge many of those gaps and take a fresh look at the couple's complicated, three-year relationship and its influence on almost a quarter of the poems in Federico's landmark collection, *Poet in New York*.

PART ONE

Prelude to Eden

CHAPTER ONE

Madrid, July 1928

Passing stranger! You do not know how longingly I look upon you,
You must be he I was seeking, or she I was seeking.

—Walt Whitman, "To a Stranger"

IT WAS JUST AFTER lunch on a hot July afternoon, the time of day when most citizens of Madrid rose from the table, closed their curtains against the sun, and lay down for a short siesta. Spain, indeed all of Europe, was in the middle of a heat wave, but Philip Cummings was unfazed by either the temperature or his midday meal. Striding out of the dining room with all the restless energy of a healthy twenty-one-year-old "not given to the pattern of afternoon naps," he set off in search of something to do until classes resumed later in the day.[1]

As he took in the commanding view of the city from the main terrace of the Residencia de Estudiantes, Madrid's famed residential college, Philip was surprised to hear music in the distance. Intrigued, he followed the sound to the Residencia's spacious conference room, a popular gathering spot for students and faculty. In the dappled afternoon light, he could see a group of people clustered around a grand piano in the corner, listening intently as a dark-haired young Spaniard played a haunting, minor-key melody with great vitality and passion. Fascinated by the unfamiliar music, Philip walked in and joined the others.[2]

By happy accident, he had stumbled upon an event normally reserved for the Spanish occupants of the Residencia: the poet Federico García Lorca giving an impromptu concert for a select audience. These intimate performances were so memorable that, decades later, Federico's friends could still recall them in vivid detail:

> Not far from his room, in the so-called "piano corner" in the great hall of the Residencia, was an old Pleyel that Federico used to play, alone or surrounded by friends who listened to him. Federico was tireless at the piano. He would begin with his favorite composers—Chopin, Schubert, Mozart, Beethoven, Debussy, Ravel, Falla, Albéniz—but from them he went on to "tonadillas" from the eighteenth and nineteenth century and folk songs from Castile, Galicia, Andalucía.[3]

The music that so enchanted Philip came from the second part of Federico's concert, when he had moved on from his favorite classical pieces to the regional folk songs and Romani ballads he loved. Federico played beautifully, with a level of showmanship guaranteed to keep his audience engaged: "Federico sat at the piano as a master, with full control. Never mind that between pieces he made jokes and played boyish pranks; he regained mastery whenever he placed his fingertips on the keys."[4]

Federico's great charm and presence, paired with his musical talent, invariably drew people in and made him the center of every gathering. One observer claimed that even those who sensed Federico's "defect"—his romantic and sexual interest in men—and generally avoided him could never resist his music.[5] In Philip's case, if anything had made him suspect that the unknown pianist shared his attraction to men, his interest would have only been further piqued. But how did Philip, a newly arrived American on his first visit to Spain, happen to be there in the first place?[6]

Figure 3. Federico García Lorca at the piano in the Residencia de Estudiantes, Madrid. Drawing by José Moreno Villa, 1928. From José Luis Cano, *García Lorca: Biografía Ilustrada* (Barcelona: Ediciones Destino, 1962), 65.

That July, Philip was one of 150 students enrolled in the annual summer program for foreigners at the Residencia de Estudiantes.[7] The name means simply "student residence," but the "Resi" (as the students affectionately called it) was much more than a dormitory. In addition to accommodations for up to 250 students, faculty, and visitors, its four elegant buildings housed offices, lecture halls, scientific laboratories, and a full library, all surrounded by poplar trees, formal gardens, and athletic fields.[8] The campus was situated on a hillside in what were then the northern outskirts of Madrid, a location carefully chosen to isolate students from the temptations of city life as well as the politics and intrigue of the royal court.[9] As a

Figure 4. The Residencia de Estudiantes, affectionately known as the "Resi," in Madrid, ca. 1925. Commercial postcard.

fortuitous side effect, residents enjoyed a peaceful setting with beautiful vistas, fresh breezes, and more moderate temperatures than in the city center, making it, by one account, "the healthiest spot in Madrid."[10]

During the regular academic year, the Residencia functioned much like a small, private college for young men from well-to-do families who showed unusual promise in the humanities, arts, or sciences. Potential students were recruited from across Spain in an attempt to overcome the entrenched provincialism that tended to limit scholarly exchange on a national level. As one famous example of the success of this endeavor, Federico and his fellow students Salvador Dalí and Luis Buñuel came to the Residencia from the widely separated regions of Andalucía, Cataluña, and Aragón, respectively. The three became close friends, at least for a while, and actively encouraged each other's artistic endeavors.[11]

Though students took most of their classes at other institutions, they were drawn to the Residencia by its appealing mix of comfortable housing, academic support, world-class cultural events, and personal freedom. In contrast to traditional Spanish universities, where students had minimal contact with faculty or each other outside the classroom, the relaxed atmosphere of the Residencia encouraged intellectual curiosity and informal collaboration among Spain's best and brightest. It was an exciting place to be.

Founded in 1910, the Residencia had great success in attracting applicants from the outset, but it soon became clear that the income from regular student fees alone would not be enough to keep the staff paid and the school solvent during vacation periods. To help address this problem, in 1912 the nearby Centro de Estudios Historicos (Center for Historical Studies) launched a special summer program at the Residencia for foreign students and teachers of Spanish.[12] For a fixed fee, the program offered participants a series of intensive short courses on the Spanish language and Spanish literature, history, and culture, all taught by distinguished faculty from Spain and the United States, as well as lodging, meals, special events, and excursions.[13]

Besides generating badly needed funds for the institution, the summer program's designers hoped it would provide an additional benefit for the many regular students who remained at the Residencia over the summer. Their goal was to bring Spain's most promising young men into close contact with their well-educated peers from other parts of the world, thereby expanding their cultural horizons and widening their circle of friends.[14]

For their part, the regular students looked forward with great eagerness to the annual return of the *golondrinas* (swallows), as they playfully called the summer students, but not for the same high-minded reasons. The source of their enthusiasm was the prospect of sharing their campus, if only for a month, with a bevy of pretty young women deeply interested in the language and culture of Spain. Who better to assist these damsels in their studies than the chivalrous young Spaniards who already happened to be there?[15]

Of course, each year's flock of golondrinas also included many young men. The regular students were typically too distracted to pay much attention to male arrivals, but a tall, fair-haired American with an athletic build and confident manner would have been hard to miss. This would have suited Philip, who did not mind being noticed. But even as he pretended to share his comrades' romantic interest in women, he kept watch for a kindred spirit, a young man who might return his casual glance with a smile of recognition.

The 1928 summer program had been under way for about a week on the day that Philip followed the sound of Federico's music into the conference room.[16] By chance, one of the faculty members around the piano that afternoon was Pedro Salinas, a well-known Spanish poet and professor of Spanish literature who had just begun his first term as director of the summer program. Although Salinas was seven years older than Federico and living a much more settled life, the two were good friends and had long admired each other's work.

Salinas also knew Philip, at least by name, as a student in one of his classes, while Philip was certainly well aware of his teacher's prestige and influence. Tall, elegant, and charming, Salinas was a particular favorite of the female golondrinas that July. As one observer noted, "At every moment, beautiful young ladies with his book *Presagios* (Omens), recently bought, stop and give him, with a pleading smile, the first page of the book to write a dedication."[17] Philip, too, managed to acquire his own autographed copy of *Presagios*, inscribed "Al Sr. Cummings, estudiante en Madrid el verano de 1928, Pedro Salinas" (To Mr. Cummings, student in Madrid in the summer of 1928, Pedro Salinas).[18]

When Federico's afternoon concert came to a close, Salinas, with his customary courtesy, introduced Philip to Federico and the other faculty members clustered around the piano. The group may have included the Spanish poets José Moreno Villa, Rafael Alberti, Dámaso Alonso, and Concha Méndez, all of whom were teaching at the Residencia that summer, but Philip noticed only Federico.[19] He surprised Federico by offering him a poem he had composed on the spot in honor of his performance. This gesture so impressed Federico that he told his parents about it and expected them to still remember the story a year later.[20]

We know nothing about the content of Philip's poem, whether he wrote it in Spanish or English, or whether he read it aloud or simply handed it to Federico. But if Philip was at all aware of Federico's status as an established poet, it was a bold move, a way of saying, "I am a poet myself. I understand and appreciate what you do."

And this was true. Though Philip intended to become a teacher of modern languages, a vocation that promised a decent salary and good job security, at some point he had also begun to think of himself as a poet. That spring, as he traveled across Europe and northern Africa,[21] he recorded some of his impressions in unpunctuated free verse—a practice he may have begun some time before. The poem below is an example:

> Slow spiral smoke
> In tented darkness
> Brazier of steaming coals
> Bearded Arab smokes
> Closed eyes under high forehead
> Tiptoeing veiled women
> Pass like sable ghosts
> I inhale and look out
> Big warm stars
> Way up too far up
> Unmindful of
> The old wrinkled face of the desert
> Slight movement and supplications
> Night intensity
> Algeria[22]

In keeping with this new sense of himself, Philip was preparing to transfer to Rollins College in Winter Park, Florida, for his senior year. He had spent his first three undergraduate years at Stetson University in nearby DeLand, Florida, dutifully taking the language and education courses required for his chosen profession, but now he wanted a change.[23] Rollins was a smaller and more prestigious school, well known in academic circles for its progressive approach to higher education.[24] Philip was especially drawn to its highly regarded program in modern poetry, but he was also a realist. However much he believed in his poetic potential, in the absence of any family money to support his literary ambitions, he knew he would always need a reliable way to make a living. He began his summer classes at the Residencia fully focused on preparing for his future teaching career, intent on gaining the greatest possible academic benefit from his time in Madrid.

Life, however, does not always go as planned. Philip was apparently captivated by Federico from the moment they met, because he wasted no time in signaling his interest. Giving Federico a poem was the perfect way to start a conversation, reveal a few details about himself, and listen attentively to whatever Federico said in return. This type of interaction came easily to Philip, who had a remarkable ability to draw people out and make them feel at ease. And although he had been studying Spanish for less than a year, he learned new languages quickly and enjoyed putting his skills to the test.[25]

The two made quite a pair. Philip was a rangy six-footer with wavy auburn hair that reflected his Scottish ancestry. By the time he reached Spain that summer, his face had been tanned a deep brown by the North African sun, making his blue eyes even more striking.[26] Federico was a full six inches shorter, with the olive skin, dark eyes, and raven hair of a true Andalusian, but perhaps their physical differences only heightened their appeal to each other.

At some point in their first conversation, Philip showed Federico a few photos of his native Vermont and invited him to see others that he kept in his room. Whatever else was said or implied, Federico accepted his invitation, and once the two were safely alone together in Philip's room, they had their first sexual encounter.[27]

Philip may have obliquely described the experience in a poem he wrote later that summer:

Youth
Urgent
A thing that reaches out
Pulls me close
And plays me music
It stands feet wide apart
Strength
Fine brutality
But fierce
Humanity[28]

Federico wrote his own, more explicit poem about a sexual liaison between male companions later that fall, as discussed in chapter 2.

Even in conservative, Catholic Spain in the early twentieth century, it is not surprising that two young men who recognized their mutual attraction might take advantage of an unexpected opportunity to enjoy casual sex in the privacy of a dorm room. However, it seems far less likely that a brief liaison between an established Spanish poet and an unknown American student would evolve into a complex relationship that spanned three years and two continents. Philip's own explanation for his unexpected affinity with Federico, told to an interviewer many years later, is almost certainly true, but it is also woefully incomplete: "Federico was extremely interested in the fact that I, as an American speaking Spanish, seemed to understand him. Most of the students who were there were much more interested in the señoritas of the moment, and I was there definitely for study."[29] Philip conveniently failed to mention why women were the last thing he and Federico had on their minds. But in addition to their shared attraction to men, there were numerous other similarities in their histories and interests, parallels they may have been startled to discover.

They both loved music, especially classical music, which served almost as another common language. Both were voracious readers who loved to discuss history, art, and literature, but their favorite topic, poetry, dominated their conversations. They delighted in sharing their favorite poems and debating fine points of word choice, style, and syntax.

Further, both had grown up in small rural communities—for Federico, the farming villages of Fuente Vaqueros and Asquerosa (now known as Valderrubio) outside Granada, and for Philip, the small town of Hardwick, Vermont—that offered children ample opportunity to spend time surrounded by nature. As Philip later put it, they found they were both country folk, "and friendship stemmed from that."[30] Neither fit the established mold as young boys, and both were bullied by their classmates for being different.[31] Almost certainly as a result, both Federico and Philip viewed the natural world as not only a source of endless beauty and fascination, but also as a cherished escape from the confusing and judgmental society of their peers.

In later years, Philip did his best to look back on these incidents philosophically, but the hurt and humiliation remained:

> I tried to assume the part most desired by the others, but when I had become as one of them, I was less than ever really one of them, and I felt the futility even if I could not label it, while they felt me a joke. The older boys [on a camping trip] one night dumped me in my pajamas into the creek and I was mad and perplexed, for I had done nothing. I did not know then, as I do now, that it was a tiny gesture of the mob trying to level an individual who did not or could not conform.[32]

The two may have also discovered that Federico's mother, Vicenta Lorca Romero, and Philip's mother, Addie Smith Cummings, were born within a few months of each other in 1870. Both Vicenta and Addie were unusually well educated for their time, worked as schoolteachers as young women, and transmitted their love of the written word to their verbally precocious sons.

Federico's father, Federico García Rodríguez, born in 1859, was fifteen years older than Harry Foster Cummings, Philip's father, but both were practical, business-minded men. However, Harry was decidedly less supportive, financially and emotionally, of his son's ambitions. There were many reasons for this difference, but the relative wealth of Federico's family played a primary role. For García Rodríguez, the financial security that came with his success as a landowner and sugar beet producer made it much easier to be an indulgent father to his eldest son, Federico, and his three other children.

Philip was an only child, but growing up in a strict, adult-oriented household, he had to share his mother's affection and attention with a series of ailing older relatives who came to live with the family.[33] His father struggled to establish himself, changing jobs

Figure 5. Federico García Lorca, age fourteen, with his family in Granada, 1912. Archivo Fundación Federico García Lorca, Centro Federico García Lorca, Granada.

Figure 6. Philip Cummings, age three, with his parents, Harry and Addie Cummings, 1909. Private collection.

several times before finding his niche as a real estate and insurance salesman. Though most of Vermont was in economic decline during Philip's boyhood, the family's situation did eventually improve; by the time Philip was a teenager, they were considered well-off by local standards, although this prosperity did not last. Perhaps Harry's financial insecurity accounts in part for the harsh treatment and mocking criticism he directed at his son.[34]

Federico's father's prosperity and influence granted Federico not only a comfortable existence, but also access to writers, musicians, and scholars at the highest levels of society in their home city of Granada. Philip could claim no such privilege, but despite their eight-year age difference, he was in many ways more self-reliant and sophisticated than Federico. Philip had been forced to learn how to make his own way in the world. He paid close attention to the habits and mannerisms of others, adopting those that suited him, and moved easily among various levels of society—useful talents for such an ambitious young man.

In Madrid, being so far from home gave Philip the latitude to invent any background he wanted for himself since it was virtually certain that any untruths or exaggerations would never be discovered. For example, later events suggest that Philip overstated his father's wealth and prestige, perhaps to keep pace with Federico. While it was true that Harry Cummings had once been an affluent and respected member of his community, this was no longer the case by the time Philip went to Spain.[35] Under the circumstances, it is not surprising that Philip might choose to highlight his father's past successes rather than mention his more recent failures.

Philip's presence at the Residencia in July 1928 is easy to understand, but what was Federico, at thirty (long past his student days), doing there? Federico was never much of a student, even though he was continuously enrolled in one or more institutions of higher education from the age of sixteen to twenty-seven. He read widely on a broad range of topics and was particularly well versed in classical and modern literature, philosophy, and religion, but he preferred to pursue his own interests at his own pace, ignoring the actual requirements of his classes. This was a source of endless frustration for Federico's long-suffering father, who admired his son's poetic talent but felt sure that he would never be able to support himself without an established, practical career to fall back on.

Federico had begun his higher education at the University of Granada, but after five years of lackluster performance, in 1919 his father finally allowed him to transfer to the Residencia in Madrid. Away from his family and on his own for the first time, the twenty-one-year-old took instantly to the heady mix of intellectual, artistic, and personal freedom he found there. He enjoyed himself immensely and was always much too busy socializing to worry about such mundane details as grades or classes.

His father tolerated Federico's indifference to his studies for a while, but he finally lost patience and insisted that his son come back to Granada and complete a law degree. It took Federico eighteen unhappy months to accomplish the task, but he finally managed to pass his exams in February 1923. Satisfied that his demands had been met and his son possessed at least one marketable skill, García Rodríguez relented and gave permission for Federico to return to his beloved Resi, where he was still enrolled as a student. Federico's father continued paying his room and board for two more years.

Despite his misgivings about the educational value of Federico's time at the Residencia, García Rodríguez clearly understood that living in the cultural heart of Madrid served a larger purpose for his son. In fact, it was an essential factor in Federico's growing reputation as one of Spain's most promising young poets. The Resi celebrated its students, offering them frequent opportunities to showcase their talents, and Federico was always happy to oblige. His poetry readings, performed with great drama, emotion, and humor, attracted a loyal following and soon brought him to the attention of the city's leading intellectuals. They in turn introduced him to an increasingly wide circle of influential writers, critics, journalists, and publishers, who applauded his work and helped facilitate his progress.

In June 1925, Federico left the Residencia and returned to Granada for the summer as usual, but when fall came, he chose to stay. At twenty-seven, he seemed finally ready to give up the distractions of Madrid and student life to focus on his writing. At home in either the family's spacious downtown apartment or their summer retreat outside Granada, he was both protected and indulged, left undisturbed whenever he wanted to write but assured of pleasant company when he was ready for a break: "I'm once more in the Huerta de San Vicente in bucolic surroundings, eating exquisite fruits and singing on the swing with my brother and sisters all day long and fooling around so much that at times I'm embarrassed because of my age."[36]

Despite these diversions, Federico was incredibly productive

Figure 7. Eighteen-year-old Federico García Lorca with his siblings, Concepción, Francisco, and Isabel, Granada, 1916. Archivo Fundación Federico García Lorca, Centro Federico García Lorca, Granada.

from June 1925 to June 1928. Among other projects, he finished the play *Mariana Pineda*, began several other plays, wrote numerous new poems, and organized many of his earlier poems into collections in preparation for eventual publication. However, only one of these projects came to fruition during this period: the book *Canciones* (Songs), *1921–1924*, a collection of eighty-nine short poems published by Imprenta Sur in Málaga in May 1927. Though the publisher printed only 115 copies, the book found its way to leading literary critics in Madrid, who praised the poet and his poems in glowing reviews.[37]

Most importantly, during this period Federico finished the eighteen poems in his collection *Romancero Gitano* (Gypsy Ballads), the work that would seal his reputation as Spain's most important and popular young poet. He based many of the poems on the folk ballads he had learned over the years from the Romani of Granada, social outcasts whose rich musical heritage and passion for life had always impressed him.[38] In the early spring of 1928, Federico made his final edits to the collection and sent the manuscript to his publisher in Madrid, Revista de Occidente, where the owners were eagerly awaiting its arrival.

However, Federico's retreat from Madrid was not driven solely by a desire to focus on his writing. At the Residencia, he had become enamored with Emilio Aladrén Perojo, a handsome young sculptor of ambiguous sexual orientation, who was living there while taking classes at the School of Fine Arts. At first, Emilio pursued Federico, overcoming the poet's customary caution with a barrage of flattery and attention. But once Federico allowed himself to be drawn in, the games began: Emilio would speak and act seductively, then quickly pull away. Federico yearned for a true romantic commitment and wanted to believe that Emilio shared that desire, so the constant uncertainty about exactly where he stood kept him in agony. To escape the emotional turmoil he felt around Emilio and the jarring ups and downs of their relationship, Federico fled to Granada to recover his equilibrium: "Here in Granada I feel calm and somewhat sad, cleansed of fleeting rhythms and at peace with myself. Madrid confuses me a lot and, although I do not live, at all, what is called the literary life, several emotional conflicts, opposite and extremely difficult, assault me continually, which I have been bearing for two or three years, under the sun and under the snow. Here I rest."[39]

But Federico could not avoid Madrid forever. If he was serious about building his reputation and promoting his poetry, he knew he had to maintain his contacts and visibility there. Besides, his *Romancero Gitano* was scheduled for release in Madrid on 20 July 1928, and he wanted to be within easy reach of his publisher to help shepherd things along.[40]

Federico returned to Madrid in late April 1928 and once again began living at the Residencia, where he had a standing invitation to stay whenever he wished. Although the dormitory rooms were generally reserved for students and faculty, the administration also decreed that "by exception, some people devoted to intellectual work, whose cohabitation with the students is a salutary example for them and a source of prestige for the Residencia, live there."[41]

Federico clearly fell into this special category. He was grateful for the treatment he received, as he had explained to his parents two years earlier: "I have a room, thanks to the kindness of the director, who said to me, 'It's nothing, it's nothing; you are ours and must come work here.' And the Resi is the best place in all of Madrid, and also I'm used to living in it. One has the feeling that one is at home."[42]

The Residencia was the perfect place for Federico to live while he waited for his book launch. Some of his friends were already there, others were coming soon to teach in the summer program, and of course the new flock of golondrinas arriving in early July would keep things lively. Federico was no longer a student—after all, he would be thirty on 5 June—but he happily accepted his new role as "the official poet of the Residencia."[43]

Yet despite his friends' warnings and his own best intentions, Federico could not stay away from Emilio. Perhaps he had convinced himself that he was no longer vulnerable to Emilio's charms or that Emilio might finally accept him as a true romantic partner. For his part, Emilio was more than happy to resume their relationship as long as it was advantageous to him, so, for a while, the two were once again the best of friends, spending time together almost every day in public and in private. That spring, Emilio sculpted a bust of Federico that delighted the poet, who talked up the piece and its creator wherever he went. Of course, the fact that such favorable publicity might generate new interest in his work was not lost on Emilio.[44]

Federico tried to remain happy and hopeful, but by midsummer he could no longer ignore Emilio's duplicity. Emilio had been involved with a young woman when he and Federico first met, though he had quickly ended the relationship to focus solely on Federico.[45] Federico wanted to believe that his young friend's interest in girls had been only a passing fancy, so when he began hearing rumors that Emilio was once again seeing a woman, he ignored them. However, it soon became clear that the rumors were true, and

Emilio's involvement with the woman in question was in fact quite serious.[46]

Federico felt doubly betrayed and completely devastated. He later described his emotional turmoil in a letter to a friend he had visited just after things came to a head with Emilio: "You know that in Zamora I was quite upset, and with reason. I've been going through one of the most profound crises of my life. It's my poetic destiny. We cannot gamble with what life and blood gives us, because we become enchained when we least desire it. . . . You had never seen me so bitter, and it's true."[47]

It was against this backdrop that Philip Cummings strolled into the conference room of the Residencia that fateful July afternoon, unaware that the haunting, minor-key music that drew him there mirrored the pianist's own private melancholy. What a pleasure it must have been for Federico to meet Philip and find himself the object of seduction, especially when his seducer was a handsome blond American, unabashed about expressing either his admiration or his sexual interest. Federico's affair with Philip provided a welcome distraction from his sadness and despair, though he would not be able to escape those emotions for long.

Although Federico was busy with his frenetic social life and book launch, and Philip with classes and studying, they still found time to be together. During the hottest part of the day, they would often retreat to the shady conference room of the Residencia, where they played records of "musical tone poems . . . of the Arabs that had never been written down," which almost certainly came from Federico's private collection.[48] Federico must have been delighted to find a fellow music aficionado who enjoyed them as much as he did.

When they were ready for a change of scene, they walked or rode the streetcar from the Residencia to downtown Madrid. Philip later boasted that Federico took him only to special, out-of-the way places frequented by locals, rather than to typical tourist attractions and busy public squares: "Down beyond the Rastro [public market] where the strangest oddments of the most questionable origin were sold, there were cafes of muleteers and market gardeners, and in these together the young men found a quality not known in the Plaza Mayor or the Puerta del Sol."[49]

Philip viewed these trips as a sign that Federico recognized his ability to appreciate the less touristy aspects of Spanish culture, but it is possible that Federico chose obscure locations for a very different reason: to avoid running into anyone he knew. Even though Federico's relationship with Aladrén was in shambles, the poet may have still held out hope that Emilio would relent. But if an acquaintance were to see Federico out and about with a tall, handsome stranger and report that news to Emilio, it could destroy their relationship completely. If this was indeed Federico's strategy, it changed nothing with Emilio, but it may explain why neither Federico nor his friends mentioned Philip in their correspondence during this period. Philip himself seemed unaware of Federico's maneuvers and their possible intent.

On 20 July, Federico's *Gypsy Ballads* appeared in bookstores right on schedule and became an immediate success. His friends and admirers had been waiting for the collection for years, creating a ready market, and a series of positive reviews from prominent critics drummed up even more interest from the general public. The publisher had printed a typical print run of 2,000 copies, but sales were so brisk that the book quickly became very hard to find.[50] The phenomenon even generated a joke in Madrid, in which a disappointed would-be buyer, informed that no copies were available but more were expected soon, urged his bookseller to "save one for me . . . under your table, under a rock!"[51]

Federico was as surprised as anyone by the book's reception and initially delighted by his sudden fame and popularity. Writing to his parents on 26 July, he explained how the happy bustle of his days in Madrid had delayed his return to Granada:

> For two days I've had my foot in the stirrup and I have not left because the success of my book is so fantastic that different

> groups of friends have already given me two or three meals. The copies put up for sale are sold out and it can be said that for many years a book did not raise this great enthusiasm. I am dedicating copies and preparing the press releases for here and in America. Even if this book does not bring millions, it is a book that establishes my prestige as a poet and I am nothing more than that.[52]

When Federico finally made it to Granada in early August, the local paper proudly announced the return of their native son and the critical success of his new book, *Gypsy Ballads*.[53]

Unfortunately, Philip was not there to witness the triumph and celebration. Although the summer program at the Residencia continued until 3 August, by then Philip was halfway across the Atlantic, one of 773 passengers aboard the French ocean liner SS *Paris* en route to New York City.[54] It is unclear why he had booked passage on a ship that required him to leave the program early, but the *Paris* set sail from Le Havre, France, on the evening of 1 August 1928. Getting there from Madrid was no easy feat; the 835-mile journey took at least thirty hours by rail, with additional time required for going through customs and waiting for connecting trains.[55] By this reckoning, Philip had to leave Madrid no later than 29 July to reach the ship on time, meaning that he and Federico had at most three weeks together at the Residencia before his departure.

When the two said their last good-byes in Madrid, Federico may have assumed that he would never see Philip again. If so, he had failed to recognize the resourcefulness and determination of his American friend.

CHAPTER TWO

Intermedio

> It is a great piece of skill to know how to guide your luck even while waiting for it.
>
> —Baltasar Gracián, *The Art of Worldly Wisdom*

PERHAPS TO RELIEVE ANY doubts that Federico might be feeling, Philip made his interest in continuing their relationship clear as soon as opportunity allowed. The day after the *Paris* set sail from Le Havre, Philip wrote to Federico in Spanish on stationery bearing the letterhead of the ship's owner, Compagnie Générale Transatlantique:

S.S. Paris
le 2 agosto 1928
Sr. Don Federico García Lorca
Granada, España

Muy querido amigo mio:

Aqui estoy sobre el gran mar y pensiendo mucho de usted—amigo tan simpático—en España la simpática—la graciosa si [tan] lejos.

Salimos de La Havra [*sic*], *Francía, anoche a las diez y llegaramos a Nueva York el 7 agosto por la noche.*

Nunca olvidaré España, la gente española y especialmente mi poeta español— usted—mi querido Señor Lorca. Espero a ver unas versas de su poesia alguno vez por favor.

Hago usted el favor de mi escribir cuando el conviene y por favor perdona mís faltas en la lengua castellana que yo sé deber de ser muchas.

Su amigo siempre,
q. b. s. m.
Philip
Philip H. Cummings
Box 71
Hardwick Vermont
Estados Unidos

S.S. Paris
2 August 1928
Sr. don Federico García Lorca
Granada, Spain

My very dear friend:

Here I am over the great sea and thinking a lot about you—friend so charming—in Spain the charming—the gracious, so far away.

We left Le Havre, France, last night at ten and will arrive in New York the 7th of August at night.

I will never forget Spain, the Spanish people, and especially my Spanish poet— you—my dear señor Lorca. I hope to see a few verses of your poetry sometime please.

I ask you the favor of writing to me when it is convenient and please forgive my mistakes in the Castilian language, that I know must be many.

Your friend always,
who kisses your hand
Philip
Philip H. Cummings
Box 71
Hardwick Vermont
United States[1]

Considering the intimacy of Philip's relationship with Federico, the tone of this letter is surprisingly formal and deferential. He uses the Spanish pronouns *usted* and *su*, typically reserved for elders, social superiors, and others who are not close friends or family. He phrases his requests very politely and apologizes for any grammar or spelling mistakes. He ends with a very traditional, courtly closing—*q. b. s. m.* (*que besa su mano*, "who kisses your hand")—and signs his letter as "Philip" rather than "Felipe," the Spanish equivalent preferred by Federico.

There are several possible explanations for these choices. The most likely is that Philip had no way to know who might see his letter when it arrived at Federico's family home in Granada. Anyone in the household—servant, sibling, or parent—could conceivably open and read it before passing it along to its intended recipient. Philip therefore might have been careful to avoid any hint of undue familiarity or impropriety that might compromise either Federico or himself in the eyes of the household. Or perhaps Philip was continuing a private joke he had with Federico, adopting an obsequious tone that was the opposite of their typical style of interaction, or simply wanted to flatter Federico by addressing him as a superior. Or it may have been some combination of all three.

Philip's request to "see a few verses of your poetry sometime please" is also somewhat mysterious, since he was in Madrid at the time of Federico's book launch and would surely have been among the first to snap up a copy of *Gypsy Ballads*. In all likelihood, he was referring to Federico's *future* poetry, rather than his newly published collection.

Whether Philip bought a copy of *Gypsy Ballads* himself or was given one by Federico, he clearly had it in his possession later that fall when he translated two of Federico's poems into English for one of his Spanish classes at Rollins College.[2] But before that could happen, Philip first had to gain admission to Rollins for his senior year—a remarkable achievement considering the way he went about it.

Philip had graduated from Hardwick Academy in June 1924 and

completed his freshman and sophomore years at Stetson University. But after his father encountered unexpected financial difficulties and could no longer afford his tuition, Philip was forced to take a leave of absence from Stetson for the 1926–1927 academic year. Instead of enjoying student life in sunny Florida, Philip spent that year as the principal and sole teacher of thirty schoolchildren in the tiny village of Walden Heights, Vermont—as well as the custodian of its rustic, one-room schoolhouse.[3]

The sudden change in status must have come as quite a shock, but it gave Philip the incentive he needed to get back on track. He managed to save or otherwise acquire enough money to return to Stetson as a junior in September 1927 and completed the fall and winter terms as expected. Then, for unknown reasons, Philip abruptly left the university and skipped the spring term altogether, instead traveling by steamship to Glasgow, Scotland, in April 1928. He spent the next two months exploring Europe and North Africa with Ronald Duncan, the teenage son of wealthy friends in Glasgow, reaching Madrid in early July 1928 for the start of the summer language program at the Residencia.

Philip spent less than four weeks in Madrid, a very short time to acquire any meaningful academic credentials from a Spanish university. However, having decided that he wanted to spend his senior year at Rollins College, Philip refused to let such details deter him. Upon returning home, he immediately applied to Rollins for admission as a transfer student—not from Stetson University, as might be expected, but rather from the University of Madrid—and his plan succeeded. He was approved as an entering senior at Rollins for the fall 1928 term and was in fact identified as one of five "American students who have transferred from foreign universities" in a Rollins *Alumni Quarterly* article touting the college's many international students that academic year.[4]

How did Philip manage to convince the admissions staff at Rollins that he had completed nine full-semester courses at the University of Madrid during the spring of 1928, for a total of 38.5 credits, as listed on his Rollins transcript?[5] In all likelihood, Philip relied on the formal certificates awarded to students in the Residencia's summer program for each lecture series they completed successfully.[6] If the Rollins admissions officers did not speak Spanish or understand Spanish academic conventions, Philip could have passed them off as evidence of completion of semester-long courses. And, of course, the admissions staff had no way to know that Philip did not actually spend the spring term studying in Madrid, as he must have told them, but was instead elsewhere in Europe and North Africa from April through June. It was a huge gamble, but Philip was clearly willing to take the risk, confident in his ability to appear so earnest and accommodating that no one would bother to examine his credentials too closely.

It is also possible that the college's admissions officers were complicit in Philip's scheme to some degree. Rollins prided itself on being a progressive, outward-looking institution that welcomed and initiated cross-cultural exchange. Perhaps they were willing to overlook any misgivings about Philip for the sake of adding one more "international" student to the student body that year, knowing how much this evidence of the college's reach and reputation would please both their president and their alumni donors. Their decision certainly suited Philip.

From the moment he arrived at Rollins, Philip caught the attention of his fellow students. When junior Stella Weston first saw him striding across campus in his dramatic black cape, she assumed he was a young Spanish nobleman. (If she ever told Philip this, he would have surely been delighted.) Stella and Philip enjoyed a brief romantic relationship that fall, but decades later she described him with some bitterness as a "very strange" person.[7]

It is easy to imagine the disappointment a pretty, popular co-ed with her own poetic ambitions might have felt when she discovered that her apparent soul mate had no interest in any real commitment. Philip clearly enjoyed playing at romance; he wrote heartfelt poems to Stella and may have even believed he was in love.[8] Her family's wealth, social prominence, and frequent interactions with Rollins president Hamilton Holt may have interested him as well. But at some level, Philip must have understood that he was a poor candidate for a serious, long-term relationship with a young woman and conveyed that message to Stella—even at the risk of inciting her wrath. Withdrawing from Stella may also have been self-protective, given Philip's tendency to embroider the truth. It's quite likely that he had inflated his parents' wealth and social standing to Stella and others at Rollins, as he almost certainly had with Federico, and knew that any sustained close contact, let alone an engagement, risked revealing his family's true circumstances.[9] For her part, after her breakup with Philip, Stella moved quickly to rekindle her past relationship with Harry Tuttle, grandson of pioneering Miami benefactor Julia Tuttle, and married him three years later.[10]

Philip made an immediate impression on others at Rollins as well. Soon after the semester began, the campus newspaper featured an account of the lively, multilanguage bull sessions he hosted in his dorm room every night.[11] Philip's knowledge of Europe and his talent for public speaking were also noticed by college administrators, who invited him to give a series of talks about his travels in Scotland, France, and Spain on the Rollins radio station, WDBO—the only student accorded this honor that academic year.[12]

Most importantly, Philip established a place for himself in Rollins's poetry program, including its prestigious winter seminar for "those who show a special aptitude in this art."[13] The seminar was the brainchild of poet and critic Jessie Belle Rittenhouse, a founding member of the American Poetry Society and the Poetry Society of Florida, who joined the Rollins faculty as a poetry instructor and editor in 1927.[14] Philip apparently managed to establish his poetic credentials with the English faculty early on. Before the winter term had even begun, Rollins Press published a collection of his work under the title *Mother-Tongue*. The slim paperback contained fifty-six short poems grouped into three sections—"Florida," "Silver Bell-Notes of Europe," and "Life Impressions"—and received a glowing review from the book editor of the *Tampa Tribune*.[15]

The publication of *Mother-Tongue* not only validated Philip's sense of himself as a serious poet, it also gave him a new way to reconnect with some of the people he had met in Spain. In one stellar example, he sent an inscribed copy to King Alfonso XIII of Spain; the book is still housed in the Real Biblioteca (Royal Library) at the Palacio Real de Madrid (Royal Palace of Madrid).[16] This gesture may have been inspired by Philip's claimed introduction to the king in Madrid the previous summer, perhaps as part of a special event for all the foreign students staying at the Residencia that July. But the royal response to his gift—a gracious thank-you note from the king's personal secretary, handwritten on elegant palace stationery—led to some favorable publicity as well. Rollins immediately issued a self-congratulatory press release about Philip, his book, and the letter, adding, "It is another gratifying indication of the value of the Rollins' conference plan that this work of an undergraduate has found favor with the King of Spain."[17] The press release was subsequently picked up by the *Orlando Sentinel* and reprinted in full.[18]

This degree of interest in a single letter sent to a local college student may seem a bit surprising at first, but it happened at an opportune time in Florida's history. In recent decades the state had begun to actively celebrate and promote its Spanish heritage, both as a point of pride and as a lure to attract northern tourists seeking a touch of Old World romanticism along with their sunshine.[19] Seen in this context, the receipt of a personal letter from the private secretary to the king of Spain was a very big deal indeed, no matter who received it.

This new emphasis in Florida was just one facet of the "Spanish craze" that swept the entire country following the US victory in the Spanish-American War of 1898. With Spain comfortably vanquished in the New World, North Americans were free to celebrate all things Spanish, from art to architecture to housewares, without guilt or conflict.[20] Even the Spanish language enjoyed a huge increase in popularity in the United States during this era. Bolstered by a growing antipathy to all things German during World War I, the demand for classes in Spanish (and teachers of Spanish) increased dramatically. In October 1918, *The New York Times* reported that, of 505 colleges and secondary schools surveyed in a recent national study, 400 had substituted Spanish language classes for German. In New York City, Spanish was offered at every high school and had eclipsed both French and Latin in overall student enrollment.[21]

Philip's own progress as a language learner seems to reflect this trend, at least in part. He studied French and Latin in high school then continued Latin and added Greek during his first two years at Stetson University. He did not begin studying Spanish until 1927, during his junior year at Stetson, but later clearly decided that Spanish was important enough to merit enrolling in the intensive summer language program at the Residencia. He continued taking Spanish when he transferred to Rollins for his senior year and also took two semesters of German.[22] Whatever the political implications, his knowledge of these languages served him well when he later began applying for teaching jobs.[23]

After the publication of *Mother-Tongue*, Philip's recollection of when and where he had written the poems was subject to change depending on his audience. He told the *Orlando Sentinel* that he was so inspired by the creative atmosphere at Rollins that he had composed all the poems in the book during his first term there.[24] But in the inscribed copy he sent to King Alfonso, he specifically noted that five of the poems were "escritos en España" (written in Spain).[25] As always, Philip was acutely aware of what would most flatter his intended audience and was happy to provide it.

There is no indication that Philip also sent a copy of *Mother-Tongue* to Federico that December. (In fact, other than Philip's shipboard letter, there is no direct evidence that the two communicated at all in the months following his return to the United States, though later events strongly suggest that they did.) However, it is hard to imagine Philip passing up such a golden opportunity to share his work and his success with his favorite Spanish poet. But even if he did send the book, Federico may have paid little attention, having been distracted and depressed since his return to Granada in August 1928.

It is not hard to understand why Federico felt the need to retreat to the relative peace and stability of his family's summer home outside Granada that fall. Everything that mattered most to him seemed to be going wrong. He had finally accepted the fact that his relationship with Emilio Aladrén was over, leaving him not only brokenhearted, but also embarrassed at having fallen for a man who wanted only to benefit from his association with a rising literary star. His brief fling with Philip had provided some respite, but now Philip too was gone. As Federico struggled to come to grips with his longing for an authentic, committed relationship with another man, his task was made even harder by the need to keep the source of his emotional distress to himself.

He tried to put up a brave front, writing to his friend Sebastian Gasch, "I'm vexed and afflicted by passions which I have to vanquish, but I'm beginning to emerge, free, alone, in my own creation and effort."[26] Among his other creative endeavors of the period, sometime between August and December 1928, Federico composed three prose poems in apparent homage to the unfettered free association being championed by Dalí and other surrealist friends at the time.[27] (As Federico explained to Gasch, "Naturally they're in prose because verse is a confinement they can't understand.")[28] However, despite Federico's highly original use of language and his sometimes startling images, one of these poems, "Two Lovers Murdered by a Partridge" (Amantes asesinados por una perdiz), may not be the product of free association at all, but rather a relatively straightforward description of his recent sexual encounters with Philip disguised as free association.

In the poem, the two lovers of the title are first described as "man and woman," then "two young men," then "the terrible boatmen of the Guadiana," a river that runs between Spain and Portugal.[29] Their affair involves a sexual relationship that both lovers clearly want, as attested to the speaker by two different witnesses. In the poem, the speaker describes the couple's first intimate contact with each other, touch by touch, leaving no doubt about their intent:

> Right hand
> with left hand.
> Left hand
> with right hand.
> Right foot
> with right foot.
> Left foot
> with cloud.
> Hair
> with sole of the foot.
> Sole of the foot
> with left cheek.
> Oh, left cheek! Oh, northwest of little boats and ants of mercury!
> Give me the handkerchief, Genoveva; I'm going to cry . . . I'm going to cry until a bunch of immortelles emerge from my eyes . . . They were going to bed.
> There was no other spectacle so tender . . .
> Did you hear me?
> They were going to bed!
> Left thigh
> with left forearm.
> Closed eyes
> with open fingernails.
> Waist with nape,
> and with shoreline.
> And the four little ears were four angels in a snowy cabin. They yearned for each other. They made love. Defying the law of gravity. The difference between a rose thorn and a Star is very simple.
> When they figured this out, they left for the countryside.
> They made love.[30]

The rest of the poem includes several clues that suggest Federico wrote it to memorialize his experiences with Philip at the Residencia in July 1928. First, the poem's references to museums, chemists, and professors all suggest an academic setting. There is also mention of a "departing ocean liner" that causes concern, perhaps an allusion to the ship that took Philip back to the United States after he left Madrid. Then there is the tragic and unexplained death of the lovers "at the age of twenty rivers and a single shredded winter," a possible reference to the fact that Philip was twenty-one years old when they parted—effectively dead to Federico, who did not expect to see him again. A sense of loss resurfaces in the last line of the poem, in which the speaker reveals the emotional toll of the whole sad affair: "That is the reason, my dear captain, for my strange melancholia."

Finally, there is another, especially telling clue in the name that Federico chose for one of the people present when the speaker of the poem begins his story. In his original autograph of the poem, Federico named that person "Emilio," as if to say to Emilio Aladrén, "Take note: You may have rejected me, but another young man actually wanted me and happily went to bed with me." To reinforce the point, in the next line the speaker adds, "In order to make that name bearable, I need to restrain my painful memories." But Federico later thought better of his choice, crossing out "Emilio" and replacing it with the far less weighted name "Luciano."[31]

The literary journal for which Federico originally wrote "Two Lovers" ceased operation in the fall of 1928 before the poem could be published, but it finally appeared in another short-lived journal, *DDOOSS*, in 1931.[32] The work is uncharacteristic enough that it could easily have been dismissed as an anomaly and largely forgotten. It might well have been, had not Federico chosen to revisit it at a key point later in his life (see chapter 10).

In a letter to his friend Jorge Zalamea from this same period, Federico wrote, "It grieves me to know you're passing through bad times. But you should learn to overcome them, one way or another. Anything is preferable to being eaten up, broken, crushed by them.

By sheer will power, I've resolved these past few days one of the most painful periods I've experienced in my life."[33] Despite these bold declarations, those closest to Federico could see that he was in deep despair—for reasons they didn't fully understand.

His unhappiness was all the more confusing since the publication of *Gypsy Ballads* had brought Federico both fame and financial success almost overnight. But his initial delight evaporated after Salvador Dalí, whose opinion meant more to Federico than anyone else's, sent him a long, critical letter deriding the work for being too traditional and conformist.[34] Adopting an air of detachment, Federico wrote to Gasch, "Yesterday Dalí wrote me a long letter concerning my book. . . . A sharp, arbitrary letter that sets forth an interesting poetic problem. Of course, the *putrefactos* do not understand my book, although they say they do. In spite of everything it holds no interest for me anymore, or hardly any. It died on my hands in the most tender way."[35] Somehow this response does not ring true. But even if Federico had actually lost interest in the book, its continuing popularity with the Spanish public created its own problems. With so many people talking about his work, Federico felt as though his whole life were under scrutiny. He hated the intrusion, writing to Jorge Zalamea, "I desire and demand my privacy. If I fear stupid fame, it's precisely because of this."[36]

Federico also railed against the tendency of the book's reviewers to refer to him as a "gypsy poet" or even assume that he was Romani himself. He had been feeling boxed in and stereotyped by the label ever since the first poems from his *Gypsy Ballads* collection began appearing in literary magazines. In a January 1927 letter to his friend Jorge Guillen, he wrote, "This gypsy myth of mine annoys me a little. They confuse my life and character. This isn't what I want at all. The gypsies are a theme. And nothing more. . . . Besides, this gypsyism gives me the appearance of an uncultured, ignorant and primitive poet that you know very well I'm not. I don't want to be typecast. I feel as if they're chaining me down."[37]

As 1929 began, Federico threw himself into writing new poems and essays that had nothing to do with the Romani or their folklore. He began making regular trips to Madrid again, where he gave talks on various subjects, attended literary meetings, and spent time with close friends whose emotional support helped him hold himself together. But then came a further blow. In February, Federico learned that Dalí had begun collaborating with Luis Buñuel on an experimental script for a movie that a few months later would become the world's first surrealist film, *Un Chien Andalou*.[38]

During their student days together at the Residencia, Buñuel had seemed to be a good friend to both Federico and Dalí, but over time he grew increasingly jealous of Federico's closeness to Dalí and did everything he could to diminish Federico's influence and drive them apart. Dalí himself became complicit in this rift following the publication of *Gypsy Ballads*. Unwilling to visit Federico in Granada when the poet was at his lowest, Dalí did not hesitate to travel to Paris to work with Buñuel; he also ignored his promise to publish a letter written by Federico in a journal Dalí helped edit. Federico may have wondered if he was imagining these slights, but he was not. Decades later, Dalí confessed that he felt great hostility and jealousy toward Federico at that time and studiously avoided being with him.[39] For Federico, still reeling from the end of his affair with Aladrén, the loss of Dalí's friendship must have been devastating.

Federico's parents noticed his growing despondency and quietly took steps to try to help him. In the early spring of 1929, Federico's father made a surprise visit to Rafael Martínez Nadal, one of his son's close friends in Madrid. With unusual directness, García Rodríguez said that he had come from Granada to ask Rafael if he knew what was troubling Federico and whether he thought some time outside the country might help ease his son's suffering—whatever might be causing it. Rafael was circumspect about the source of Federico's pain, attributing it to depression or the strain of sudden success, but he agreed that being away from Spain for a while might give Federico some relief. Satisfied, García Rodríguez rose to leave—but not before asking Rafael to never tell his son or anyone else about their conversation.[40]

García Rodríguez was almost certainly debating the idea of a trip abroad for his son because just such an opportunity had recently presented itself. Fernando de los Ríos, Federico's much-admired former professor in Granada and a trusted family friend, had been invited to travel to New York in early June to give a series of lectures at Columbia University. Federico's father clearly hoped that if his son, who had never left Spain, accompanied don Fernando (as Federico called him) on his journey, two goals might be accomplished: Federico would be distracted from his worries by the multitudes of new people, places, and experiences he would encounter, and he might even gain a working knowledge of English in the process. In addition, Federico would be with an experienced companion who could help him manage the details of international travel and deliver him safely to New York, allowing his parents to relax on that score. Once there, if all went according to plan, Federico would stay on for a few months to study English at Columbia under the watchful eyes of Federico de Onís, a distinguished Spanish expatriate who chaired the Department of Spanish and Portuguese at the university, and his much younger colleague, Ángel del Río. Both men had previously met Federico in Spain and were well aware of his literary status there.[41] García Rodríguez clearly trusted that they would do their best to preserve his son's good reputation while he was beyond his parents' reach.

Not long after his father's meeting with Rafael Martínez Nadal, Federico began telling his friends that he would soon be going to New York with don Fernando and that his father was paying for the entire trip.[42] The prospect of such a grand adventure brightened his spirits considerably. In a letter to his friend Carlos Morla Lynch written shortly before he left Granada in early June, Federico happily described his plans:

I will be in Madrid for two days to take care of some last minute

> things and leave immediately for Paris, London, and there I will embark for New York. Are you surprised? I'm also surprised. I'm going to die laughing over this decision. But it suits me and it's an important one in my life. I will stay in America six or seven months and will return to Paris for the rest of the year. New York seems horrible, but for that very reason I'm going there. I think I'll have a very good time. I'm taking the trip with my good friend Fernando de los Ríos, my old teacher and an extremely charming person who will get me over the initial rough spots, since, as you know, I am restless and foolish when it comes to practical life. I am very well, with a new restlessness concerning the world and my future. This trip will be very useful to me. My papa gave me all the money I need and is happy with this decision of mine.[43]

On 5 June, Federico celebrated his thirty-first birthday in Granada and received his Spanish passport the same day. On 9 June, he took the train to Madrid, where he was wined and dined by his many friends in the days leading up to his departure. Finally, on Wednesday, 12 June 1929, Federico, don Fernando, and the latter's niece Rita María (surname unknown), who would be traveling with them as far as London, boarded the overnight train from Madrid to Paris, at least a twenty-four-hour trip in those days.[44] Federico seemed happy at the time, ready to take on whatever lay ahead. But with no previous exposure to life outside Spain, and only rare excursions outside his familiar settings inside the country, he had no way to know how much his trip to America would challenge and change him.

Meanwhile, Philip was once again in Europe. The exact circumstances of his departure from Rollins several months before the end of the academic year are somewhat murky. Sometime in the early spring of 1929, he apparently convinced the administration that he was desperately needed in Spain to help teach the English classes that were being canceled at the University of Madrid due to ongoing faculty strikes and antigovernment demonstrations.[45] Philip's Rollins transcript notes that he left the school before the start of the spring term, but graduated in absentia with the rest of his class that June—a clear indication that his early departure had received official approval.

In a letter dated 16 May, Alfred J. Hanna, assistant to college president Hamilton Holt, wrote to Philip (whom he clearly thought was in Madrid), "I hope this finds you comfortably settled in Spain and making good progress in your duties there. At your convenience, won't you let us know how you are getting along?"[46] In his 7 June reply, Philip told Hanna that his work at the university was almost complete and he would soon be leaving Madrid. He then provided a detailed account of a train trip he had taken through mountainous regions of Switzerland and Austria "during Holy Week of Corpus Christi" (24–31 March in 1929), a vacation period in Spanish universities.[47]

But Philip had been nowhere near Spain in March. He did not even leave the United States until 21 April, when he sailed from New York on the SS *Caledonia*, bound for Glasgow.[48] Various stamps and seals on his passport indicate that he arrived in Glasgow on 29 April and stayed in Scotland until 22 May, when he entered France at Calais and proceeded directly to Switzerland. He received a visa to enter Spain at the US consulate in Paris on 6 June and officially registered his presence with the authorities in Madrid on 8 June. What in the world was going on?

The most likely explanation is that Philip had once again been hired by John Duncan, a well-to-do printer in Edinburgh, to tutor his seventeen-year-old son, Ronald. The plan was apparently for the two to stay in Edinburgh for a month or so, then embark on a tour of the Swiss Alps. It is unclear how Philip knew the Duncan family, but the previous spring he had taken Ronald along on his travels across the continent and northern Africa.[49] In all likelihood the Duncans covered Philip's expenses on that first trip and promised to do the same this time, and Philip could not resist the opportunity.[50]

Philip must have known that a tutoring job in Scotland would not be considered an acceptable reason to leave Rollins early, so he made up an excuse that was plausible enough to satisfy, and perhaps even please, the college's administrators. Having one of their students be asked to teach classes at a Spanish university was prestigious indeed, and in fact a notice to that effect was published in the *Orlando Sentinel* that April.[51] Once again, Philip seems to have discerned what really mattered to the Rollins administrators and adjusted his messaging accordingly, achieving exactly what he wanted in the process.

There is no proof that this theory is correct, but several clues, including the dated stamps in Philip's passport, strongly support it. In addition, Philip asked the college to address all letters to him during his entire time abroad to "J. F. Duncan, Esq., 16 Easter Road, Edinburgh, Scotland," supposedly to avoid any mix-ups as he moved from place to place. Hanna dutifully sent his 16 May letter to that address, and it did successfully reach Philip. But Philip never corrected Hanna's false assumption that he received the letter while teaching in Spain, rather than exploring the Alps with Ronald Duncan, and there is no indication that anyone at Rollins ever questioned his story.

As mentioned, Philip finally made it to Madrid on 8 June, but he left again a mere four days later. The reason for his rapid turnaround seems obvious. When Federico boarded the overnight train to Paris with Fernando de los Ríos and his niece in Madrid on the evening of 12 June 1929, he was delighted to find that Philip was not only a passenger on the same train, but also traveling all the way to Paris. Federico later told his parents that running into Philip on the train happened purely by chance, and that is possible.[52] Beyond the letter Philip wrote to Federico while aboard the *Paris*, there is no other known correspondence between the two young men during this time period. But considering the pair's prior history and Philip's arrival in Madrid just a few days before Federico's departure, it seems much more likely that they had been in contact that spring and secretly planned their "accidental" encounter. As long as Federico let Philip know the details of his upcoming trip, as he almost certainly did, Philip could ensure that he ended up on the same train. And though Federico was ultimately headed to New York and Philip would soon be returning to Vermont, both would have been happy to focus on the immediate pleasures of their reunion, including the opportunity to spend a whole night together in a private sleeping compartment as the train made its long journey north.

In a 1948 essay, Philip said that he and Federico barely slept during the trip, instead talking "for hours to the rhythmic click of the wheels over the rails, of what life was for and that man was always playing hide-and-seek with death."[53] Almost forty years later, he finally revealed that he and Federico also took advantage of the privacy afforded by their sleeping compartment to renew their sexual relationship.[54] This outcome seems both natural and predictable from a modern perspective, especially in light of Philip and Federico's previous attraction and their long separation; it would be more surprising if it had *not* occurred. But considering the many hazards they faced as same-sex lovers in that era, including serious legal and social consequences, we can instead marvel at the risks they took to be together and applaud the success of their subterfuge.[55]

At some point during their relaxed, wide-ranging conversations on the train, Philip invited Federico to visit him in Vermont later that summer, after the poet had settled in at Columbia, and Federico happily accepted.[56] When they finally reached the Paris station, Federico and Philip parted ways once more, but this time with the confidence that they would soon see each other again in the United States.

CHAPTER THREE

Plans and Preparations

Alternate the cunning of the serpent with the candor of the dove.

—Baltasar Gracián, *The Art of Worldly Wisdom*

AFTER SPENDING THE NIGHT in Paris, Federico, don Fernando, and Rita María crossed the English Channel by boat.[1] They spent the next few days exploring London together before leaving Rita María at the school where she had been hired to teach that summer. The two men continued on to Oxford, where don Fernando planned to visit an old friend. In addition to sight-seeing, the Oxford visit gave Federico an opportunity to do some last-minute shopping before he set sail for New York. It was almost certainly there that he purchased the white cricket sweater with navy trim that would later serve him so well in Vermont.

Following their short stay in Oxford, Federico and don Fernando made their way to Southampton, where on 19 June 1929, they boarded the White Star Line's SS *Olympic*, a sister ship to the *Titanic*. The voyage went smoothly, though Federico frequently found himself beset by homesickness and questioning his decision to make the trip.[2] But when the massive ocean liner arrived in New York harbor six days later, he was delighted to find a delegation of Spaniards waiting at the pier to welcome him and don Fernando.[3]

Figure 8. The SS *Olympic* entering New York harbor, June 1911. Library of Congress, Prints and Photographs Division, no. LC-DIG-det-4a27498.

The group included several leading members of the city's Spanish expatriate community: Columbia University professors Federico de Onís and Ángel del Río, artist Gabriel García Maroto, poet and translator León Felipe, and newspaper publisher José Camprubí. Some of these men already knew Federico, but even those who did not were well aware of his reputation as Spain's most important young poet, the rising star of his generation.[4]

Three days after arriving in New York, Federico wrote a long, chatty letter to his parents—the first of twenty known missives (including one postcard and one telegraph) he sent to his family during his eight months in the United States.[5] The letters make fascinating reading. Full of amusing anecdotes and observations, they not only document what was on Federico's mind at the time but also reveal his care in choosing which stories to share with his anxious parents back in Granada. He knew from long experience that they would worry most (and not without cause) about his spending habits, his attention to his studies, and his choice of companions, so he carefully shaped and embellished his accounts with reassuring details designed to relieve their fears.

In his first letter, dated 28 June, Federico described his ocean voyage and arrival in New York, his first impressions of the city, and how Professor Onís had arranged for his enrollment and lodging in a dorm at Columbia, where he now lived "surrounded by American students." Near the end of the letter, he casually mentioned his recent encounter with the "young American poet" he had met in Madrid the previous summer and his friend's gracious invitation to come for a visit. Well aware that his parents would not want him to leave the city on his own, especially to stay with an unknown American, he was quick to assure them that Philip came from a respectable family. Not only that—he claimed that don Fernando himself had approved the plan:

> Here's another strange thing. Do you remember my telling you about a young American poet who wrote a poem to me in the Residencia after hearing me play the piano? I met him again on the train from Madrid to Paris, and he invited me to spend the month of August (the hottest month here) in his house in Canada [*sic*]. His father is a railroad broker, and he will send me the tickets free. Don Fernando told me not to miss this opportunity to visit one of the most beautiful places in North America; to get there, one passes by Niagara Falls.[6]

Federico got many facts wrong in this part of his letter—Philip actually lived in Vermont, not Canada; getting to his house did not involve passing by Niagara Falls; and Philip's father was a real estate and insurance agent, not a railroad broker—but these are understandable mistakes, especially for someone newly arrived in the country. While Federico may have discussed Philip's invitation with Fernando de los Ríos, as he claimed, he took some liberties with the truth in his next paragraph: "He is a fine boy; he has studied at

Columbia and Onís knows him. Last year, as an exercise in his Spanish class, he translated two of the 'Gypsy Ballads' into English. In other words, he knows me and hasn't invited me for just any old reason. I've accepted and, God willing, if all goes as planned, I'll spend the month of August in Canada. American customs are nothing like Spanish ones. Here they invite you places at the drop of a hat."[7]

While it is true that Philip had translated two of Federico's poems for a class at Rollins, he had never studied at Columbia University nor met Onís. Federico clearly thought that these invented details would bolster his friend's standing in his parents' eyes and help convince them that Philip was a suitable host for their son. Should they still object, Federico also made it clear that he had already accepted Philip's invitation, so there was no going back on it now.

With his family advised of the general plan, the challenge was to bring it to fruition within the next six weeks. This would of course require working out the details of the trip with Philip, a task made more complicated by the fact that Philip was still on his way home from Europe on the Boston-bound SS *Albertic* when Federico first wrote to his parents.

After saying good-bye to Federico in Paris, Philip had spent the next week in Scotland, probably with the Duncan family, before boarding the *Albertic* in Liverpool on 22 June. He disembarked in Boston on 1 July and reached his hometown of Hardwick, Vermont, some 200 miles to the northwest, the following day.[8]

Based on their subsequent correspondence, Philip must have mailed a letter to Federico almost as soon as he walked in the door of his parents' home; he may even have sent it from Boston. At that point Philip knew only that his friend was somewhere at Columbia University, so he must have addressed his letter accordingly. The fact that it actually reached Federico seems almost miraculous, but the Columbia mailroom must have been accustomed to tracking down new campus residents based on very little information.

This first letter from Philip to Federico has been lost, but two others that the friends exchanged over the next several weeks have been preserved and provide a window on the progress of their arrangements. Federico wrote on 6 or 7 July and was clearly responding to the initial letter from Philip:

My dear friend:

I was overjoyed to receive your letter. I've found a place in New York. I want to see you soon and think of you constantly but on the advice of Professor Onís, I've registered at Columbia University, and for this reason I can't be with you until six weeks from now.[9] *Then, if you still wish me to, I'll be delighted to come.*

If you won't be at home at that time I invite you to come to see me in New York. What do you say to that? Write me in all confidence if this is possible.

I'm bewildered by your great generosity in sending me the money for the ticket and, of course, if my trip isn't arranged within the next six weeks I'll return it to you with eternal gratitude and noble friendship which is the most a Spaniard can offer.

Write me immediately and tell me what you think of the postponement of my trip. Since I'm registered I must take this course in English. Later on I could spend a few days with you and they will be delightful for me.

I hope that you will answer me and will not forget this poet from the South now lost in this Babylonic, cruel and violent city, filled on the other hand with a great modern beauty.

I live at Columbia and my address is:

Mister Federico G. Lorca
Furnald Hall
Columbia University
New York City

I hope that you will answer me right away.

Adiós, dear friend. An embrace from Federico.

My respects to your parents.[10]

In his letter, Federico sounded enthusiastic about making the trip, but he was also clearly ready to call it off if Philip asked him to. He may have simply wanted to ensure that the visit was still possible, considering the six-week delay in his departure, or perhaps he wanted to offer Philip a way out if he had changed his mind. But it seems most likely that, after his first heady excitement at finding himself in New York, Federico was starting to feel a little less certain about his ability to manage alone in an unfamiliar place where he did not speak the language and may have been having second thoughts about thc wisdom of traveling outside the city on his own.

At this early stage in his visit, Federico would have still been coming to grips with the sheer number of people in New York—Manhattan alone had over 1.6 million residents in 1929, almost twice as many as Madrid and over sixteen times as many as Granada—and the dawning realization that, without fluency in English, he had no way to communicate with the vast majority of its citizens.[11] This left him completely reliant on his English-speaking friends to help him navigate the city's boroughs and serve as translators. Fortunately for him, New York's Hispanic community was thriving in 1929 and included not only many Spaniards, but also a growing number of immigrants from Cuba, Puerto Rico, and other Latin American countries.[12] As long as he stayed within that orbit, he could converse exclusively in Spanish to his heart's content.

Still, for someone as sociable as Federico, it must have been incredibly hard to find himself unable to understand or participate in all the other conversations taking place around him, let alone ask a simple question of a non-Spanish speaker. He would have gotten a taste of this type of linguistic isolation during his brief stays in France and England, but it had probably had little impact since he was just passing through. Now, as he contemplated voluntarily leaving his safe haven in the city, he must have felt much more vulnerable.

Figure 9. Lorca *(far right)*, María Antonieta Rivas (*next to Lorca*), and two unidentified friends on the campus of Columbia University, New York, October 1929. Archivo Fundación Federico García Lorca, Centro Federico García Lorca, Granada.

In addition, unlike Philip, Federico was not an experienced solo traveler. Even in Spain, the few times he had ventured outside familiar territory, it was almost always as part of a group. Federico also did not seem to share Philip's persistent drive to see and explore new places, nor his boundless confidence that he would be able to get by wherever he went. But however much Federico may have privately considered canceling the trip, he told Philip that he was still willing to attempt it.

Many details remained unresolved, however. The next extant letter was written by Philip (in Spanish) on 31 July, just before he left Hardwick for the month of August. It seems clear from his agitated tone that Philip feared Federico might fail to send him critical details about his travel plans far enough in advance or, worse yet, change his mind and not make the trip at all:

Don Federico Lorca
New York City

Dearest:

Listen! Tomorrow we will go to our country house and wait for you there. But we will not be near the mail, so telegraph five days before you arrive; write to us, so we can meet you. I await you with impatience. Come! Come, man!

With strong and eternal embraces,
Felipe Cummings
31 July 1929
My address until 31 August
Philip Cummings
Camper
Eden Mills
Vermont[13]

Federico's more relaxed view of the situation comes through in a letter to his parents. On 8 August, he wrote:

> In a few days I leave for the Canadian border, the state of Vermont, where I'm going to spend fifteen or twenty days with a boy I met at the Residencia. He has a farm in the mountains on Lake Eden, and that is where I'm going. I'll write you from there, and you write to me there. Fifteen days is nothing. This trip is like going from Granada to Loja, and yet it involves a twenty-hour train ride. You simply can't imagine the immensity of the United States.[14]
>
> This boy, who is a poet, was so eager to have me visit him that he sent me the $20 train fare. I've asked my friends if this is normal, and they tell me it is the custom here. When an American invites you, he treats you to *everything*. So next week I take the train to Burlington, and I expect to have a good time. This boy is extremely kind, and in his house only English is spoken, which will be very good for me.[15]

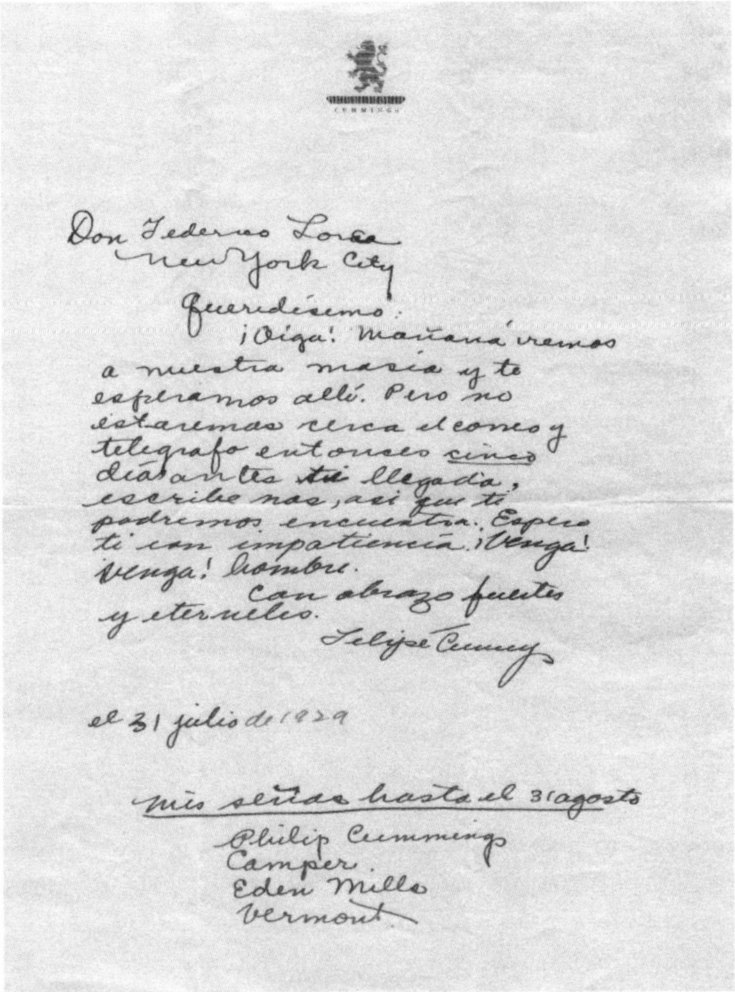

Don Federico Lorca
New York City

Queridísimo:

¡Oiga! Mañana vamos a nuestra masía y te esperamos allí. Pero no estaremos cerca el correo y telégrafo entonces cinco días antes tu llegada, escribe nos, así que te podremos encuentra. Espero ti con impatiencia. ¡Venga! ¡venga! hombre.

Con abrazo fuertes y eternales.

Felipe Cumming

el 31 julio de 1929

mis señas hasta el 31 agosto

Philip Cummings
Camper.
Eden Mills
Vermont.

Figure 10. Handwritten letter from Philip Cummings in Hardwick, Vermont, to Federico García Lorca in New York City, 31 July 1929. Manuscripts and Rare Books, Hispanic Society of America, New York.

These paragraphs suggest an additional lost letter, or perhaps a phone call, from Philip, in which he must have described Lake Eden and advised Federico to travel there by way of Burlington, Vermont. Philip's full instructions were probably quite specific: Once his departure date was set, Federico should reserve a sleeping berth on the Rutland Railroad's *Mount Royal* train, which stopped in Burlington on its daily overnight run from New York City to Montreal—the most convenient and efficient way to make the trip.[16]

The contents of Federico's 8 August letter are intriguing for other reasons as well. For cxample, he repeated what he had already told his parents about his initial meeting with Philip at the Residencia, perhaps to remind them that Philip was a known quantity with a genuine connection to Spain. He also included a new point in Philip's favor: In his house, "only English is spoken," suggesting that Federico would therefore be forced to practice his English. This would have been true in most households, but of course, since Philip also spoke Spanish, Federico would always have an interpreter on hand. In addition, Federico implied that Philip's family owned the place where he would be staying, which was not the case. It's not clear whether this was simply a false assumption on Federico's part or if Philip deliberately misled him about it; either way, Federico must have thought the additional detail would please his parents.

Federico's next task was to finalize his travel dates. He rarely if ever attended classes, but since the Columbia summer session continued until Friday, 16 August, staying in the city until then would help maintain the fiction that he was still an active student.[17] But if he left immediately after that, he would not be able to say good-bye to his old friend and mentor don Fernando, who was away until 19 August. Federico had also been invited to join don Fernando and other leading members of the city's Spanish expatriate community at a gala dinner featuring poetry readings and music the following night.[18] In the end, Federico decided to take the overnight train from New York City on the evening of Tuesday, 20 August 1929, and thus arrive in Burlington on the morning of 21 August.[19]

Federico's only remaining responsibilities were to notify Philip of his expected arrival time, buy his ticket, pack his clothes, and get himself to the train station at the appointed time. Philip had a great deal more to do to prepare for his friend's visit, especially after deciding not to bring Federico anywhere near his hometown of Hardwick.

It is possible that Philip made this decision out of concern that Federico would find Hardwick too boring, but this seems unlikely. In 1929, Hardwick was a lively town of 2,700 people that served as the commercial and cultural hub for the entire region.[20] Its downtown streets were lined with banks, shops, hotels, and other businesses patronized by local tradespeople, farmers, business owners, and their families. Telephone service was available to those who could afford it, and the St. Johnsbury and Lake Champlain Railroad made six daily stops in Hardwick on its regular east-west route.[21] The town even had its own hospital.

The Vermont granite industry was still thriving then, and Hardwick was a granite town. The Woodbury Granite Company operated stonecutting and finishing sheds within the town limits, a quarry on a mountainside eight miles away, and a railroad line connecting the two. The company was world famous for both the efficiency of its operation and the quality of its granite; its Woodbury Gray and Vermont White granites were the preferred stone for monuments, state capitols, and other public buildings across the United States. In 1913, the company was the largest granite business in the world under single management, employing many hundreds of skilled workers.[22]

The granite industry made Hardwick a surprisingly cosmopolitan place, with stonecutters from Scotland, Ireland, England, Italy, Spain, Sweden, and Austria sharing the streets with native Vermonters and French-Canadian immigrants.[23] While some in the town resented the influx of strangers, for a curious boy like Philip, the multiplicity of cultures was exhilarating.[24] His early exposure to the diverse customs and dialects of the stonecutters and their families led to a lifelong fascination with other countries and languages, a perfect fit for someone with his auditory memory and talent for mimicry. In his later years, he told journalist Mildred Adams that the melodious speech of the Spanish workers had particularly captured his attention, sparking the interest that would later lead him to Madrid.[25]

However, from Philip's perspective, there were multiple reasons to keep Federico as far away from Hardwick as possible. Growing up there had been a painful experience for him.[26] From a young age, he had been teased by other children for being different. This happened initially because of his precocious use of language—the result of being the only child of a well-educated mother in a house full of adults. But as he grew older, his preference for history, science, and literature over sports, girls, and other typical adolescent male preoccupations made him an object of new taunts and pranks.

The fact that Philip matured into a tall, muscular teen made it particularly galling to his classmates that he had no interest in playing football or basketball. (Philip attributed his aversion to these sports to his father's mockery of his throwing skills as a young boy, after which he never threw a ball again.)[27] He was restless and enjoyed physical exercise but preferred to spend his energy hiking alone in the wooded hills around Hardwick, a welcome escape from the pressures he felt in school and at home. In a journal entry written a few years after his father's comment about his athletic skill, Philip acknowledged his lack of "that something which makes one love group competition." Resigned to the difficulty of his situation, he added, "I find that the average fellow can't comprehend this, so I just accept it and wish it were otherwise."[28]

The June 1924 issue of his high school newspaper, which doubled as the senior yearbook, provides a window on how seventeen-year-old Philip was viewed by the other twenty-two students in his class. In the nickname section, Philip was given two: "Sister" and "Brassy." "Sister," the term from which the pejorative "sissy" derives, indicates that his peers perceived him as less than fully masculine, as does the prediction that he would become "the athletic coach at a girls' private college."[29] His senior profile was somewhat kinder. Though it poked fun at his hobbies and fresh-faced good looks, it also acknowledged his well-honed verbal skills: "Brassy's favorite sports are learning and collecting—witness his ever present memorandum pad and his admirable assortment of curios, precious gems, and bugs. But the strenuous life seems to agree with him; for just notice his wonderful wavy hair and rosy cheeks which are the envy of all the girls. Brassy's hobby is arguing, but we have to hand it to him for being a good debater, all the same."[30]

Interestingly, unlike many teased and bullied children, Philip never tried to fade into the background. He was sensitive to slights and felt them acutely, but he also loved attention, especially from adults, and was even a bit of a show-off. Perhaps this confidence stemmed from some inherent sense of his own abilities, reinforced by his mother's support and encouragement.

It would have been hard for him to avoid the spotlight in any case. As the only child of Harry Cummings, a prominent local businessman, and his wife, Addie, a former teacher and active churchwoman, Philip and his family were often in the news. Even their minor activities—the installation of a telephone, an accident on the school playground—were reported in the local *Hardwick Gazette* on a regular basis.[31] Of course, other leading families received the same type of attention, as was the custom then. People in small towns everywhere expected the newspaper to tell them what their neighbors were up to.

However he might have felt about his local notoriety, Philip left Hardwick as soon as he could. After graduating from high school, he jumped at the opportunity to leave Vermont and join the freshman class at Stetson University. (His enrollment there was almost certainly due to his father's business interests in Florida.) Philip said good-bye to his hometown that fall and rarely looked back; over the next ten years, he returned to Hardwick only for occasional winter holidays and summer visits with his parents. The *Hardwick Gazette* published regular updates on his various travels and achievements, but Philip himself was seldom around.

Yet now he was back in Hardwick again, mulling over Federico's impending visit. Most people would want to show a visiting friend, especially one from far away, the place where they grew up, even if some of their experiences there had been unpleasant. But Philip must have felt that the risks of bringing Federico to Hardwick were simply too great. Philip knew he was already viewed with considerable curiosity—some kind, some less so—by people in the town and may have feared attracting even greater scrutiny if Federico were with him. Their chances of finding any privacy there were almost nil. In addition, if Philip had misled Federico about his father's degree of financial success and influence, he may have realized how impossible it would be to maintain this fiction if Federico actually spent time in Hardwick.

Harry Cummings's fortunes had declined dramatically and publicly over the previous few years. His ambitious land development project in Florida had collapsed in 1926, and a similar initiative in nearby Greensboro, Vermont, was on the brink of failure. As a result, the many friends and neighbors he had persuaded to invest in these ventures were losing their hard-earned money, and Harry was facing financial ruin.[32] News items in the *Hardwick Gazette* chronicled his fall from grace, reporting first that Harry had moved his real estate business into much smaller quarters, then that he had sold the family home.[33] By the summer of 1929, Harry and Addie were reduced to living in rented rooms on the second floor of his brother's house in Hardwick. Harry had given up his business completely and lost the respect of his community.

Philip' s decision to avoid Hardwick is understandable, but it also left him in urgent need of an alternative place to vacation with Federico. A few summer cottages were available to rent near Hardwick, but their proximity to the town would make it all too easy to spend time there. The ideal location would be close enough to feel familiar to his parents, but far enough away to discourage casual trips back home. And since Federico's travel dates were still uncertain, a place that could be reserved for the whole month of August was also essential.

We don't know how Philip discovered the rental cottage on Lake Eden, but it had been advertised for sale in the *Burlington Free Press* in the summer of 1926, a time when his father was still active in local real estate, so perhaps Harry knew about it.[34] However Philip found the cottage, it fit the bill perfectly. Though the town of Eden was only in the next county, getting there from Hardwick required twenty miles of difficult driving over rough roads and hilly terrain, a trip not to be undertaken lightly. The cottage itself was located in Eden Mills, a village within the town limits, and was just a short walk from the combined post office and general store where they could get their provisions. It was available for the entire month of August, meeting Philip's date requirements. Best of all, it was in a place where no one knew Philip or his parents, promising a level of anonymity he could never achieve in Hardwick. To the villagers, they would simply be more "summer people," strangers who flocked to the cottages along Lake Eden when the weather turned warm and just as quickly disappeared at the first hint of frost.

It's unclear how much it cost Philip to rent the cottage for a full month, but ads for similar cottages in the Burlington paper showed weekly rental rates ranging from $15 to $25, depending on amenities. Whatever the amount, Philip later told Mildred Adams that he paid it himself using money earned from teaching.[35] He also told Adams that the primary goal of the vacation was to give his mother a break from her regular household duties—a somewhat dubious claim. In keeping with this theme, he invited Addie's younger sister Carrie Southwick and her daughter, Edna, who lived outside Boston, to join them for the month. This was supposedly another treat for Addie, but it seems equally likely that Philip wanted his aunt and cousin there to distract his sharp-eyed mother from paying too much attention to whatever he and Federico might be up to.

It is easy to imagine Philip working out these arrangements with all the anxiety and suppressed excitement of someone engaged in a secret love affair and delighting as everything fell into place. Convincing his parents to leave Hardwick for Eden, apparently the only local vacation the family ever took, may have been the hardest part. Once that was accomplished, he must have breathed a sigh of relief. Including them in the plan for his reunion with Federico was a calculated risk, but there is no indication that his parents ever suspected their son's ulterior motives.

On 1 August, the Cummingses packed up the family's Model T Ford with all their supplies and headed off to Lake Eden with Harry, the only driver in the family, at the wheel. By that time, Philip knew that Federico would not be leaving New York for another three weeks, but he may have realized that the delay was a blessing in disguise. For one thing, it reinforced the myth that Federico's visit played only a minor role in the timing of the vacation. More importantly, it gave Philip time to get to know the cottage, the lake, and the village of Eden Mills, and begin to determine which local people and places would be most likely to please and entertain his friend. He had much to do to prepare for Federico's arrival, but as the August days rolled by, Philip happily rose to the challenge.

CHAPTER FOUR

The Journey to Eden

Not I, not any one else can travel that road for you,
You must travel it for yourself.
It is not far, it is within reach,
Perhaps you have been on it since you were born and did not know.

—Walt Whitman, "Song of Myself"

DESPITE ALL HIS TREPIDATIONS, Federico arrived at New York's Grand Central Terminal in time to board his train on the evening of Tuesday, 20 August. The group of friends who accompanied him did their best to keep him calm and bolster his courage—with limited success. In a letter to his parents written a few days later, Federico tried to put the best face on his behavior at the station: "The day before yesterday I went to the station and said goodbye to Maroto, Mr. Brickell, Ángel del Río, Flores, and others. They were all in stitches. It was my 'moment of truth' in English, and the first trip I've made by myself on this enormous continent. Grand Station Central [*sic*] is enough to frighten anyone, but even an idiot could find his way around this country."[1]

Twenty-five years later, Ángel del Río still recalled the scene with considerable amusement:

> Typical of Lorca's reaction to the new atmosphere was the panic, half simulated and half in earnest, that possessed [him] on entering the bustle of Grand Central. On boarding the train, he was genuinely worried by his removal from all means of communication, for he could not speak a word of English. He dramatized the incident by shouts and gestures and was not at ease until the friend who had taken him to the train assured him, after talking with the conductor, that he would be left safely at his destination in Vermont.[2]

It was obvious to all concerned that Federico was deeply anxious about traveling to Vermont on his own, and yet he did it anyway. How did he explain his uncharacteristic resolve in the face of such a difficult personal challenge? His friends knew only that Federico had been invited to Vermont by an American acquaintance named Cummings whom none of them had ever met—hardly a compelling reason to put himself through such agony. Perhaps Federico told them he had accepted the invitation as a way to escape the summer heat of the city, or so that he could see a part of the country he might not otherwise visit. Whatever explanation he gave, he successfully concealed the nature of his relationship with Philip from everyone there, at least initially.

The person who learned the truth not long after was Federico's friend Ángel del Río, but del Río had little inclination to share what he knew. He never mentioned Cummings in any of his writings about Lorca until 1955, and even then described Federico's host in Vermont as simply "a fellow poet, according to [Federico], a Mr. Cummings, whom he had met a few months before in the Residencia at Madrid."[3] As later events made clear, del Río knew exactly who Philip was when he wrote those words in 1955, even if that was not the case when he was helping to calm Federico as he began his journey north. (Del Río's pattern of omissions and the reasons behind it are discussed more fully in the epilogue of this book.)

Once safely on board the train, Federico was in for a treat. The

Mount Royal was one of the Rutland Railroad's premier passenger trains, known for its modern amenities.[4] It made far fewer stops on its overnight trip from New York City to Montreal than other northbound trains, making it a favorite of politicians and lobbyists traveling to the state capitol in Albany. It boasted an opulent club car for those who wanted to smoke, drink, and socialize on the way north, and travelers who preferred to sleep could reserve a private room, a cleverly designed compartment with a real bed, on one of the train's brand-new Pullman cars.[5] Pullman passengers had the option to go directly to their room when they boarded the train, and Federico chose to do so.[6]

On the first leg of its evening run, the *Mount Royal* traveled north along the east bank of the Hudson River on tracks owned by the New York Central Railroad. Federico described his impressions of the experience in a letter to his parents:

> This was also my first trip on an American Pullman (which you've seen in the movies), and it is a true prodigy of comfort and technical inventiveness. I lay down, put out the light, and opened the windows. I wanted to sleep, but the sight of the moon and the boats on the Hudson River was so wonderful that it filled my head with ideas and kept me from sleep, which wipes out everything. At times we heard the great eastern express trains, in contrast to the mute little boats nodding at the riverbank with their almost imperceptible lights.[7]

As Federico settled into his berth, the bright moon and busy traffic on the river clearly occupied his mind at first. But as the train moved away from the city into the quiet of the countryside, other thoughts may have begun to intrude. He had survived the first phase of the trip and could breathe a small sigh of relief, but now he was entering completely new territory. There were so many things to worry about.

To begin with, Federico may have wondered what kind of creature comforts he would find at Philip's country house. What if it were as rustic as the isolated compound in Daimuz (now Daimús), the farming village where his family used to spend the summer, with its bleak aspect and lack of basic conveniences? Federico must have hoped that Philip's place would be more like his family's newly acquired country estate outside Granada, the Huerta de San Vicente (Orchard of St. Vincent), named in honor of his mother, Vicenta. The family and their servants now spent much of the spring, summer, and fall there, shielded from the heat by shade trees and thick plastered walls. The Huerta had no running water, despite his father's best efforts to arrange it, but the newly installed electric lights allowed Federico to keep reading or writing in his room as late into the night as he wished, just as he could in their elegant apartment in Granada. And of course the Huerta had a piano for him to play whenever the mood struck him.[8]

He may have worried about his wardrobe, wondering if he had packed the right kind of clothes. Philip must have warned Federico that August in Vermont could be surprisingly cool, since Federico brought long pants along with his regular knee-length knickers and a suit jacket. He also threw in the white cricket sweater he had bought in Oxford just before he and don Fernando sailed for New York.[9] The sweater was bulky and much too warm for the sweltering New York summer, but it might be just right for Vermont.

The rhythmic sound and motion of the train may also have brought to mind his night alone with Philip on their overnight trip from Madrid to Paris a mere two months earlier. He must have wondered how it would be to see Philip again after so many weeks apart, and whether their attraction to each other would still be as strong. Federico knew that Philip saw and appreciated him for exactly who he was, unlike Emilio Aladrén. Emilio had brought him only pain and suffering, but perhaps Philip would turn out to be the young man Federico had been seeking, a true romantic partner who would return his feelings in kind.

There were other pleasures to anticipate as well. Federico appreciated Philip's athletic build and masculine appearance, such a contrast to the effeminate dandies who frequented Riverside Drive, just a few blocks from his Columbia dormitory, at night—with their rouged cheeks, tweezed eyebrows, and flamboyant outfits. He was shocked by the brazenness of their behavior and appalled by the occasional gawkers who laughed and pointed like visitors at a zoo. These men did not even seem to mind being mocked as "pansies" or "fairies"; they sashayed and primped and called out to every male who walked by, then disappeared into the bushes with any willing taker.[10] Federico was clearly disgusted by their womanly mannerisms. If a man couldn't take pride in his masculinity, why bother to live? Perhaps Philip could explain it all in a way that made sense. As the train lumbered on, Federico closed his eyes at last and slept.

The *Mount Royal* continued north along the river, making stops in Poughkeepsie and Albany before reaching Troy, New York, at 12:42 a.m. Crossing into Vermont, the train made brief stops in North Bennington and Manchester, then a longer stop in Rutland, before finally pulling into Burlington at 4:49 in the morning, eight hours after leaving New York. The *Mount Royal* spent a relatively long time at the Burlington station before continuing to Montreal, giving departing passengers fifteen minutes to collect their belongings and disembark before it pulled away.[11] For a late riser like Federico, waking up that early would have been a real challenge, but fortunately conductors kept track of each person's itinerary. They typically woke travelers up well in advance of their arrival time, so no one was likely to sleep through their destination.

Still, Federico must have been barely awake as he followed the other passengers up the covered stairway from the platform, across the elevated bridge, and into the spacious central hall of Burlington's Union Station. The building had been designed by Alfred Fellheimer, the same architect responsible for Grand Central Terminal, but happily for Federico it was much smaller and easier to navigate than its New York cousin.[12] Despite his fatigue, he would have easily found his way to the men's waiting room at the north end of the building. Once there, all he had to do was put down his bags, settle into a comfortable chair, and wait patiently for Philip to come and get him. Even so, Federico may have been feeling considerable anxiety at that moment. He had placed his fate in Philip's hands and must have hoped he had decided wisely.

In later years, Philip gave differing accounts of the actual place where he and his father met Federico's train. In 1955 he told Ángel del Río that he and his father took Federico to the Burlington station at the end of his visit, which strongly suggests that he had also arrived there.[13] However, in 1967, Philip told Mildred Adams that they met the train in Waterbury, Vermont. This option would have shortened their drive from Lake Eden by about sixteen miles, but it would have also required Federico to find and board the connecting train from Burlington to Waterbury on his own at a very early hour, a challenge Philip would have surely wanted to spare him.[14] Further muddying the waters, in 1974, Philip told scholar Daniel Eisenberg that they met Federico at Montpelier Junction, and he said the same thing to biographer Ian Gibson in 1986.[15] But the overnight train from New York to Montpelier Junction took a more easterly route; it departed from Pennsylvania Station, not Grand Central Terminal, and it traveled along the Connecticut River, not the Hudson, putting this version of events at odds with Federico's own description of his trip.[16] So, although Philip's memory of the event clearly wavered over time, all of Federico's contemporaneous statements indicate that his train trip ended in Burlington.[17]

In spite of Federico's worries, in due time Philip and his father arrived at the station as planned in the family's Model T Ford. It is easy to imagine Federico's relief at seeing his friend's face appear at the waiting-room door and the sheer joy of their reunion. No doubt they greeted each other warmly and were soon conversing in rapid-fire Spanish, peppering each other with questions as they made their way to the car. Philip would have introduced Federico to his father and perhaps explained that Harry was a quiet man, given to prolonged periods of introspection, so they could speak Spanish as much as they wished around him.

Philip almost certainly did not add that his father had not always been this way, that until recently he had been an energetic, sociable fellow. In the past, Philip and his father had often been at odds, but they had at least enjoyed an occasional conversation. Now Harry was silent and withdrawn and had little interest in engagement. Some people may have assumed that he was in a state of depression, the result of the string of business failures that had cost him the trust and confidence of many friends and associates who had invested in one of his ambitious real estate schemes.[18] With so many in Hardwick turned against him, it would have been difficult to continue on as usual.

But depression was not the cause of the change in Harry's behavior. Rather, his symptoms at the time are explained by the cause listed on his death certificate when he passed away a mere five years later: "general paralysis of the insane." This carefully chosen euphemism for late-stage tertiary syphilis was routinely used by doctors in that era to shield families from the true cause of their loved one's condition.[19] There is no evidence that either Philip or his mother ever knew what actually afflicted Harry, but at that point in the course of his disease, he was still relatively capable and could handle driving a car.

Leaving the station, Harry would have driven through Burlington to State Route 15 and then headed east across open farmland toward the western edge of the Green Mountains. For Federico, the verdant landscape must have felt almost surreal after the looming skyscrapers and endless pavement of New York. As in Granada, he could see tall mountains in the distance, but these were unlike the windswept Sierra Nevada he knew. Everything was just so *green*, perhaps bringing to mind the opening lines of a poem from his *Gypsy Ballads*, "Sleepwalking Ballad" (Romance sonámbulo):

Verde que te quiero verde.
Verde viento. Verde ramas.
El barco sobre la mar
  y el caballo en la montaña.

Green, how I love you green.
Green wind, green branches.
The boat on the sea
  and the horse on the mountain.[2]

Onward they went, through Essex, Jericho, and the village of Underhill, nestled at the base of Mount Mansfield, Vermont's highest peak at 4,393 feet. The road turned north as it skirted the foothills, then east again at Cambridge, following the meandering path of the Lamoille River through the mountains. Reaching the eastern side of the range, they entered a wide river valley full of small farms, their fields ripe with corn and wheat, their meadows full of sheep and cows grazing in the luxuriant grass. At Johnson, they left Route 15 and turned north onto Route 100, an unpaved highway that ran the whole length of Vermont. After just a few miles, they came to the little town of Eden, then the even smaller village of Eden Mills.

Federico must have been completely captivated. He had grown up in a little farming village on the *vega*, the fertile plain west of Granada, with its cluster of homes, shops, and public buildings surrounded by a wide expanse of carefully tended farmland. Though the topography of Vermont was completely different, he may have noticed a few familiar elements: the little store in the center of town where old men smoked and lounged in the shade, the unpretentious town hall, the simple white church with its pointed steeple—not exactly a cathedral, but it served the same purpose. A less familiar sight was the series of water-powered mills perched along the banks of the little river that ran through the village, clearly the source of its name.

There was no sign of the promised lake until Harry made a sharp right turn onto a narrow dirt road barely visible among the trees. And suddenly, directly before them was Lake Eden. The scene was astoundingly beautiful: the dark blue lake sparkling in the sunshine, its far shore rimmed by stands of pine trees and gently sloping hayfields that reached all the way to the water's edge. Beyond the fields and trees, the rounded hills of the Lowell range extended northward, and above the hills, a clear blue sky completed the glorious panorama.

Lake Eden is a glacial lake, forty feet deep at its deepest point and about two and a half miles long, with an unusual, H-shaped configuration. It would be two separate lakes were it not for the channel that connects its two parallel bodies of water, known locally as the "front lake" and the "back lake." Along its western edge, water flows out of the lake through a small dam and spillway into the narrow gorge of the Gihon River. At the time of Federico's visit, the outflow from the lake provided waterpower for the mills downstream. The lake was a boon to the villagers in other ways as well: a source of fresh fish in the summer and as much ice as they wanted to harvest in the winter.[21]

Harry followed the narrow dirt road along the shore and stopped at the second cottage, their home away from home for the month of

Figure 11. Aerial view of Lake Eden, Vermont, from the south. Commercial postcard.

August. In a letter to his parents, Federico described his first impressions of the lake and cottage:

> I'm now in the prettiest place in the US, next to a huge lake in the midst of a northern forest. . . . The ferns, toadstools, and moss come spilling down from the mountains to the lake, and the birds (very few of them) sing delicately and distantly about the tangled briar patches. . . . Outside [the cottage], over the totally American-looking portico, with its little columns, is a sign saying "Dew-Kum-Inn," which means, more or less "Venga aquí, por favor." It is truly naive and delightful.[22]

Federico's brief description of the Dew-Kum-Inn (named by the owners long before the Cummings family stayed there) did not do it justice. The cottage sat on the western side of the lake almost twelve feet above the shoreline, providing magnificent views to the east. The surrounding trees and steady breeze off the lake kept it comfortably cool on all but the hottest days. The cottage was painted a dark burgundy, with fascia and windows trimmed in white, bringing the distinctive architecture of the building into sharp relief. A series of flat stone steps led up the hillside to a spacious front porch that provided extra covered living space for the household in almost any weather. Graceful Tuscan columns supported the porch roof, giving the cottage an air of elegance unmatched by any other on the lake.

A few of the plainer wooden cottages nearby dated as far back as the 1890s. They were originally built as boardinghouses for the lumberjacks who descended on Eden Mills every year, when logging was still a profitable enterprise there. At that time, logs were routinely floated from the north end of the lake over the dam to the mills along the river. Trees that were felled when the lake was frozen were simply piled up on the ice, then guided across the lake to the dam after the spring thaw.[23] (Most of the primitive logging and fishing camps once common in northern New England are long gone, but they still survive in spirit. Even today, the word "camp" is used to describe almost any summer home in the region, however lavish it might be.)

The Dew-Kum-Inn itself was constructed around 1905 and was one of the first places on the lake built exclusively as a vacation cottage—a novel concept in Eden at the time. Even in 1929, the idea of spending an extended period away from home during the summer months made no sense to most residents in the agricultural regions of rural Vermont. For them, summer was the time to get as much done as possible around the house, barn, and fields before winter arrived. Philip was well aware of the social and economic differences between the hardworking locals and the transitory summer people who came to the village only during the warmest months.[24] The villagers, he noted in the journal he kept at Lake Eden, were "rather suspicious of us who have the leisure of a month, anyway. Their idea of a vacation is a day's trip on an excursion, or more likely a day's trip to some distant relative."[25]

The larger cottage just south of the Dew-Kum-Inn had a very different history. The original owner was a doctor whose daughter suffered from tuberculosis. He built the cottage—which had screened porches on all three floors—as a summer convalescent home for her, eventually renting rooms to others with the same pernicious disease.[26] At that time, the lower incidence of so-called consumption among people in rural settings was attributed in large part to their frequent exposure to cold fresh air, which was thought to have both preventive and curative effects. The popularity of screened and unscreened sleeping porches in cottages across New England, including those at Lake Eden, was a testament to this widely held belief.[27] The Dew-Kum-Inn itself had two screened sleeping porches.

As he climbed out of the car, Federico must have felt as though he was entering a new, almost magical world. After weeks of inhaling the grime and dust of New York, he may have forgotten that air could be so fresh and clean. The smell was intoxicating, a combination of pines and ferns, warm earth and pure water. After the heat of the city, the unexpected coolness of the breeze must have delighted him.

As Federico unloaded his bags, the other three members of the household emerged from the cottage to welcome the travelers. Philip would have introduced them to Federico one by one: his mother, Addie Cummings; his aunt Carrie Southwick; and Carrie's daughter, Edna Southwick. And Federico would have greeted each woman in turn, bowing deeply as he addressed them in his most respectful Spanish: "Encantado de conocerla [I am delighted to meet you], Señora Cummings, Señora Southwick, Señorita Southwick." They must have been completely charmed.

In all likelihood, the women would have soon moved beyond these formalities and begun peppering Philip with questions about the trip—in English, of course, since none knew any Spanish. Did they have any trouble finding Federico? Were the roads still in good shape after last week's rain? How recently had they eaten? Federico may not have minded being excluded from this conversation, since it gave him an opportunity to study the women more closely. They looked comfortable but old-fashioned in their long white cotton dresses, especially compared to the stylish women he was used to seeing in New York. Cousin Edna, even at age twenty-six, still had the air of a teenager. Though not a conventional beauty, she looked lively and alert. Philip's mother, Addie, and his aunt Carrie were tall and fair-haired and had similar facial features, as might be expected of sisters. At age fifty-nine, Addie was the elder by two years, but while she stood straight and strong, Carrie emanated sorrow. Even when she smiled, her eyes were filled with sadness. Philip had almost certainly told Federico about the unexpected death of Carrie's beloved husband, Frank, some eighteen months earlier, which left her consumed with grief and Edna without a father.[28]

At some point, someone brought out a camera—almost certainly Harry, and almost certainly at Philip's request. Philip was an inveterate maker of scrapbooks and was probably already thinking ahead to the one he would make to commemorate Federico's visit. It may also have crossed his mind that having photos to send to Federico later, after he left Lake Eden, would be an ideal way to stay in touch. Creating a visual record of his friend's first day at the cottage was important for both purposes.

As Harry positioned himself with his back to the lake, the other five posed obligingly. One photo from that session shows the group directly in front of the Dew-Kum-Inn, their eyes squinting in the bright sunlight. Philip stands at the back, with Federico, Edna, Addie, and Carrie lined up in front of him. Federico is seated on a stump, which at first glance makes him appear far shorter than he actually is. In contrast to Philip's casual, short-sleeved T-shirt, Federico is wearing a crisp white shirt and dark tie under his cricket sweater, a more formal look appropriate for a recent traveler.[29]

Another photo shows the same group arranged along the

Figure 12. Family group in front of the rented cottage at Lake Eden. Rear: Philip Cummings; *left to right*: Federico García Lorca, Edna Southwick, Addie Cummings, and Carrie Southwick, August 1929. Archivo Fundación Federico García Lorca, Centro Federico García Lorca, Granada.

lakeshore. The water level is low, revealing a wide, sandy beach. Edna and Addie sit on the prow of a rowboat resting on the beach, while Carrie, Philip, and Federico stand behind them. The distinctive profiles of Mount Norris and the Three Sisters foothills are visible in the distance. Philip rests one hand on Addie's shoulder and the other on Federico's.[30]

A third photo shows Federico and Philip together by the lake. They stand stiffly, each with a hand in his pocket, right beside each other but carefully making no physical contact; perhaps they adopted this pose to avoid any hint of a stronger attachment. In the final photo from the session, Federico stands by himself with his back to the lake, shoulders square to the camera. He later sent a copy to his family with the humorous inscription "Me on the lake, half sportsman and half altar boy" on the back.[31] His obvious enjoyment of the photo suggests that, at least at the time, having a visual record of his Vermont visit was important to Federico too.

In a long letter to his parents from Eden Mills, Federico described the Cummings family as "three very tall people, Puritans, with blond hair, like the people one sees in Tom Mix movies, but very gentle and very affectionate, in a serious distinguished way."[32] Although he would come to know Harry, Addie, Carrie, and Edna much better in the days that followed, he provided no further information about them in his letters except to say that they were treating him very kindly.

The initial photos taken, Philip would have shifted his attention to showing Federico around the cottage. This required ascending the stone steps up the hillside to the spacious front porch and passing through the screen door into the first floor of the cottage proper, which contained the sitting room, dining area, and kitchen. The charms of the place may not have been apparent to Federico at first. To someone accustomed to buildings with thick stucco walls that blocked out the heat, the contrast between the cottage's elegant exterior and its rustic interior must have been startling. The nine-and-a-half-foot ceilings gave the rooms a spacious feel, but there

Figure 13. Family group at Lake Eden. *Rear*: Carrie Southwick, Philip Cummings, and Federico García Lorca; *front*: Edna Southwick and Addie Cummings, August 1929. Archivo Fundación Federico García Lorca, Centro Federico García Lorca, Granada.

Figure 14. Federico García Lorca and Philip Cummings on the shore of Lake Eden, August 1929. Archivo Fundación Federico García Lorca, Centro Federico García Lorca, Granada.

Figure 15. Lorca alone on the shore of Lake Eden, August 1929. Archivo Fundación Federico García Lorca, Centro Federico García Lorca, Granada.

was no plaster or any other finish on the inside walls, which were just the unpainted back sides of the exterior siding. And since the cottage was intended only for summer use, no one had bothered to seal the occasional small gaps between the planks of siding, allowing breezes to pass through freely.[33]

Federico told his parents that the cottage was made of "unpainted wood," a clear reference to the interior walls.[34] He may even have wondered if the building was still under construction. Of course, any New Englander would know that this type of bare-bones architecture was the norm for a summer cottage. Owners seldom spent much money on structures used exclusively for recreation during the few warm months of the year.[35]

One saving grace was the expansive picture window in the sitting room, which measured a full three-and-a-half-feet wide by five-feet high. The window faced due east across the lake, framing an ever-changing tableau of water, hills, and sky. And the room was certainly homey, with upholstered chairs flanked by small tables and shelves for books and knick-knacks. There were no electric lights, since Eden Mills—in fact, most rural areas of Vermont—still had no electrical service in 1929, even though it had been available in more populous parts of the state since the 1890s.[36] Instead, the cottage came equipped with a collection of portable, glass-globed oil lamps, ready to be lit when night fell.[37] For vacationers eager to leave their everyday lives behind for a while, the old-fashioned charm of the lamps must have been particularly appealing.

Federico may have given the kitchen a quick glance as they passed by. In a well-to-do Spanish household, the kitchen would be the domain of the domestic help, but there were clearly no servants in attendance here. This may have been a disappointment to Federico, but it would not have been much of a shock; even in New York, he had observed that the lack of a "serving class" meant that "only very rich Americans have maids."[38]

As was typical for the times, responsibility for the cooking, cleaning, and laundry fell to the women of the household, though the men may have been enlisted to help from time to time. The kitchen contained a cast-iron woodstove for cooking and an icebox for storing food, which would have been familiar appliances to Addie, Carrie, and Edna. There was no indoor plumbing, as was still common in rural areas, but the kitchen had a cast-iron hand pump mounted beside the sink that allowed fresh water to be drawn directly from the lake through a pipe below the cottage.

There were more surprises in store for Federico on the second floor, beginning with a full-size door in the wall at the top of the long staircase. The door opened onto a narrow wooden bridge with handrails that spanned the gap from the back of the house to the steeply sloping hillside behind it, where a wooden outhouse perched on a flat spot carved into the hillside. (Federico was fascinated by the outhouse, which he nicknamed the *rincón de los sacerdotes*, or "priests' corner.")[39] A trip to the outhouse was clearly not for the faint of heart, especially at night. Fortunately, each upstairs bedroom was also outfitted with a chamber pot, so no one was forced to make the perilous journey in the dark.[40]

The second floor also included a wide hallway furnished with dressers and a tall wardrobe for storing clothes, two bedrooms along the back wall, and an upstairs sitting room with a picture window exactly like the one below it, which provided an even better view across the lake. On this floor, the bones of the cottage were even more exposed. The bedrooms had no ceilings, just free-standing walls with empty space above them, providing an unimpeded view straight up to the rafters and the underside of the hip roof. The lack of ceilings certainly made the cottage cheaper to build, but it also meant that there were virtually no barriers to sound or light traveling from room to room. The fact that the bedroom "doors" were just long curtains compounded the effect. The resulting lack of privacy was a typical condition of cottage life, but it was almost certainly not what Federico expected.

He must have been relieved to learn that the two upstairs bedrooms were reserved for Philip's parents and aunt Carrie. Edna and Philip, on the other hand, were each assigned one of the screened sleeping porches located on either side of the upper porch. With every sleeping space already spoken for, it made perfect sense for Federico to bunk with Philip, exactly as Philip must have planned from the outset. The sleeping porches were so small (just seven feet square) that two people would have no choice but to lie right next to each other. Better yet, each porch had a solid wooden door that could be completely closed, effectively isolating the inhabitants from the interior rooms. Perhaps cottage life would be everything Federico had hoped for after all.

PART TWO

Lake Eden Days

CHAPTER FIVE

Paradise Found

We have circled and circled till we have arrived home again, we two,
We have voided all but freedom and all but our own joy.

—Walt Whitman, "We Two, How Long We Were Fool'd"

WITH THEIR SURVEY OF the cottage completed, Philip could at last offer Federico an introductory tour of the lakeshore and village. As Federico followed Philip from one new place to the next, he paid close attention to the unfamiliar sights, sounds, and scents all around him, forming the impressions that would later emerge in his poems. Other than his wonderfully descriptive letters to his family, he had produced almost no new writing during his eight weeks in New York, perhaps because of the sheer mental energy required to adapt to life in a new country, but that would soon change.[1]

Showing Federico the sights was not just a hospitable gesture on Philip's part; it also gave him his first chance to be alone with Federico. The rest of the household would have thought nothing of it; they would have fully expected the young men to head off on their own as soon as opportunity allowed. The two were free to go wherever they wished whenever they wished, as long as they were home in time for dinner.

From the front steps of the Dew-Kum-Inn, Philip and Federico could stroll southward along the narrow lakeshore road and soon be out of both sight and earshot of the family. They had so much to catch up on, but in all likelihood a top priority would have been to agree on a code of conduct when they were around other people. In case Federico had not already absorbed this lesson, Philip probably reminded him that, unlike in Spain, American men never held hands in public, no matter how close their friendship. It might be acceptable to drape an arm around a friend's shoulder from time to time, but the arm should not remain there for long. It would be safest to simply avoid physical contact altogether unless they were absolutely certain they were alone.

As for conversation, though they had the luxury of being able to say whatever they wished to each other in Spanish without being understood by the others, there was always the chance that a family member would ask for a translation on the spot. To forestall this danger, Philip might have asked Federico to avoid using terms of endearment or discussing their more intimate activities when they were around other people. He had good reason to plead for this type of caution. As the only bilingual person in the household, Philip was thus the only translator. If anyone asked him to interpret a word or phrase that was meant to be kept private, it would fall to him to quickly invent a plausible alternative.

As they continued their walk, Philip may have occasionally stopped to point out a few of the places he planned to take Federico in the coming days. Some of the destinations were close by, and others required more time and effort to reach, but Philip had done his homework and knew just what was needed for each expedition. He had clearly used the three weeks prior to Federico's arrival to learn as much as he could about the natural features around Eden Mills and its more interesting human inhabitants. He was determined to keep his friend well entertained during his visit, just as Federico had entertained him in Madrid the previous summer.

From the south end of the lakeshore road, it was an easy walk to Route 100, the main thoroughfare in the village, and the iconic, multipurpose establishment at the center of Eden Mills that was one of Philip's favorite haunts:

> The Post Office, barber shop and general store, and whatever other functions the building may serve, is a white business-dwelling house with a front porch so laden with the et cetera of a country store that were all the rest of the house to blow away it would not budge an inch! It is a country store dubbed as typical and having its share of homespun, cornbread philosophy and the interested gossip which makes all that is social of life in such a community. The Government has its pigeonholes in a corner across from the barber chair and the tall bottles of green liquids. Over and around, yes and under are: thread, onions, lamp globes, iodine, crab meat, gloves, dishes, brooms, spices, cinnamon bark, flour, veterinary medicine, fishhooks, canned peaches, rice, and soap flakes. There seems to be one specimen of every known commodity of the last decade and somewhat previous.[2]

From the general store, Philip and Federico could amble north along Route 100 to the Wayside Inn, a restaurant and gas station on the edge of the lake that offered travelers food and fuel—and even music and dancing in the newly constructed pavilion on weekend evenings. Over the previous three weeks, Philip had become acquainted with John Frank Ruggles (known as Frank), the twenty-year-old son of the Wayside's owners, and the two had become friends.[3] A West Point cadet home on leave for the summer, Frank loved hiking and was always up for an adventure. He was also a handsome, athletic young man with a fine military bearing, none of which was lost on Philip.[4] If Frank happened to be at the Wayside Inn that afternoon, Philip would have jumped at the opportunity to introduce him to Federico. And Frank, as befitted a future senior officer of the US Army, would surely have done his best to make Federico feel welcome despite their lack of a common language.[5]

Figure 16. Eden Mills general store, August 1936. Photo by Carl Mydans, Library of Congress, Prints and Photographs Division, no. LC-USF33-000807-M3. Some damaged elements of the photo have been restored.

Figure 17. The Wayside Inn, owned and managed by Albert and Agnes Ruggles, parents of Frank Ruggles, Eden Mills, Vermont, ca. 1925. Commercial postcard.

Figure 18. John Frank Ruggles, "the Soldier" in Cummings's journal, in his West Point uniform, 1929. Private collection.

Their next stop was a long-neglected farmhouse owned by the Tyler sisters, two remarkable women unlike anyone else in Eden Mills. The Tyler house was over a mile away on North Road, and getting there required hiking up a steep, heavily wooded hillside for much of the way. In a letter to his parents, Federico described what turned out to be one of the most significant encounters of his time in Vermont:

> This morning, after rowing for a while around the lake, we went to visit two ladies who are unimaginably picturesque and amusing. We found them dressed in pants, doing some plastering. They are two intelligent old maids, and in their old age they are doing something truly extraordinary. I don't remember whether I

> mentioned to you that the cruel winters and poor soil have made many of these farmers abandon their farms and move away. Well, here are these two ladies, who bought an old ramshackle wooden house and are fixing it up all by themselves with no help from anyone. They are putting on the roof, raising walls, putting down floors, and finding sensible uses for second-hand furniture. From a millstone they have made a stove, and from the bin where bread was once kneaded they have made a kitchen table, and so on. Eventually they will have a magnificent home.[6]

Thus began Federico's friendship with Elizabeth and Dorothea Tyler, former city dwellers who had only recently taken up country life. The Tyler sisters were elderly by Philip and Federico's standards—Elizabeth was sixty-three, and Dorothea was almost forty-two—but they possessed enormous energy and drive.[7] To Federico, the simple

Figure 19. Home of Elizabeth and Dorothea Tyler, Eden Mills, Vermont, 1929. Archivo Fundación Federico García Lorca, Centro Federico García Lorca, Granada.

fact that two older, unmarried women had chosen to live by themselves in a remote, tumbledown house, doing their own repairs and wearing men's trousers as they worked, was fascinating. "In Spain," he told his parents, "this would be considered madness, and people would make pilgrimages to see these ladies, but there is nothing unusual about them here."[8]

In truth, the sisters were just as mysterious to the other residents of Eden Mills as they were to Federico. The townspeople simply didn't know what to make of two city women with no experience in country living who insisted on trying to revive a decrepit house and farm without even a hired hand to help. The Tylers were a frequent topic of conversation among the men at the general store, where Philip noted that "local comment has the ladies in all stages of insanity." In his journal, he recorded a few of the more pointed remarks he overheard there:

> "What did they want that old place for?"
> "They must be funny, wanting to fix up that old farm!"
> "City folks are always doin' the golramdest things a body ever thought of."
> "Think of two women doin' sech a fool thing! You'd think they'd want comfort instead of workin' all the time around that old place, but they don't seem to do nothin' sensible. The idea of walkin' up to the top of them rocks jest to see the sun set. My sakes, they can't be very busy!"[9]

The local farmers had good reason to question the sisters' sensibility. The Tylers had officially assumed ownership of their abandoned farm with its falling-down house and 17 acres of land in October 1928, then purchased another 140 acres of forested land three months later to expand their "sugar bush," the New England term for a stand of maple trees suitable for harvesting sap. Collecting sap and boiling it down to maple syrup might have been easier than coaxing crops out of the rocky Vermont soil, but it was still a very hard way to make a living. What could have motivated the sisters to leave their city lives behind and take on such a challenging new way of life?

The Tyler sisters were among tens of thousands of people nationwide drawn to the back-to-the-land movement of the early twentieth century. Proponents of this movement were rightfully concerned about the plight of low-level professional and clerical workers in the cities—who could lose their jobs at any moment at the whim of their employers but typically had no savings or other support systems to fall back on. The solution to this problem, according to movement leaders, was for city workers to give up their stressful, precarious lives, buy a cheap house and a few acres of land somewhere in the country, and learn how to grow whatever crops were profitable in that region. There were no guarantees, of course, but if they and their families applied themselves wholeheartedly to the effort, proponents claimed that this new generation of homesteaders could become truly self-sufficient. By keeping a garden and animals for their own food supply while producing cash crops for income, they could secure their financial independence even into old age.[10]

It was an appealing concept to a great many people, including, as it turned out, unmarried working women.[11] The movement's founders had expected the male heads of traditional households to be most inclined to take up country life, envisioning husband, wife, and children working together to make their farm a success. But single women faced an even greater threat of poverty if they suddenly lost their jobs or became too old or sick to continue working. To a close-knit pair like the Tyler sisters, the idea that they might escape this fate and achieve true independence by taking up farming, even in a limited way, would have been hard to resist. They were no longer young, but they still had their strength and intelligence, so why should they not succeed at making a living from the land as well as any man?

In her landmark book on the back-to-the-land movement, historian Dona Brown described a 1904 letter to Edward Payson Powell, a well-known movement authority, from a Philadelphia schoolteacher, who raised some of the same questions and concerns the Tylers must have debated some twenty years later:

> If she could work on her own terms, she wrote—"have a school and carry out my own ideas"—she would enjoy teaching. Because she lacked that autonomy and was required to "carry out other people's feelings and views," she had decided to seek it elsewhere—to go "into the country to make a home for mine own self." What this correspondent wanted was precisely the autonomy and independence usually called "manhood" in the back-to-the-land literature. "Why cannot I keep bees, or raise chickens for broilers, or have a greenhouse, or grow small fruits?" she asked, listing the kinds of farming that seemed most suited to women. She pressed Powell directly: "Can a woman make a living in the country without a man to take care of her?"[12]

The sisters had clearly decided that, for them, the answer was yes. After decades of teaching children in urban private schools, the idea of moving to a home of their own in the country must have been both exhilarating and frightening. When they began contemplating this possibility, the sisters were living and working at a unique, progressive boarding school called the Carson College for Orphan Girls (now Carson Valley School) just outside Philadelphia.[13] As part of their general education, Carson girls (and quite possibly their teachers) learned how to care for animals and grow crops in the school's dairy and vegetable gardens, use weaving looms, and even operate a printing press.[14]

The Tylers had been working at Carson College since September 1921, Dorothea as a primary-level teacher and Elizabeth as a housemother.[15] They created quite a stir by bringing their elderly father, Casper William Tyler, to live with them at the school. Colonel Tyler, a decorated Civil War veteran and former leading citizen of Meadville, Pennsylvania, where the sisters grew up, had been in their care for two years and had nowhere else to go. Under pressure from school administrators, they finally moved him to a nearby nursing home, where he died in October 1922.[16] Were it not for the money they inherited after his death, Elizabeth and Dorothea could have never afforded a farm of their own.

But of all the locations they might have chosen for their new enterprise, how did the sisters pick Eden Mills? The decision arose from an invitation from fellow teacher Amy Proctor Bingham, a Vermont native, to join her on a visit to her brother in Waterbury, Vermont, in July 1927. During their visit, the three women made a side trip to Eden Mills, where they stayed for several days.[17] The sisters clearly fell in love with the place, since they subsequently chose it as the site for their experiment in rural living.

The Tylers' decision to buy a farm in northern Vermont dovetailed perfectly with several newly implemented initiatives intended to help the state stay solvent. From the 1870s onward, alarming numbers of Vermont residents had abandoned their hillside farms and picturesque villages to pursue new opportunities in industry and agriculture in other parts of the country. With both the population and the economy in serious decline, state politicians and planners developed a grand strategy to reinvent Vermont as a summer destination for well-to-do outsiders, especially those who might actually purchase property in the state, not just visit there. With farms and land available at rock-bottom prices, many middle- and upper-class families had the resources to buy an old place and restore it to its former glory or even build their own summer home in the country. State planners distributed scores of books, pamphlets, and ads that promoted Vermont as the ideal place for such a venture—with considerable success.[18]

The rural residents who remained on their farms welcomed the extra income they could earn from their seasonal neighbors, but they were not always pleased with the resulting influx of strangers. They particularly resented those who treated them as quaint curiosities, but in the Tylers' case, the situation was reversed—the sisters were treated as quaint curiosities by the locals, as Philip had discovered on his visits to the general store.

In July 1928, a year after the sisters' first trip to Eden Mills, the local paper reported that the "Misses Elizabeth and Dorothy [*sic*] Tyler of Chicago have purchased and taken possession of the house vacated by George Whittemore . . . to be used for a summer home."[19] After spending the winter away, the Tylers returned to their farm in Eden Mills in June 1929 and were busily engaged in their summer routines when Philip first met them in early August.

The fact that Philip took Federico to meet the sisters almost as soon as his friend arrived suggests that Philip not only understood how special the Tylers were, but also how much they all might enjoy each other's company despite their age differences. And he was right. The sisters and Federico took to each other immediately. It might have seemed strange to some in the village that the sisters were more comfortable socializing with two young men than with local women their own age, but the four actually had a great deal in common. They were all far better educated and more widely traveled than the other inhabitants of Eden Mills and shared a love of classical music, fine art, poetry, and the beauty of the natural world—refinements that few other residents had the time, money, or interest to pursue.

Figure 20. Philip Cummings and Elizabeth Tyler at the abandoned village. Archivo Fundación Federico García Lorca, Centro Federico García Lorca, Granada.

But there was more to their mutual affinity than common cultural interests. The sisters had long ago chosen to live outside the norm for women of their generation and had surely experienced some degree of social isolation and discrimination because of it. This experience would have prepared them to recognize Philip and Federico as fellow travelers: people who, like themselves, did not conform to society's expectations and paid a price for being different. Rather than passing judgment, the sisters welcomed the pair without reservation, and their genuine warmth and interest made a profound impression on both young men. Philip wrote about them with affection in his journal and later said that wherever he and Federico rambled during the day, they almost always ended up at the sisters' house in the late afternoon.[20] Federico's reaction was perhaps more personal; he told his parents, "I can tell you that their house is in the middle of a forest and is difficult to get to, but the peace I felt there is a rare experience."[21] He was particularly struck by the sisters' determination to live exactly as they pleased, regardless of what other people thought—a choice that may have seemed both astoundingly brave and hopelessly out of reach to the young Spaniard.

It is also possible that Elizabeth and Dorothea had long been living a lie and felt some kinship with Philip and Federico in that respect as well. The Tylers always referred to themselves as sisters but, if this were true, it would mean that their mother, Lucy, had given birth to Dorothea when she was forty-five years old, after a fourteen-year break from bearing children. The timing is not impossible, but this pattern of childbearing would have been highly uncommon for a well-educated woman like Lucy Tyler in the late 1800s.[22]

An alternative explanation is that Dorothea was actually Elizabeth's daughter, identified as Elizabeth's sister by the family to avoid the shame and scandal of a child born out of wedlock. Census records show that, in later years, both women routinely gave census-takers false ages that reduced their twenty-one-year age gap. Elizabeth claimed to be as many as fourteen years younger than she actually was, while Dorothea claimed to be six or seven years older than she was. The two women lived together almost continuously from the time Dorothea was born, and neither ever married, when it would have been far more typical for them to marry and lead separate lives. But this is all speculation. In the absence of any definitive proof to the contrary, Elizabeth and Dorothea shall remain sisters in this book.

Despite the somewhat compromised state of their beloved old farmhouse, the Tylers entertained Philip and Federico in grand style, as Federico described to his parents:

> Birds were nesting inside the house, but the two old ladies haven't disturbed them, so that there are ten or twelve under the eaves where the dining room is. "We've made a bird gallery," they said, where the little creatures can rest peacefully. I didn't know whether to laugh or pat them on their fannies. It was strange and very moving. . . . They gave us a truly exquisite Chinese tea with dried jasmine blossoms. And they looked very delicate and very feminine with their silvery hair once they changed into their simple white dresses. We must have had fifteen cups of tea: I lost count. Cummings, the young man who is my friend here, translated my poems for them. They understood them very well and were really touched (something I can always judge). I told them I descended from a very ancient Arabic family, and they showered me with all sorts of courtly attention, which I bore with a certain melancholy and a touch of humor.[23]

The sisters spoke no Spanish, but they, Philip, and Federico all knew enough French to converse fairly easily in that language.[24] Whenever French proved insufficient, Philip could translate from Spanish to English and vice versa, as needed. They also shared music as a common language. The sisters had a piano among their few cherished possessions and played "songs from the heroic age of

Washington" for Federico. He in turn improvised "a few songs just for them at the spinet."[25]

When this first soirée ended, Philip and Federico said good-bye to the sisters and made their way back to the Dew-Kum-Inn. Federico was charmed to see both a US and a Spanish flag on display by the door when they arrived and gratefully thanked his hosts for their consideration. At that hour, the household would often gather on the spacious front porch, which was almost as big as the whole first floor interior. In good weather, the porch served as a natural extension of the indoor living space. It easily accommodated the long outdoor dining table and chairs, a row of comfortable rocking chairs, and a swinging canvas love seat suspended from the porch ceiling—all positioned to take maximum advantage of the view and the breezes off the lake. The porch was almost always a pleasant place to be, at least until sunset when the mosquitoes came out in full force. Happily, the sun didn't set until 7:45 p.m. on the evening of Wednesday, 21 August, so there was plenty of time for a relaxed evening meal.[26]

Since this was Federico's first dinner at the cottage, the women of the household would have laid out the best that they and the season had to offer. Even if typical cottage fare was nothing more elaborate than sandwiches and iced tea, this was a night for pulling out all the stops. The temperature had been a comfortable seventy-two degrees that day, so spending hours cooking over the woodstove would not have been as onerous as it could be in really hot weather. And with so many locally grown fruits and vegetables available to combine with meat, butter, milk, and eggs from nearby farms, it was the perfect time of year to assemble a feast.

Federico had told his parents that the food served in his dining hall at Columbia was very good,[27] but whatever he was used to eating in the city must have paled in comparison to the freshness and bounty of the Dew-Kum-Inn's late summer cuisine. The dinner on that first night might have begun with an appetizer of sliced tomatoes and homemade pickles, followed by a main course of roast chicken served with steaming bowls of green beans, summer squash, and potatoes—all accompanied by warm biscuits and butter. Dessert, the grand finale, would almost certainly have been a fruit pie topped with whipped cream. Blueberries, blackberries, and raspberries grew wild near the cottage and were free for the picking, and peaches, plums, pears, and apples were also easy to obtain. There was water to drink, of course, and perhaps milk, tea, coffee, or fruit punch.[28] Federico later told Ángel del Río that he was disappointed to find no wine or other alcoholic beverages on offer, in contrast to some of the special dinners he had attended in New York.[29] However, this would not have come as a surprise to anyone who knew his hosts. Prohibition was still in effect in America in 1929, and Philip's parents were not inclined to flout the law. Even if the legal constraint against alcohol did not exist, Addie, a devout Congregationalist, would surely have frowned on its consumption.[30]

Philip and Federico would have been on their best behavior during their first evening with the family, but it is unclear whether they were ever in any real danger of being found out. If Harry were still capable of questioning his son's sexual orientation, he might have been on the alert for any hidden undercurrents between the two; however, by that time, he was so compromised by his illness that he would have noticed very little. Addie and Carrie, Philip's mother and aunt, were less worldly than Harry and inherently disinclined to believe that Philip, the pride and joy of the family, could ever do anything that might embarrass or distress them. And since Federico was Philip's close friend, they would have granted him the same latitude and treated him as they would any honored guest. Besides, Federico was obviously foreign, a convenient explanation for anything about his way of speaking or acting that might strike them as odd. Even so, being in such close quarters with the rest of the family for so many days posed a unique challenge. There could be a heavy price to pay if anyone's suspicions were aroused, as both Philip and Federico surely understood.

Addie and Carrie seemed safely unaware of the two men's

relationship, but Edna may have been more skeptical. Edna worked for an insurance agency outside Boston and was still single at the time.[31] Though she was three years older than Philip, several clues suggest that she had developed a romantic crush on her younger cousin. One photo in particular, taken a day or two after Federico's arrival, shows Philip, Edna, and Federico in front of an abandoned building. Philip stands stiffly with his arms by his side, his face expressionless, while a smiling Edna leans back against him in a surprisingly intimate, almost possessive, pose. Federico is on their left, looking less uncomfortable than Philip, but he is definitely not smiling. If Edna was trying to make Federico feel like the odd man out, she may have succeeded—at least at that moment.

Edna's attraction to Philip is understandable; after all, in addition to being tall and handsome, he was well educated, well traveled, and poised to make his mark on the world. She and Philip had been the only two young people at the cottage during the first three weeks of August, so they must have spent considerable time together. Philip may have even taken Edna on trial runs to some of the places he planned to take Federico. But once Federico arrived, Philip would have turned his full attention toward his friend, abandoning Edna to her own devices. Even if she didn't fully understand the men's attraction to each other, it would be only natural for her to view Federico as an unwanted interloper who had ended her happy idyll with Philip.

Edna's resentment seems to have persisted long after she married and had a family. Forty-five years later, when scholar Daniel Eisenberg contacted her to ask about her time with Philip and Federico at Lake Eden, she initially denied having been there at all. But after Eisenberg showed her photos of the three of them together by the lake, Edna crisply replied that she could not help him in any way and ended all further communication.[32] Considering these later actions, it is probably safe to assume that Edna kept a watchful eye on Federico during his first dinner with the family as she tried to gauge the strength of his hold on Philip.

After dinner, Federico wrote a long, exuberant letter to his parents, telling them all about his trip to Eden Mills and everything that had happened since he first arrived—or almost everything. In addition to sharing his adventures and impressions, he clearly wanted to reassure them that their beloved son was in a safe place surrounded by trustworthy people and completely content.[33]

By then, Federico must have been exhausted. He and Philip would have bid everyone good night as soon as circumstances allowed and retired to their private sleeping porch, free at last to embrace as long as they wanted. It may not have struck them until that very moment that Philip's plan had actually succeeded. It had cost him considerable time, effort, and money to arrange, but he had found a way for them to be left alone for hours on end to pursue their sexual relationship in relative safety.

The sleeping porch was just large enough to hold one double bed or two narrow cots. It is unclear which arrangement was in place that summer, but Philip told Kessel Schwartz, the first scholar who interviewed him in later years, that he and Federico had been bedmates.[34] In either case, though they were hidden from view by the door and the darkness, they still needed to be careful. In the deep quiet of the evening, virtually anything they said or did might be heard not only by others in their own cottage, but by those in neighboring cottages as well. They were apparently cautious enough, since everyday life continued undisturbed.

It had been a long day for Federico and far more physically demanding than his usual city pursuits. The unaccustomed exertion would have helped him sleep soundly that night and may have also begun to prepare him for the even more strenuous excursions Philip had in mind for the coming days. New York City, Federico told his parents, seemed "infinitely remote," but after such a pleasant afternoon and evening, that must have felt exactly right.[35]

The sun rose at 6:12 a.m. on Thursday, 22 August—Federico's first full day at the cottage. The air was a crisp forty-three degrees that morning, but Federico and Philip would have been warm and snug under a generous pile of quilts.[36] Though their beds faced due east, the sleepers were shielded from the morning sun by the trees surrounding the cottage, allowing them to greet the day gradually. As Philip explained: "We have also learned the art of lying half-awake in bed and enjoying the morning. The sleeping porch opens onto the fresh bosom of a woodland. It touches the house with the soft boughs of the spruces. That reverie which is popularly reserved for the twilight we get as the natural course of our first view into the pure perspective of the morning. Every moment seems a cornucopia of possibility!"[37]

In addition to the sheer pleasure of waking up beside each other, the morning had other delights in store. The lake itself was out of sight from the bed, but they could see the open sky above it and the tops of the hills on the other side. Below the hills a shroud of fog drifted over the lake, as it did every cool morning, adding a dreamlike softness to the air. (According to Philip, Federico loved the fog, especially the idea that everything beneath it was hidden yet still there.)[38] If they listened closely, there was music all around: water gurgling in the sluice gate up the road, waves lapping quietly on the shore, leaves rustling in the breeze. There were animal voices as well: birds singing, frogs croaking, and the low hum of insects. After eight weeks in the ceaseless noise of the city, Federico must have been delighted to hear the natural world again. Most of what he heard would have been comfortably familiar, but the haunting calls of the loons were new to him. He was fascinated by the plaintive, almost otherworldly sound of their cries echoing across the lake, and the memory stayed with him for years.[39]

Despite these wonderful distractions, they eventually dressed and headed downstairs for breakfast. The morning meal might feature bacon and eggs, or perhaps blueberry pancakes and maple syrup. If they were really lucky, Addie would have made the fried doughnuts that quickly became Federico's favorite treat. In the days that followed, whenever he detected that Philip's mother had started another batch, Federico would perch on a wooden stool beside the stove, watching her work and chattering away in Spanish while he waited for a sample. Although Addie could not understand a word he said, the two developed a great fondness for each other in the warm companionship of the kitchen.[40]

With a hearty breakfast under their belts, Philip and Federico were finally ready to begin the day in earnest.

CHAPTER SIX

Two Translations

And I swear I will never translate myself at all,
only to him or her who privately stays with me in the open air.

—Walt Whitman, "Song of Myself"

BY EITHER CHANCE OR shared inclination, Philip and Federico had both come to the cottage with a specific literary project in mind that required the other's participation: They had each brought along a book of poems that was not yet available in the other's language but that they believed was supremely worthy of translation. As they began telling each other about their respective goals and how they might achieve them together, they had no way of knowing how profoundly both projects would affect Federico's sense of himself and his place in the world.

The first translation project, conceived by Philip, was private, intended for just the two of them to share. Philip would have known from his long talks with Federico in Madrid the previous summer that his friend was largely unfamiliar with American poets and poetry, not least because so little of their work had been translated into Spanish. Eager to remedy that situation, Philip must have packed his reading material for the month at Lake Eden accordingly, making sure to leave room for a certain volume that was especially dear to his heart.

The work in question was *Leaves of Grass*, the magnum opus of American poet Walt Whitman. Of all the editions in print at the time, it is most likely that Philip had the popular Modern Library edition (1921) in his personal collection. The Modern Library series was created to give a wider range of American readers the opportunity to own attractive, hardbound copies of select American and European classics. To this end, the publisher kept its books inexpensive and made them widely available to the public in department stores as well as traditional bookshops.[1]

Philip would have had several reasons to find the Modern Library edition of *Leaves of Grass* particularly appealing. For one thing, it cost only ninety-five cents, a price well suited to a student budget. Second, it included an introduction by Carl Sandburg, another of Philip's favorite poets.[2] As a final point in its favor, the book was designed to be portable; at only 6 1/2 inches tall by 4 3/8 inches wide by 5/8 of an inch thick, it was small enough to slip easily into a pocket or knapsack. Unfortunately, to achieve this compact size, the book's editors left out the last 192 of the 383 poems in Whitman's 1881 edition of *Leaves of Grass* and crammed the remaining 191 poems onto 311 printed pages. The small font size required to accomplish this feat may have challenged older eyes but would have been no obstacle to younger ones.

Philip's role in the project was threefold: He would select a set of poems from the book, translate part or all of each poem into Spanish, and explain its meaning to his friend. Federico's part was much easier, at least on the surface. All he had to do was listen attentively as Philip spoke and ask questions if anything was unclear. In all likelihood, Philip had already decided to begin with the section (or "cluster," to use Whitman's term) of the book titled "Calamus." But why choose Whitman in the first place, and why those particular poems?

Walt Whitman died in Camden, New Jersey, in 1892, at the age of seventy-two, and by the end of the 1890s he had become an icon to gay men across the English-speaking world for his unabashed celebration of romantic and physical love between men in *Leaves of*

Grass. The homoerotic aspect of Whitman's poetry was virtually ignored by scholars and critics for decades, but it was unmistakable to men who shared his attraction to men.[3] In fact, in that era, anything to do with Whitman—photographs of the poet, gifts of his books, specimens of his handwriting, or even admiring references to him—could serve as a secret signal, a "badge of homosexual recognition" between like-minded strangers.[4]

In *Leaves of Grass*, Whitman grouped his most explicit poems of praise for both male and female bodies and the pleasures of sexual congress into a cluster he titled "Children of Adam." The opening lines of the cluster's second poem, "From Pent-Up Aching Rivers," get straight to the point:

> From pent-up aching rivers,
> From that of myself without which I were nothing,
> From what I am determin'd to make illustrious, even if I stand sole
> among men,
> From my own voice resonant, singing the phallus,
> Singing the song of procreation,
> Singing the need of superb children and therein superb grown people,
> Singing the muscular urge and the blending,
> Singing the bedfellow's song, (O resistless yearning!
> O for any and each the body correlative attracting!
> O for you whoever you are your correlative body! O it more than all
> else, you delighting!)[5]

Whitman clearly expressed his delight in the male physique throughout the "Children of Adam" poems, but he gave almost equal time to the female form and was also effusive in his accolades for heterosexual union. However, he chose to separate his poems about the deeper emotional lives of lovers—more specifically, of men in same-sex relationships—into a different cluster, the one he called "Calamus," which comes immediately after "Children of Adam."

Whitman named the "Calamus" section after a common aquatic reed (*Acorus calamus*, or sweet flag), which has an unmistakably phallic central flower stalk. However, it is likely that the mythical origins of the plant's name meant as much to him as its physical structure. The Greek word *kalamos*, meaning "reed" or "stalk," comes from the name of a tragic figure in Greek mythology. Young Kalamos loved another youth so much that when his beloved drowned during a swimming race, Kalamos allowed himself to drown as well. Upon his death, the gods turned Kalamos into a water reed and deemed that, forever after, the sound of the wind in the reeds at the water's edge would echo his endless sighs of grief.[6]

In the fifth poem of the "Calamus" cluster, "These I Singing in Spring," Whitman explains the special role he assigned to the plant: "O here I last saw him that tenderly loves me, and returns again never to separate from me, / And this, O this shall henceforth be the token of comrades, this calamus-root shall, / Interchange it, youths, with each other! Let none render it back!" And in case a reader might think that the exchange of calamus roots was meant to express mere friendship between men, the last line of the poem clarifies the speaker's intent: "I will give of it, but only to them that love as I myself am capable of loving."[7]

In keeping with this theme, many of the thirty-nine poems in the "Calamus" cluster describe the emotional highs and lows of a man who is deeply in love with another man. Whether the speaker's overtures to his beloved are joyfully returned or casually rejected, it seems clear that these were not abstract concepts for Whitman but rather defining elements of his own life. And rather than concealing or disguising his true feelings, in these poems he chose to be honest with his readers, present and future:

> Recorders ages hence,
> Come, I will take you down underneath this impassive exterior, I
>   will tell you what to say of me,
> Publish my name and hang up my picture as that of the tenderest lover,

The friend the lover's portrait, of whom his friend his lover was fondest,
Who was not proud of his songs, but of the measureless ocean of
love within him, and freely pour'd it forth,
Who often walk'd lonesome walks thinking of his dear friends, his
lovers,
Who pensive away from one he lov'd often lay sleepless and dissat-
isfied at night,
Who knew too well the sick, sick dread lest the one he lov'd might
secretly be indifferent to him,
Whose happiest days were far away through fields, in woods, on
hills, he and another wandering hand in hand, they twain apart
from other men,
Who oft as he saunter'd the streets curv'd with his arm the shoulder
of his friend, while the arm of his friend rested upon him also.[8]

For many men struggling to understand and accept their homosexuality, Whitman's straightforward descriptions of his emotions and desires validated their own experiences and made him a cherished role model. He served as a source of comfort, hope, and affirmation in their lives, as well as an imagined, accepting father figure. The diary entries below, for example, written in the 1920s by a young gay man living in Washington, DC, illustrate the importance of both Whitman and the "Calamus" poems in his life:

July 5, 1923: I walked home rather happily and settled into my leather-seated rocker and read in "Calamus"—the heart of *Leaves of Grass*. What a noble, lovable man old Walt was! And he was a government clerk too, like myself. Often, I yearn toward Walt as toward a father, look up at his picture, then close my eyes and feel him beside me, rugged and strong with his gentle hands caressing and comforting me.

December 9, 1929: Walked home deeply wretched. Got out my Whitman and read all of "Calamus." It seems that all my strength and vitality have gone toward loving Dash.

> August 25, 1930: Tonight is the anniversary of the first sexual experience I ever had—with Randall, ten years ago. It was then that I thought I had finally joined forever with a loving friend and companion. I still cherish the memory of that beautiful moonlit night. No matter what happened afterward, "that night I was happy."[9]

The quoted phrase in the last entry is from the "Calamus" poem "When I Heard at the Close of the Day," which had particular resonance for many gay men. In it, Whitman describes the elation he felt at his lover's return after a long absence, leaving no doubt about the gender of his beloved. The last two lines read in full: "In the stillness in the autumn moonbeams his face was inclined toward me, / And his arm lay lightly around my breast—and that night I was happy."[10]

From what we know of Philip, it is not surprising that he, too, revered Whitman and his work. Perhaps as a signal to future readers, he included high praise for the poet in the very first entry of the journal he kept during Federico's visit:

> The lake was rough-shod this afternoon and the gusts of wind swept in on us, lying beside a big log, and trying to understand the infinite beauty of Whitman. Where better could we enter into a familiar companionship with this great Interpreter than in the outdoors of a mountain landscape? The storm clouds and the wind movement gave a scenic background, making a living vitaphone of the words of our great Walt. We are all so prone to discuss the work of the day, the sunset, the storm—everything which has particularly moved us, in the terms: "If I could only put that on paper!" Whitman has put it all down for all of us. He has grasped a whole humanity and made significant gestures at those forbidden subjects which we usually cast aside as "quite beyond us"—a sort of mental shrugging of the shoulders on our part. Nothing seems to have been beyond the pen of Walt

> Whitman, though he may only have touched some subjects in a curious reverent mood.[11]

It seems clear from Philip's entry that he had brought a copy of *Leaves of Grass* with him to Eden to share with Federico. It also suggests that his translations began with the poems that directly addressed the "forbidden subjects" of greatest interest to them both, including love and longing between male comrades. (The 1921 Modern Library edition of the book preserved the full "Children of Adam" and "Calamus" clusters exactly as printed in Whitman's 1881 edition.) And for his very first poem to translate, Philip may well have chosen this one, tailor-made for Federico:

> This moment yearning and thoughtful sitting alone,
> It seems to me there are other men in other lands yearning and
> thoughtful,
> It seems to me I can look over and behold them in Germany, Italy,
> France, Spain,
> Or far, far away, in China, or in Russia or Japan, talking other dia-
> lects,
> And it seems to me if I could know those men I should become
> attached to them as I do to men in my own lands,
> O I know we should be brethren and lovers,
> I know I should be happy with them.[12]

Whitman's poetry was almost unknown in Spain at that time, so it is unlikely that Federico was already familiar with *Leaves of Grass*. Only 85 of the poems in the 1881 edition had been published in Spanish, including just two from the "Children of Adam" cluster and seven from the "Calamus" cluster.[13] Even if Federico had seen a few of those translations, Philip would almost certainly have wanted to share all the poems in which Whitman described his physical and romantic attraction to men.[14]

We can imagine the pair seated side by side in a secluded clearing somewhere in the woods near the lake, their backs against a fallen tree, the book of poems open before them. Philip may have translated a few of Whitman's poems in advance and brought the translations with him, or he may have worked his way through the chosen poems on the spot. How amazed Federico must have been to learn that one of America's most revered poets had written so openly and candidly about his same-sex relationships and not been shamed or shunned or imprisoned because of it.

But Whitman's words would have meant more to Federico than just the prospect of poetic honesty. Despite his ever-cheerful demeanor, he was still dealing with the private despair that followed his rejection by Emilio Aladrén the previous summer. The loss of that particular dream was hard enough, but as time passed he had begun to fear that he would never experience a deep, committed relationship with any man, let alone have that relationship accepted by society. Whitman, on the other hand, seemed to offer a different way forward. In Whitman's world, emotional attachments between men were both real and respected, and male couples had as much right as anyone to long-term happiness.

At first Federico may have found it hard to imagine a world in which everyone was free to live and love as they chose, but the Tyler sisters gave him proof that it was possible. The sisters' insistence on making their own choices and their calm acceptance of being different seemed to affect him deeply. He had not expected to find kindred spirits, let alone role models, in such an unlikely setting. As he wrote to his parents after their first meeting, "The afternoon I spent with these ladies was really wonderful. It taught me of the dream of life and reminded me how differences in character disappear thanks to identical things that lie below the surface."[15] Whitman would have surely agreed.

As he struggled to reconcile Whitman's message of acceptance with his own fears of exposure and scandal, Federico may have begun to question his long-held assumptions about what might be possible in his own life and work. But these new thoughts came at a price. Along with a glimpse of greater freedom, they brought all his suppressed pain and anguish to the surface. Unwilling or unable to share his distress with Philip, Federico poured out his feelings in his poetry (see chapter 8).

But why might he have hesitated to share these thoughts with Philip? It is possible that in the course of their discussions about Whitman, Federico began to suspect that he and Philip were on very different paths. Whitman's message that committed relationships between men were both legitimate and attainable would have given Federico new hope that he, too, would find the life partner he was seeking. Philip, on the other hand, seemed satisfied simply by Whitman's willingness to say out loud what had long been kept silent—that some men were sexually and romantically attracted to other men. The disparity in their expectations and aspirations would become ever more evident in the days to come.

The second translation project was initiated by Federico, who had finally realized that he was unlikely to ever gain an American audience for his work if it was available only in Spanish. He had given little thought to the whole issue of translation before coming to New York, but once there, he could no longer ignore it. After achieving so much fame and recognition in Spain for *Gypsy Ballads*, it must have come as a shock to discover that only a handful of people in all of New York City had ever heard of him or his poems. As Federico's friend and biographer Mildred Adams recalled: "Several times that year Federico, who had no skill in any tongue but his own, showed an insistent desire to have his work put into English. To a man as gregarious and vocal as he was, the frustration of being surrounded by people who could neither understand nor respond to his poems . . . was repeated torture."[16]

Federico felt sure that Americans would love his poems if only they could read them and was determined to make that possible. There were at least two ways to address the problem: He could find someone to translate his previously published works into English or could compose new poems of particular interest to American readers with future translation in mind.[17] The trip to Lake Eden gave him an opportunity to do both.

For translating his published poems into English, Federico apparently considered Philip his best option. From their previous time together, he knew that Philip had a decent command of Spanish, loved Federico's poetry, and was always happy to talk about Federico's previous work or listen to something new. Philip was also well aware of Federico's literary reputation in Spain, so he would not take the assignment lightly. Perhaps most importantly, Philip was a poet himself, with his own recently published book of poems.[18] He would surely have the sensitivity to language, sound, and rhythm that would be necessary to bring Federico's poems to life in English. Philip also happened to be the only American poet Federico knew, which must have simplified his decision.

Philip's Rollins College transcript shows that he took several advanced Spanish classes in the fall and winter of 1928–1929, which aligns with Federico's note to his parents that Philip had translated two poems from *Gypsy Ballads* for one of his classes. Of course, the transcript provides no details about specific assignments, but evidence suggests that those same two translations were later published in the August 1929 issue of the New York literary journal *Alhambra* as an adjunct to a feature article about visiting Spanish poet Federico García Lorca.[19] The article did not identify the translator of the poems but, based on an in-depth textual analysis of the work, scholar Andrew Samuel Walsh concluded that it was almost certainly Philip.[20] If true, this would make Philip Cummings the first person to have their English translations of Lorca's poems published anywhere in the world.

But how did Philip's translations end up in *Alhambra*? It is quite possible that Philip sent Federico copies of his translations for the poet's interest or amusement while he was still at Rollins College and that Federico later brought them to the United States. In New York, Federico could have shown them to *Alhambra* editor Ángel Flores, who could have decided that they were good enough to include with his planned article about Federico. Federico and Flores had several friends in common in the city's Hispanic community and were in the same place at the same time on at least one occasion before the August 1929 issue of *Alhambra* was published, so there is a clear possible line of transmission supporting Walsh's conclusion.[21]

Walsh determined the translator's identity based in large part on the clumsy, amateurish nature of the translations, as well as their many outright errors and oddly archaic use of English. He concluded that the translations were a "disservice" to Federico because they gave the English-speaking world such a flawed introduction to his work. But it is unfair to fault Philip for this perceived transgression. If the published translations were indeed the ones he had done for his Spanish class, there is no indication that Federico ever asked his permission to share them with Ángel Flores or even told him about their publication. Philip was a college student, not a professional translator. Any damage, perceived or otherwise, to Federico's poetic reputation must lie with Flores, an experienced translator who must have recognized the problems with Philip's renditions but decided to publish them anyway.

With no way to assess the quality of Philip's translations himself, Federico had no qualms about asking him to take on more—but he had a different set of poems in mind. When Federico first broached the topic of translation, Philip suggested they begin with *Gypsy Ballads*.[22] Federico asked if they could instead tackle his earlier work, *Canciones, 1921–1924*.[23] This collection of eighty-nine short, relatively simple poems must have seemed like a reasonable target for the amount of time they would have together.

However, the simple act of obtaining a copy of the book to take to Vermont had proven far more difficult than Federico had imagined. The first edition, published in 1927, was long out of print, and in an unfortunate case of bad timing, the second edition did not arrive at bookstores in Madrid until after Federico had already left for the United States.[24] In the letters he wrote to his family from New York in the weeks leading up to his trip to Vermont, Federico repeatedly urged his brother Francisco, known as Paco, to buy multiple copies of the book and ship them to him as quickly as possible. As late as the second week of August, they had still not arrived: "Today I received Mother's letter, so I know Paco is back at the Huerta. Why doesn't he write me? I wrote him a long letter, and haven't gotten a reply. I asked him to send me books. I still haven't seen my 'Songs' and to me that doesn't seem right. Of course I haven't written to the Revista [de Occidente, publisher of the second edition], for I thought Paco would send it."[25]

Paco must have ultimately purchased and sent the books, because Federico arrived at Lake Eden with a copy in his suitcase. At the end of his visit, he gave the book to Philip as a memento with the inscription: "A mi querido amigo Felipe Cummings. Recuerdo cariñoso de la estancia en una cabaña de Vermont. Federico García Lorca" (To my dear friend Philip Cummings. A fond remembrance of the stay at a cabin in Vermont).[26]

The two worked on the project every day and managed to translate all eighty-nine poems by the end of Federico's visit. But as the days progressed, Federico seemed to develop mixed feelings about the project. In a letter to Ángel del Río, he described the effort in a detached, offhand way, as though he had nothing to do with it: "My young friend Cummings translates my songs and gazes at me with the tenderness of a wounded cow."[27] Philip, however, had only happy memories of their collaboration, as he expressed in a 1974 letter to Daniel Eisenberg: "To my mind the best product of those days, besides my several picture records of Federico García Lorca and my personal memories, is the translation of *Canciones* [Songs] which I pecked out on my father's old Oliver typewriter on the porch of our camp at Eden Lake. . . . We read all those poems and argued as to their meanings which I gained very well. He could get the nuances of my translation even if he didn't get the exact words."[28]

Two photographs in the archives of the Fundación Federico García Lorca depict the very scene that Philip described to Eisenberg. In the first, Philip and Federico are seated on the front porch

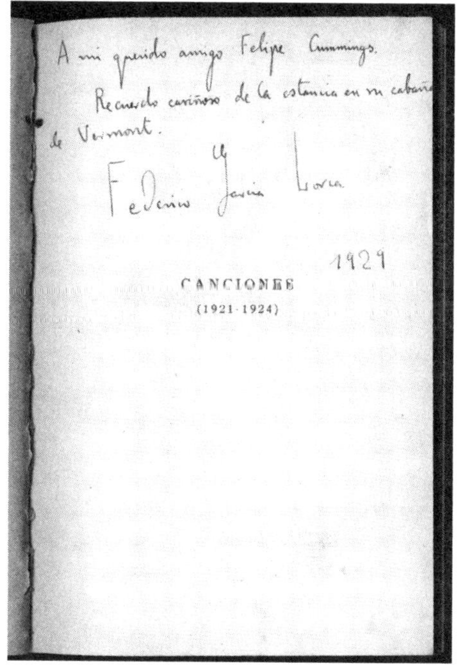
A mi querido amigo Felipe Cummings.
Recuerdo cariñoso de la estancia en su cabaña
de Vermont.
Federico García Lorca
1929
CANCIONES
(1921-1924)

Figure 21. Lorca's inscription on the copy of *Canciones (1921–1924)* he gave to Cummings, whom he called "Felipe," in 1929. Manuscripts and Rare Books, Hispanic Society of America, New York.

of the cottage, bathed in morning sunlight. Lorca is perched on the wide porch railing facing Philip, while Philip sits in a rocking chair, his fingers on the keyboard of a typewriter balanced on the same railing, a stack of paper visible to the left of the typewriter. The two are deeply involved in their work, unaware of the person standing at the other end of the porch holding a camera. In the second photo (not reproduced here), it is clear that Philip and Federico were startled by the click of the shutter, as both have turned their heads to look at the photographer. These two photos are the only known candid shots of Philip and Federico at Lake Eden and the only depictions of the two at work together on the *Songs* translation project.[29]

Though Federico and Philip both enjoyed discussing "words and their visible and invisible meanings" at great length, the actual translation of each poem was a difficult and painstaking process: "a

Figure 22. Cummings and Lorca at work on their *Canciones* translation project on the front porch of the Lake Eden cottage, August 1929. Cummings's typewriter is balanced on the railing. Archivo Fundación Federico García Lorca, Centro Federico García Lorca, Granada.

mental wrestling match," in Philip's words.[30] Adding to the challenge was Federico's unique approach to his native Spanish, in which, as Philip explained, "he coins new words when he chooses, he uses words not in the popular vocabulary, and his images are his own."[31]

Philip was not alone in finding Federico's use of language both dazzling and confusing. The poet Edouard Roditi, recalling an encounter with Federico in Paris in June 1929, reported, "Federico's speech, in particular, puzzled me. He expressed himself with such a rich vocabulary and such a wealth of imagery and idiom that I was often left struggling to follow him."[32]

Considering the mismatch between Federico's highly sophisticated knowledge of Spanish and Philip's much more limited understanding, the fact that together they were able to complete a credible translation of all the poems in *Songs* in little more than a week is truly remarkable. But Philip had an advantage not shared by any other translator of Lorca's works: the opportunity to ask, line by line, what exactly the poet meant to say—and receive an answer directly from the source. It was clearly an imperfect process—Philip later noted that Federico often relied on the sound and rhythm of each phrase rather than its precise meaning—and yet, somehow, it worked.[33]

When Philip's translation of *Songs* was finally published in 1976, the initial reviews were decidedly mixed. Some critics pointed out the many errors in the translations but praised the book's unique contribution as a work in which Federico himself had collaborated.[34] Others made some allowance for Philip's youth and inexperience as a translator but were scathing in their overall assessment of the work.[35] In any case, few copies of the book were sold, and it soon went out of print.

More recent scholars who have examined Philip's translations take a broader view. For example, Jonathan Mayhew commented:

> Aside from the purely historic interest of these translations, I find Cummings's translations of the Canciones to be a mixed bag. Some of them are actually very good. I could go on the hunt for mistranslations or for places where I would have made different choices, but Cummings does not do as badly as many others well known for their work on Lorca, like [Stephen] Spender, [Ben] Belitt, or [Rolfe] Humphries. . . . [One can] conclude that particular poems are felicitously translated, and that the translation as a whole has both historical and aesthetic value for a 21st-century reader.[36]

D. Gareth Walters noted the same mistranslations, rhyming problems, and archaic language that bothered earlier critics, but added: "On the whole [Cummings] has a good ear for rhythm, certainly no worse than some acclaimed translators of Lorca. . . . In all fairness, there were some signal successes."[37]

Walters particularly liked Philip's translations of the seven poems in the section of *Songs* called "Songs for Children," especially

"Canción Cantada" (A Chanted Song). Philip's translation appears below beside the Spanish original:

En el gris,
el pájaro Grifón
se vestía de gris.
Y la niña Kikirikí
perdía su blancor
y forma allí.

Para entrar en el gris
me pinté de gris.
¡Y cómo relumbraba
en el gris!

In the gloaming
The Griffon bird
Clothes itself in grey.
And the little girl Kikirikí
Has lost her paleness
Has lost her form, there.

To enter into the gloaming
I painted myself with gloamy gre
And how I, myself have shone
In the gloom.[38]

It is noteworthy that at two points in the poem, Philip translated the color name *gris* as "gloaming," a poetic term for dusk or evening, rather than the literal "grey" used by other translators, including A. S. Trueblood and Walters himself.[39] Why did Philip forgo the literal translation and instead replace *gris* with "gloaming"—a more evocative and specific word associated with day's end—in those two places?

Philip may have been imposing his own stylistic preferences on the wording, but this is unlikely since he held Federico's poetic skills in such high regard. It seems more probable that the decision to use "gloaming" resulted from Philip's direct discussions with Federico as they searched for the optimal English equivalent for each Spanish word or phrase. Daniel Eisenberg observed many signs of their deliberations in the handwritten edits on Philip's original typescript.[40] But even without this direct evidence, Jonathan Mayhew noted, "I have a sense that their communication was close, and that Lorca might have clarified certain details of his poems to Philip in cases where the Spanish could have different meanings."[41] In this particular case, the choice of "gloaming" may reflect Federico's unobvious but intended meaning for *gris*, revealed only through his dialogue with Philip. If so, this is one example of the potential value of Philip's 1929 translations to today's Lorca scholars.

Revisiting the generally lighthearted poems in his *Songs*, written so many years earlier, appears to have had an unexpected but profound effect on Federico. The intense focus on the poems required for the translation project seems to have triggered in him a deep sadness, a yearning to return to a simpler, more carefree time when he was a happier person, a time when he did not yet know that falling in love, especially with another man, could be the source of so much pain. Much like the complex emotions Federico must have experienced on hearing Whitman's poetry for the first time, the feelings of loss and regret evoked by working with Philip on the translation of *Songs* may have had considerable impact on the tone and content of the poems he wrote in Vermont and in the Catskills soon after.

CHAPTER SEVEN

The Story in the Journal

Up and down the roads going, North and South excursions making.

—Walt Whitman, "We Two Boys Together Clinging"

AS THE WEEK PROGRESSED, Philip and Federico settled into a regular daily routine. They set aside part of each morning for solitary endeavors—Philip wrote new entries for his journal while Federico worked on his poems—with the remainder of the time reserved for their ongoing *Songs* translation project. In the evenings, they typically stayed at the cottage with Philip's family, writing letters or reading by the light of the oil lamps, until it was time to say good night and retreat to the privacy of their sleeping porch.

Afternoons, on the other hand, were for exploration and adventure. Most days, Philip and Federico were on their own, free to go wherever they liked as long as they could walk there. They would typically hike to some local point of interest and then, if time allowed, stop for tea and conversation with the Tyler sisters before heading home for dinner. But if Harry happened to be at the cottage with his car, as was the case on at least two different days, Philip would enlist his father to drive them to more distant locations.

In either case, since everything was new to Federico, it was up to Philip to choose their itinerary. The three weeks before Federico arrived at Lake Eden had given Philip ample time to explore the area and decide which spots he most wanted to share with his friend. Given his penchant for planning, Philip probably also worked out in advance exactly where they would go on each particular day. Of course, he could not control the weather, but fortunately it stayed dry and clear at the cottage throughout Federico's visit except for one rainy Saturday.[1]

It must have been challenging for Philip to choose a slate of activities that would keep his friend entertained throughout his stay. After all, Federico was coming directly from New York City, with its endless variety of shops, shows, restaurants, museums, and other amusements. There was no way for Eden Mills to compete in that sphere, so Philip chose instead to focus on the very different charms of northern Vermont: a scenic mix of small farms and villages nestled against the foothills and peaks of the Green Mountains, with forests stretching off in all directions.

Though it makes perfect sense from a modern perspective that Philip would choose to introduce Federico to the natural beauty of the region by taking him on a series of hikes, this was a relatively new concept at the time. For the permanent residents of Eden Mills, walking was simply part of the day's work, necessary for getting from here to there in the village or on the farm; any pastime that expended time and energy with nothing to show for it was viewed with suspicion. But starting in the 1890s, the idea of voluntarily taking a long walk in a natural setting for the pure pleasure of the experience had taken hold among those with the time and resources to afford it. And soon there was more than pleasure at stake: As the country continued its steady march toward a more urban, industrialized economy, civic leaders became increasingly concerned that male Americans were in danger of losing their masculinity in the process. To counteract this perceived threat, men and boys were encouraged to take up strenuous outdoor activities like hiking, backpacking, and camping. For the many who followed this guidance, the wilderness became not only a source of natural beauty, but also a proving ground for testing their strength, ingenuity, and fortitude.[2]

Vermont took longer than its mountainous neighbors, New York and New Hampshire, to embrace this growing trend, but the state had made great progress by the time Philip and Federico embarked on their rambles. Among other accomplishments, the volunteer members of the Green Mountain Club managed to complete the Long Trail, a continuous 262 mile hiking route that traverses the entire north-south length of the state, by 1930—the culmination of an arduous twenty-year effort to make the peaks and valleys of the Green Mountains accessible to the people of Vermont and to visitors as well.

The Long Trail was the first long-distance recreational footpath in the United States; work on its initial sections started a full ten years before the Appalachian Trail was begun. (The two trails now share 100 miles in common within Vermont.) But such a trail has little impact if hikers are unable to reach it in the first place. Fortunately, between 1910 and 1930, Vermont substantially upgraded its highway system, making the trailheads much easier to access. In addition, during that same period, large expanses of the state that were once stripped bare of trees by farmers and loggers had grown back into forest, a result of the exodus of so many Vermonters to more accommodating lands farther west in the late 1800s. This change increased both the beauty and the perceived wildness of the whole region, making it more attractive to serious hikers—though once those hikers actually entered the forest, they were very likely to come across abandoned farms and clear-cuts along the way.[3]

Whether or not a given footpath was officially part of the Long Trail, all the hiking trails located anywhere near it benefited from the same factors that made it so popular. Fortunately for Philip and Federico, the Long Trail passed right through the less populated northwest corner of Eden Mills. They took full advantage of this proximity, following an offshoot of the Long Trail on one afternoon, and hiking an actual segment of it on another.

Philip recorded detailed entries about these expeditions in a typewritten journal.[4] His journal, along with four pieces of correspondence Federico wrote in Vermont and a small number of photos taken at Lake Eden, stand as the only known contemporaneous records of Federico's visit to Vermont. The journal thus played a central role in piecing together how Philip and Federico spent their time together, but doing so was not always a straightforward process. For example, Philip did not include any dates with his thirty-one entries, but at least the order of the entries is clear. He titled each account with a roman numeral, from I to XXXI. When he was ready to start a new one, he would return to the same page where his previous entry ended, add the next roman numeral in the sequence, and continue from there—almost certainly to conserve typing paper.

In the absence of any dates on the individual entries, my first task was to map the events described in the journal to the August 1929 calendar. Since there are thirty-one days in the month of August, I initially assumed that the journal functioned like a diary, with one entry for each day of the month. However, it quickly became clear that the entry numbers for the few datable events in the journal did not match the calendar dates. I also had to account for Philip's assertion to Daniel Eisenberg that he had written all thirty-one entries during the days Federico was with him at the cottage.[5] When I viewed the journal from this perspective, the collected entries made far more sense.

It was also helpful to remember that Philip thought of himself as a writer and wanted to be perceived as such by Federico. Once Federico arrived, what better way for Philip to demonstrate his commitment to the craft than to regularly record his miscellaneous thoughts and observations in a journal, which also gave him a clear-cut task to work on while Federico was intent on his poems. In the journal, Philip typically followed an entry about a given day's activities with several additional, unrelated entries about the local landscape, history, or residents. This mixture of content is consistent with the fact that Philip must have written several entries on each day of Federico's visit, fitting them in as time and opportunity allowed, to reach a total of thirty-one. Building on this premise, I matched clusters of sequential entries to the ten calendar days from 21 to 29 August, and all the datable events fell into place. The resulting dating scheme is the one I use here.

Another task I faced was untangling Philip's inconsistent use of personal pronouns. For example, he often referred to an activity as something "we" did, without specifying who else was present. At other points he described something "I" did, when it is clear from other sources that Federico was also there. I have clarified this confusion as much as possible.

Finally, Philip never used the given names of the people he mentioned in his journal, instead referring to them only by whatever title he had assigned them. Thus, Frank Ruggles was always "the Soldier," Dorothea and Elizabeth Tyler were "the Sisters," and Federico was "the Spanish poet." He never mentioned his father, mother, aunt, or cousin at all, though they were clearly with him at the cottage. I have done my best to clarify these conventions and omissions as well.

My analysis of the journal entries and supporting information ultimately allowed me to develop the following picture of Philip's and Federico's probable activities during each day of Federico's visit.

Wednesday, 21 August 1929

When Federico first arrived at the cottage, Philip was faced with a quandary. He was a tireless wilderness hiker himself, but he knew that Federico was a man of the city—accustomed to long walks, but always on paved streets and sidewalks. The main road through the village was perhaps not so different, its treated gravel surface was generally smooth and level, especially during the summer.[6] The unpaved side roads—in Philip's words, "two sandy bands with grass between which undulate over the landscapes in twining and combining ribbons"[7]—were also easy for walkers to navigate. But the local trails and footpaths were another story. Rarely flat, they typically required travelers to scramble around rocks, through streams, and over fallen logs as they climbed uphill and down. In addition, Federico was prone to develop a limp when he was overtired, a trait that Philip had almost certainly observed during their rambles in Madrid.[8]

Accordingly, before he and Federico embarked on any significant hikes together, Philip needed a way to assess his friend's readiness for such ventures. As discussed in chapter 5, soon after Federico's arrival, Philip took him on a relaxed stroll around the lakeshore and village followed by a visit to the Tyler sisters. This excursion served two purposes: It allowed Philip to show Federico his new environs, while simultaneously giving him a way to discreetly test Federico's strength and stamina.

This dual goal is apparent from the route Philip chose to reach the Tyler house. The easiest, most straightforward way to get there was to take North Road, which climbed gradually upward from the village center for about a mile to the sisters' homestead. But instead of using the road, Philip took Federico on a shorter, much steeper footpath through the surrounding woods.[9] Federico managed to keep up, but the shortcut definitely made an impression: He told his parents that the house was "in the middle of a forest and difficult to get to."[10] He must have decided that meeting the sisters was worth the effort, however, because his overall reaction to the experience was so positive. As an added consequence, Philip clearly deemed him ready to move on to greater challenges.

Thursday, 22 August 1929

Wasting no time, the very next day Philip took Federico on a major hike to the top of Belvidere Mountain, a 3,376-foot peak northwest of the village. Just reaching the trailhead required a five-mile walk from the village center, followed by a two-and-a-half-mile climb from the trailhead to the top. The trail gained over 2,000 feet of elevation along the way, no small feat for a city dweller like Federico.

In planning their path up the mountain, Philip seems to have used a popular 1926 guidebook he may have brought with him to the cottage or perhaps found on a shelf there: *Trails and Summits of the Green Mountains* by Walter Collins O'Kane.[11] His reliance on this book is apparent from the close correspondence between his detailed account of their journey and O'Kane's description of the eastern route to the top of Belvidere Mountain (called Mount Belvidere by O'Kane) used by the fire warden, which linked to the Long Trail at the summit.

There is other evidence that Philip used O'Kane's book. In O'Kane's turn-by-turn directions for the trail, he included a cautionary note: "Near the point where the road joins the old highway there is a short branch leading to the right to a sugar house. Care should be taken to avoid this branch." In Philip's journal entry about that same part of the hike, he seemed almost in conversation with O'Kane: "Sure enough—beyond a copse of fir trees was the sugar place."[12] He was clearly aware of O'Kane's warning but also chose to

Figure 23. View from the east side of Lake Eden, September 1937. The white scar of the asbestos mine on the slope of Belvidere Mountain is visible in the distance. Photo by Arthur Rothstein, "Frank Kinney on a Hay Rake, Eden Mills, Vermont," Library of Congress, Prints and Photographs Division, no. LC-USF33- 002619-M1.

ignore it, a response that seems entirely in keeping with his usual confidence and bravado as well as his youth.

One of the goals of the hike was to locate an old talc mine that Philip had heard about in the village. But when they finally reached the spot Philip had in mind, they discovered instead a working asbestos mine, complete with busy miners and an amiable foreman who explained the mining operation to them.[13] They enjoyed this unexpected diversion, but the real reward for their efforts was the spectacular eastward view visible from the upper reaches of the trail: a verdant landscape that stretched from the Canadian border to the White Mountains of New Hampshire.

After exploring a bit further, Philip and Federico made their way back down to the trailhead, then walked the final five miles to the village. The route took them right past the Tylers' house, so odds are that they stopped in for a quick visit with the sisters and some much-needed refreshments. The pair must have been exhausted by the time they finally returned to the cottage, but Philip expressed only contentment when he summed up the day in his journal: "Our fifteen miles added to our hunger and made the soft lengths of bed most inviting, and then there was the silent starlight where we could think it all over."[14]

Friday, 23 August 1929

The next day's outing was much less strenuous, as befitted a day of recovery. Their first destination was a deserted village on the south slope of Belvidere Mountain, about six miles from the cottage, but this time Harry drove Philip, Federico, and Edna to the site in his car. The deserted village was a Vermont ghost town: a cluster of unpainted wooden houses and sheds built for the miners (and their families) who once worked in a nearby asbestos mine that had been abandoned after its vein ran out. The buildings were falling to ruin in the absence of human attention, aided in their slow decline by various woodland creatures. Philip noted, "Most of the houses are open and birds build their nests on the floors. Hedgehogs and all small animals make their regular excursions within."[15]

The "hedgehogs" that Philip mentioned here and elsewhere in his journal were actually porcupines, but he invariably used the Vermont vernacular name for the animal. In fact, this usage of "hedgehog" is enshrined in Vermont law: In 1910, the Vermont legislature passed a measure titled An Act Relating to a Bounty on Porcupines, Commonly Known as Hedgehogs. The term was later adopted by Federico as well (see chapter 8).[16]

The solitary emptiness of the deserted village seemed to dim everyone's spirits, and they did not stay long; according to Philip, they "sped away after picking a few raspberries." But the melancholy feeling aroused by the visit continued to haunt him, moving him to write: "We shall probably never visit it again but there it is—the village that is dead. Again the silent hills tolerate but slowly erase. The stars will look down still when every ridgepole has sagged to the ground and then the trees will close over the town that used to be."[17]

Figure 24. Philip Cummings, Edna Southwick, and Federico García Lorca at the abandoned village, August 1929. Archivo Fundación Federico García Lorca, Centro Federico García Lorca, Granada.

Federico never mentioned the deserted village to his parents, but this is understandable. Coming as he did from a part of the world in which the ruins of ancient buildings are simply part of the landscape, he may have been puzzled by Philip's reaction. Of course, Federico was also accustomed to contemplating his own mortality, whereas this type of rumination may have been a novel experience for Philip.

From the deserted village, Harry drove the touring party twenty-seven miles north along Route 100 to Newport, Vermont. Newport was (and is) a small town of around 5,000 people on the southern end of Lake Memphremagog, a deep glacial lake that stretches forty-five miles north from Newport across the Canadian border to Magog, Quebec. When Philip was seventeen and had just finished high school, he spent the summer working as a cook's helper on a little steamship that carried passengers and mail between Newport and various ports around the lake, so he knew the area well.[18]

Going to Newport gave Philip the chance to show Federico a significantly larger and more lively place than Eden Mills, as well as the majestic lake itself. To accomplish the latter, Harry drove them to a well-known viewpoint on a hill above the town, where they could see far across the lake and the surrounding foothills. Philip had also hoped to take Federico across the border into Canada, just eight miles away, but Federico had not brought his visa, so that part of the trip could not happen.[19]

Somewhere along the way, Federico bought a postcard of the lake with the words "Beautiful Memphremagog, Newport, VT" printed across the bottom. Before sending it to his parents, he wrote the following message on the back:

> This is the incredibly lovely landscape around Newport, which I visited. The words across the bottom of the card make it look a bit smaller, but you can see its greatness and serenity. The whole country is like this. The mountains are covered with pine trees and the lakes come one after another, giving rise to perspectives

> and patches of great beauty, though too monotonous. You wander around this place and a certain sweetness comes over you, as though you had fallen asleep in this paradisiacal light. Don't forget to write me. And so should Paquito and everyone else. Goodbye![20]

Federico was much too polite to let Philip know that he had begun to find the landscape monotonous, but his note to his parents suggests that the pressure of being a dutiful guest was starting to take its toll, despite all the benefits that came with it.

Saturday, 24 August 1929

Saturday brought the only significant rainfall of Federico's visit, resulting in a peaceful afternoon at the cottage with no outdoor activities. After the nonstop pace of the previous few days, Federico may have been privately relieved by the unexpected respite. The weather also gave him a chance to experience the special pleasure of being under the tin roof of the Dew-Kum-Inn during a rainstorm. As Philip described it, "The quiet orchestration of the rain . . . makes a whole octave on the various leaves and on the roof of our porch." During the day, Philip and Federico wrote letters to friends and otherwise kept themselves amused. When the rain finally stopped in the late afternoon, the mist lifted and the air turned beautifully clear, bringing the sweeping view across the lake back into focus. In Philip's words, "The rain has washed away the haze and the hills are ranked in true perspective for my review."[21]

But the weather wasn't quite done for the day. As evening approached, a spectacular lightning storm moved across the lake, complete with rolling waves of thunder that echoed off the hillsides. Philip captured the excitement of the moment in his journal, employing a virtual torrent of metaphors: "The sky is in the midst of a turmoil. The fierce fires of Heaven are seaming, creasing, splitting, fretting and smocking the dark garments of the Firmament. At intervals the trees and leaves are stamped in a coarse fillet against the hem of Heaven. There is the heavy droning in the distance of a thousand thundering bees. Unseen chariots are assailing the Universe of rough cobblestones. The entire sky is being reflected by the surprised lake, as it whirls in a vivid Apache dance."[22]

Federico, too, was clearly moved by the dramatic display, which almost certainly inspired the title of his bittersweet poem "Living Sky" (Cielo vivo; see chapter 8). In the autograph original, he left no doubt about exactly where and when he composed the poem, adding the following below the last line of verse:

Cabaña de Dew-Kum-Inn
Edem [*sic*] Mills, Vermont,
24 de Agosto 1929[23]

That evening, the pair attended a community square dance at the Masonic Hall in Eden Mills, an event held every other Saturday night during the summer months, discussed further in chapter 8.[24]

Sunday, 25 August 1929

On Sunday, Philip embarked on his most ambitious hike yet: to the top of nearby Mount Norris. However, this time he was accompanied by his friend Frank Ruggles, while Federico stayed behind at the cottage. It is unclear who made this decision, but it was a wise choice. The Mount Norris trail was a little shorter than the one they had hiked on Belvidere Mountain, but it was over far rockier, steeper terrain, especially near the summit.[25]

The rigors of the hike seemed to do Philip good, leaving him "scratched and tired" but with a solid sense of accomplishment, if not outright superiority. At the end of his long account of all the obstacles he and Frank had surmounted along the trail, he criticized the parade of tourists who merely glanced at Mount Norris as they passed by and were satisfied with that, unlike determined hikers like Frank and himself, who had earned the right to truly "know" it.

Philip, who was clearly somewhat enamored of Frank, gave his friend high praise for his performance on the trail: "The Soldier is a good hiker. My definition of a good hiker is a man or woman who can walk long miles over rough ground and in rough costume, who can assail the hills and then absorb a view without an explosion into adjectives, then retreat gracefully."[26] Philip did not say whether he granted the same status to Federico.

Federico thus ended up with a whole afternoon to himself. Alone by the lake, he had the space and time to begin writing a new poem that must have required deep concentration, his "Poema Doble del Lago Eden" (Double Poem of Lake Eden). Federico did not date this poem, but there is no doubt as to exactly where it was composed (see chapter 8).

Monday, 26 August 1929

Philip and Federico's next outing may have been planned in advance or may have arisen from their failed quest on the slopes of Belvidere Mountain. Although they had been unable to find the rumored abandoned talc mine there, Philip knew where they could visit an active one. Accordingly, on Monday, Harry drove Philip and Federico a full forty-five miles south on Route 100 to Moretown, Vermont, home of the primary talc mine of the Eastern Magnesia Talc Company.[27] The route took them through the town centers of Morrisville, Stowe, and Waterbury, but there is no indication that they stopped anywhere along the way.

Perhaps Harry knew a supervisor at the mine or perhaps they simply came at a good time, but soon after they arrived, they were given a guided tour of the whole operation. Philip paid close attention during the tour, as is clear from his description of the mine's interior and of one of the products made from the talc after it was extracted:

> Very cool air met us and it seemed to get colder as we walked into the shaft which is horizontal. On and on we went, along the slippery track, into the heart of the mountain. The damp talc underfoot was very tricky. The walls glistened pale greenish-white in the electric light glare. We saw the pieces being picked off with the sharp steel tools and the drills working with the savage sound of machine guns. We came back out and went to the cutting room where the talc is cut by saws into little square shapes and also into pencils for marking fine marbles. This very fine grade talc is a pale luminous green and feels like soap. Light can be seen through pieces of it a quarter of an inch thick.[28]

Federico may not have shared Philip's fascination with the mine and its mechanics, but the experience definitely made an impression. His response was simply more subtle (see chapter 8).

Figure 25. Workers at the Eastern Magnesia Talc Company in Moretown, Vermont, ca. 1925. From "Moretown Talc," *Moretown (VT) Historical Society Newsletter* 1 (Jan. 2014): 1.

Tuesday, 27 August 1929

Philip saved the most spectacular hike until Federico's visit was almost at an end. This was a moderately difficult, 1.7-mile trek to the top of Jay Peak, the most northerly of the Green Mountains and the last major summit on the Long Trail. The mountain was a good twenty miles to the north of Eden Mills, but fortunately Harry was willing to drive them to the trailhead.

Philip had only good things to say about the trail and its condition, perhaps an indication of the relatively poor state of the other trails he and Federico had hiked: "There is a fine trail up this mountain. It is the Long Trail which leads over the higher peaks of this

Figure 26. Harry Cummings at the summit of Jay Peak, Vermont, August 1929. Journal of Hispanic Philology Collection, Special Collections, Florida State University Libraries, Tallahassee.

Figure 27. Philip Cummings at the summit of Jay Peak, Vermont, August 1929. Journal of Hispanic Philology Collection, Special Collections, Florida State University Libraries, Tallahassee.

New England state. Long indeed it is, and after toiling over wet stones and muddy spots we prepared for the view from the top but alas, the top loomed up seemingly thousands of feet ahead. . . . We walked on up and up, easily following the carefully made trail; and may the trail-maker receive herewith our thanks for his foresight."[29]

When they finally reached the top, Philip was amazed by what he saw: "The view! Two countries and their districts for a hundred miles around lay out clear and pleasant before us."[30] His excitement is understandable: The mountain's relatively flat, treeless summit offered an unobstructed, 360-degree view of the surrounding countryside, far more expansive than any vista Philip and Federico had encountered on their previous hikes. On that clear, late August afternoon, they could see as far as Lake Champlain and the Adirondacks to the west, Quebec's Sutton Mountains to the north, the White Mountains to the east, and all the rivers, lakes, towns, and valleys in between. Despite his comments to his family about the monotony of the Vermont landscape, Federico, too, must have been impressed by the striking panorama that stretched to the horizon in every direction.

Wednesday, 28 August 1929

After the excitement of climbing Jay Peak, Philip and Federico spent their last full day together in more relaxed occupations, giving Federico a chance to rest and recover before his departure on Thursday. At some point that morning, he managed to gather his thoughts and compose the poem "Earth and Moon" (Tierra y luna). Below the last line, he added a postscript in an interesting mix of Spanish and English: "28 de August 1929, Cabaña de Duw-Kum-Inn, Edem Mills, Vermont."[31]

That afternoon, Philip and Federico went on a leisurely stroll through the fields and woodlands on the east side of the lake. They watched cows grazing peacefully in a pasture, and Philip took note of the many wildflowers in bloom along the roadside. They gorged on wild blackberries they found in a clearing, a local version of the berries known in Spain as *zarzamora*.

In his multiple, somewhat jumbled entries about this outing, Philip paid uncharacteristic attention to Federico's responses to events and the objects they encountered along the way. For example, after seeing a pile of dust balls beside the road, Philip reported that Federico said, "Each is a little world, with its own shadow." Describing Federico's reaction to a pair of crumbling tree stumps in the woods, Philip wrote: "One decaying stump was for him the ruin of a citadel of Babylon, another became a castle. It was soft nearly in powder and the poet, great child that he and all poets are, knelt and shaped of the white punk material a castle. He covered it with moss and there it stood—first a mere rotten birch stump, now a historic castle of the plains of La Mancha in faraway Spain."[32]

In the course of their outing, they visited a legendary spot in the woods known locally as the Garden of Eden, accessed via a trail off

East Road. The garden was a clearing deep in the forest, hidden from the roadway, where an unexpected profusion of perennial flowers grew among the ferns and grasses. They had been warned that the blossoms would be past their peak, but the flowers were still quite evident. They were also told that the perennials were originally planted by the Native Americans who once lived in the area, but after finding the foundations of several old buildings nearby, Philip concluded, "Probably in the late eighteenth century the seeds were strewn which still make for the spring time glory which many tell of but very few have seen."[33]

The visit to the Garden of Eden gave Philip and Federico one final opportunity to be completely alone together. They may have spent the time reading or discussing Whitman or perhaps enjoying their last sexual episode. Philip did not specify, saying only that in the quiet setting there, he could hear "the whispering through the soft ferns when one lies among them."[34] We know almost nothing about the details of Federico and Philip's sexual activities in Vermont except the little that Philip told Daniel Eisenberg in 1974. During a private discussion with Eisenberg at Philip's home in Vermont, Philip casually mentioned that he had performed fellatio on Federico at Lake Eden, at Federico's request, giving Federico "some release."[35]

After returning from the Garden of Eden, Philip and Federico spent the rest of the day and early evening with the Tyler sisters, celebrating their fond friendship and saying good-bye to each other. Elizabeth and Dorothea had gathered brilliant red and gold leaves from the maple trees on their property, which were already beginning to show their fall colors, and used them to decorate their dining room. Federico was in high spirits, as Philip reported: "Never is he without a joke, and he said after looking all around the adorned room that it was so significantly the farewell to the summer that his feet were cold!"[36]

While the sisters worked in the kitchen, preparing their last dinner together, Philip and Federico roamed the fields behind the house, searching for items they could contribute. They collected blackberries and blueberries, and Philip found a few wizened apples in the old orchard that were still suitable for making applesauce. But it was Federico's tour de force that stole the show:

> The poet meanwhile was making a masterpiece, not in poetry but in floral design. From a simple base of pearly everlastings he added golden sprays of goldenrod and the tall spike of a mullein, a few deep red leaves from a raspberry bush, a bunch of red elderberry and back of this a spray of pine branches, among which he put long stalks of ripe timothy grass. It was a beautiful thing to look at and appeared as a mirror of the Season. The final touch was a group of three small branches with little apples. The poet bore it as his offering to the feast.[37]

When the meal ended, Federico sang a few Spanish folk songs for Elizabeth and Dorothea, accompanying himself on their treasured spinet piano. The sisters and Philip sang a few "old songs of our country" for Federico in return, and then it was time to go.[38]

Thursday, 29 August 1929

Early Thursday morning, Federico left the cottage for the last time, setting out in the Model T with Philip and Harry for the two-hour drive to Burlington. There, he boarded a southbound train for a somewhat circuitous journey to his next destination: the town of Shandaken in the Catskill Mountains of New York state. (Because Federico had originally purchased a round-trip ticket to Burlington, he had to first return to New York City, then travel north again to Kingston, New York, the closest railway station to Shandaken.) He was eagerly anticipating spending the next three weeks in Shandaken with Ángel del Río and his wife, Amelia, good friends with whom he could freely laugh and drink and relax.

It is clear from Philip's journal that he thoroughly enjoyed his outings with Federico, and the more rigorous, the better. For Philip, a long walk over rough terrain was the perfect way to spend a summer afternoon. He knew that Federico had tended to avoid such endeavors in the past, but he must have decided early on that, given the right opportunity and incentive, Federico would come to appreciate the pleasures of hiking in the open air as much as he did. Years later, Philip expressed satisfaction in the apparent success of his strategy, writing to Ángel del Río, "Federico was not over given to physical exercise, yet he tramped all over that part of my native state with me."[39]

Philip clearly took his responsibilities as a host seriously and worked hard to ensure that Federico could experience the best that Lake Eden and its environs had to offer, at least from Philip's perspective. And while he took obvious pride in having convinced his less exertion-minded friend to join him in so much physical activity, it is unclear how Federico felt about their excursions. Did he begin to tire of the constant pace of new adventures and start to find it all a little repetitive or exhausting? If so, he was apparently careful to hide those feelings from Philip. Like any well-brought-up Spaniard, Federico would have expressed interest in anything Philip wanted to show him and gratitude for his generosity. That was simply how a proper guest behaved.

Still, it must have been hard for Federico to find himself so completely dependent on Philip's whims and enthusiasms, especially after leading his own life in the city. If he had thought more carefully about what he already knew of Philip when he accepted his invitation, Federico might have been able to predict this outcome, but at the time his mind was focused on other aspects of their relationship. As the days progressed, the mismatch between Federico's private expectations for the visit and the reality he encountered at Lake Eden found its way, consciously or unconsciously, into his poems.

CHAPTER EIGHT

The Story in the Poems

This hour I tell things in confidence,
I might not tell everybody, but I will tell you.

—Walt Whitman, "Song of Myself"

BEFORE CONTINUING FEDERICO'S STORY in the Catskills, let us take a closer look at some of the dynamics underlying his relationship with Philip and how they appear to be reflected in four of the poems he composed at Lake Eden: "Living Sky," "Death," "Double Poem of Lake Eden," and "Earth and Moon." In these poems, Federico continued to experiment with the surrealistic imagery and stream-of-consciousness techniques that Salvador Dalí had encouraged him to adopt as an antidote to his overly conventional (in Dalí's mind) use of language in the *Gypsy Ballads*.[1] Federico took this advice to heart, and as a result, the more abstract parts of these poems can seem almost incomprehensible at first. However, their meaning becomes clearer when we take his Vermont experiences into account.

Federico provided a few clues about his emotional state in his letters from Lake Eden, but the poems provide the best window on his deepest feelings. In contrast to the carefree, happy facade that he maintained with the people around him, including Philip, the poems

Federico wrote in Vermont show a man beset by a whirlwind of emotions: at times amused by the pretense he encounters or resigned to being disappointed, but ultimately unable to contain the anger, despair, and anguish of being unable to find, or even openly speak about, the authentic love he is seeking.

Philip's journal contains only two comments on Federico's mood over the course of their time together at Lake Eden. At one point Philip observed, "never is he without a joke," but he later noticed a touch of melancholy in his friend: "He sees a bush, a familiar tree and the momentary homesickness which we are all prey to takes him and he looks with saddened eyes far, far beyond the thicket."[2]

A comparison of two of Federico's letters from Lake Eden shows a marked change in his tone over time, a contrast that seems to indicate a growing unhappiness. In the long letter he wrote to his parents at the beginning of his stay, he ended on an upbeat note, with only a hint of nostalgia: "I don't have to tell you how often I think of you, particularly in these calm, quiet places, so different from Spain. But this trip is extremely important for me. And I find it wonderful to have experienced this totally American, intimate way of life. Just now they are lighting the lights. The atmosphere reminds me of my childhood in Daimuz. Not a single frog can be heard in the lake. The silence is perfect. And from this wonderfully peaceful spot I send you hugs and kisses."[3]

At that early point in his visit, Federico was still delighted by the peaceful atmosphere of the cottage; he had not yet realized how that same quiet and lack of distractions would make it increasingly hard for him to suppress the deep unhappiness he had carried with him from Spain. But later in his visit, Federico expressed much darker emotions in a letter to his friend Ángel del Río:

Dearest Ángel:

I'm writing to you from Eden Mills. Having a good time. The landscape is marvelous, but infinitely melancholy. A good experience for me. I'll tell you all about it. Now I only want to know how to find you so as to be with you in few days' time.

It never stops raining. This family is very nice, full of gentle charm, but the woods and lakes immerse me in a hardly bearable state of poetic desperation. I write all day and at night I feel drained.

Ángel: tell me by return mail how to meet you. When I think that I can drink at the house where you live it makes me very happy.

Now night is falling. The oil lamps have been lit and my whole childhood comes back to me, wrapped in a glory of poppies and grainfields. Among the ferns I've found a distaff covered with spiders and in the lake not one frog sings.

Urgently need cognac for my poor heart. Write me and I'll go to meet you.

All good things to Amelia. Kisses to the baby (on his feet), and you get a hug from your friend, Federico

(Pursued in Eden Mills by the liqueur of romanticism).

My young friend Cummings translates my songs and looks at me with the tenderness of a wounded cow.

Show me the route of the trip. If it's easier for you, send me a long telegram explaining it to me. My address for the telegraph is as follows—Cummings will type it out. I'd prefer if you would send me a telegram.

Did you ask Fernando de los Ríos for the money?

In any case, I'll have to pass through New York. It's likely I'll leave on Thursday.

This is a haven for me, but I'm choked in this mist and this tranquility brings my memories back in such a way that they burn me.

Goodbye, my dear![4]

In his letter, Federico clearly overdramatized some aspects of his situation. For example, other than one rainy day, the weather stayed clear and dry during his visit. However, he also expressed genuine emotional distress—not only directly, but also in his fervent assertion that he would surely recover his happiness if he were only among Spanish friends again—and had access to alcohol.

One striking element of the letter is Federico's statement that

Philip gazed at him "with the tenderness of a wounded cow," essentially mocking his friend as a lovesick acolyte who dutifully translates his poems. What did Federico hope to gain by portraying Philip in this way? Perhaps by presenting Philip, rather than himself, as a disappointed suitor, Federico was trying to soothe his wounded pride and recover his sense of dignity at Philip's expense. Unwilling to acknowledge that he had once again pinned his romantic hopes on an unsuitable younger man, Federico may have been trying his best to deflect attention elsewhere.

This may be yet another indication of the larger, very human dilemma that Federico faced at Lake Eden. If he had indeed made the long trip to Vermont in the hope that Philip would turn out to be the life partner he had been seeking, after several days of close contact he must have realized that he had misjudged Philip's interest in and emotional readiness for a meaningful commitment. Compounding Federico's distress, while Philip remained a willing sexual partner, he seemed to be largely oblivious to Federico's internal turmoil. Along with his private sadness and disappointment, Federico must have felt embarrassed by the wishful thinking that had left him so emotionally vulnerable. By treating Philip's obvious affection as a source of amusement in his letter, rather than something he had actively sought, Federico may have helped himself feel better. However, by portraying Philip in such an unflattering light, he also set in motion a misleading narrative about their relationship that would influence Ángel del Río's attitudes and actions toward Philip, and by extension those of his colleagues and students, for decades.

Part of Federico's chagrin may have come from hearing Philip talk about his expectation that he would someday marry a woman and have children of his own, despite his obvious preference for male sexual partners—a life choice that was the opposite of Federico's own.[5] Federico could not pretend that Philip's willingness to accept his assigned role in society was due to a lack of self-knowledge; Philip knew exactly who he was, but he also understood what was needed to succeed socially and financially in the wider world and had no interest in fighting the system. Given his own background, Federico likely did not consider the fact that, in the absence of family wealth, Philip did not have the luxury of ignoring societal norms for proper male behavior if he wished to make a living. Nine years later, Philip met his own expectations and married an accomplished young woman from a wealthy, socially prominent family.[6] The couple had two children and remained married until his wife's death in 1983, while Philip hid his homosexuality from all but a few close confidants.[7]

Federico's growing sense that he had been mistaken about Philip may have also involved questions of wealth and class. Philip had almost certainly presented himself as the son of a successful, high-powered businessman when he first met Federico in Madrid. However, the reality of Philip's social and financial status would have been obvious to Federico as soon as he arrived at the lake, where he could see for himself the modest size of the cottage, the fact that it was rented rather than owned, the lack of servants and creature comforts, and everyone's old-fashioned, well-worn clothing. (Of course, never having seen Philip's family in any other setting, it may not have occurred to him that they would dress differently for a month at a rustic cottage than they would for their regular city and town pursuits.) And after spending time with Philip's father, Federico must have realized that Harry's days as a dynamic, driving force in his community were long past, even if everyone pretended that he was still somehow a businessman.

Federico wrote the first poem that we will consider—"Living Sky" (Cielo vivo)—on 24 August 1929, the rainy Saturday that he and Philip spent stuck inside the cottage.[8] It is hard to miss the rueful tone of the poem. The speaker knows he has failed this time but is determined to continue his quest for joyful, "visible" love—a love that speaks its name:

I won't be able to complain
though I never found what I was looking for.
Near the dried-up stones and the husks of insects,
I won't see the sun's duel with the creatures of flesh and blood.

But I'll go to the first landscape
of shocks, fluids, and murmurs
that seeps into a newborn child,
and where all surfaces are avoided,
so I'll know that my search has a joyful target
when I'm flying, jumbled with love and sands.

There, the frost of snuffed-out eyes won't reach,
nor the bellowing of a tree, murdered by the caterpillar.
There, all the shapes intertwine and have
the same frenetic, forward expression.

You can't pass through the swarming corollas—
the air dissolves your teeth of sugar.
And you can't caress the elusive fern
Without feeling the utter astonishment of ivory.

There, under roots and in the marrow of the air,
you can grasp the truth of mistaken things.
The finest wave about to pounce on the chrome swimmer
and the flock of nocturnal cattle with a woman's little red feet . . .

I won't be able to complain
though I never found what I was looking for;
but I'll go to the first fluid landscape of heartbeats
so I'll know that my search has a joyful target
when I'm flying, jumbled with love and sands.

I'm used to the cool air when I fly over empty beds.

Over squalls and ships run aground.
I stumble sleepily through eternity's fixed hardness
and love at last without dawn. Love. Visible love![9]

Whatever deeper meanings "Living Sky" may hold, the poem confirms C. Brian Morris's description of Federico as "an extraordinarily porous poet [who] left clues about his readings and observations" throughout his work.[10] As Andrew A. Anderson noted in his initial analysis of the poem, many of the images Federico chose to include were almost certainly based on actual objects he had seen in and around Lake Eden. Anderson added, "Much more important, of course, is what Lorca did with these raw materials."[11]

Examining the sources of Federico's "raw materials" as fully as possible is an essential first step in understanding the deeper, symbolic meanings he gave to those materials in his poem. For example, the physical setting where Federico composed "Living Sky" may have affected his choice of images. Philip told scholar Kessel Schwartz that Federico spent much of his time beside the lake, "scribbling away on an overturned boat" that he used as a writing desk.[12] The summer of 1929 was exceptionally dry across most of New England, leading to widespread drought conditions.[13] The prolonged lack of rainfall caused Lake Eden to recede far below its usual level, revealing a secondary beach of small stones that were normally covered by water, just beyond the strip of sandy beach where Federico sat. The stony part of the beach is clearly visible in photos of Federico with Philip and his family taken beside the lake, as is the overturned aluminum rowboat "desk" that came with the cottage. Thus the poet himself was "near the dried-up stones and the husks of insects" as he contemplated his current disappointment and his hopes for a happier future.

As for the "tree, murdered by the caterpillar" in the poem, Federico almost certainly encountered nests of tent caterpillars in the branches of birch or apple trees on his excursions with Philip, who would have explained the terrible damage the voracious insects can do to their host by devouring its leaves. These caterpillars are found throughout North America but were almost certainly new to Federico, and they clearly made an impression.

Federico would have also encountered "cattle with a woman's little red feet" in his walks with Philip. Several of the farmers in and around Eden Mills had Ayrshire cattle, a breed that originated in Scotland, among their livestock. Ayrshires were first imported to New England in 1822 and are still highly valued in Vermont for their hardiness in cold weather and prodigious milk production. Most importantly, Ayrshires are predominantly reddish-brown in color and are known for their relatively small, delicate feet compared to other breeds.[14] Federico saw at least one such animal on his hike up Belvidere Mountain with Philip, who noted "a red cow, philosophically chewing some choice herbage" in his journal.[15] Given the number of dairy farms in the area, Federico surely had multiple other opportunities as well.

Finally, the speaker's statement that he is "used to the cool air when I fly over empty beds" seems to acknowledge both his loneliness and his ability to rise above it. But it may also refer in part to the chilliness of the nights Federico spent with Philip on the upstairs sleeping porch of the hillside cottage, high above Lake Eden. Overnight low temperatures for the period ranged from thirty to fifty-four degrees Fahrenheit, with the average being a brisk forty-two degrees. Perhaps this was the setting where, in the words of the poem, "you can grasp the truth of mistaken things."

The second poem we will consider is "Death" (Muerte); though undated, it is one of eight that Federico later explicitly connected to Vermont.[16] Based on the poem's mood and content, it was probably written on the same rainy Saturday afternoon as "Living Sky." As in "Living Sky," the tone of the poem is bemused, almost lighthearted, despite its disquieting title. The speaker gently mocks all those who try in vain to make themselves into something they are not, expending great energy in the process. This may be Federico's commentary on Philip's willingness to present himself to the world as a happily heterosexual young man, despite his true sexual orientation, and to accept the role that society assigned him—a posture that Federico understood but did not support.

> How hard they try!
> How hard the horse tries
> to become a dog.
> How hard the dog tries to become a swallow.
> How hard the swallow tries to become a bee.
> How hard the bee tries to become a horse.
> And the horse
> what a sharp arrow it squeezes from the rose,
> what an ashen rose rising from its lips!
> And the rose,
> what a flock of lights and cries
> knotted in the living sugar of its trunk.
> And the sugar,
> what daggers it dreams in its vigils!
> And these miniature daggers,
> what a moon without stables, what naked flesh,
> what undying and rosy skin they seek out!
> And I, on the roof's edge,
> what a burning angel I look for and am.
> But the plaster arch,
> how vast, how invisible, how minute,
> without even trying![17]

In addition to its almost playful tone, "Death" shares with "Living Sky" a speaker who is observing the other actors in the poem from above. However, this time the speaker is not flying, but rather "on the roof's edge"—almost certainly another reference to the lofty position of the sleeping porch that Federico shared with Philip.

It may also be significant that in Federico's original Spanish, the speaker of the poem is seeking not just a burning "angel," but more specifically, a burning "seraph" (*serafín* in Spanish)—one of the seraphim, the highest order of angels in the Christian hierarchy. The role of the seraphim in both the Christian and Jewish traditions is to surround God while crying out "Holy! Holy! Holy!" to proclaim his presence.[18] This was perhaps Federico's way of saying that his ideal partner would, unlike Philip, be unafraid to state the truth about himself out loud.

The day after these two poems were composed, Sunday, 25 August, must have been a difficult one for Federico. The night before, he and Philip had attended the square dance at the Masonic Hall in Eden Mills. Philip entered into the dancing with great enthusiasm despite the fact that he was completely unfamiliar with the steps, but there is no indication that Federico joined in. He may have felt a bit left out, or even jealous, as he watched Philip twirling left and right with various young women from the village or, perhaps, cousin Edna.

The events of the previous night may have led to a subdued Sunday morning, but Federico's sense of his standing with Philip soon declined even further. On Sunday afternoon, Philip left Federico behind at the cottage and went hiking up Mount Norris without him, perhaps with the excuse that the hike would be too strenuous for Federico to handle. This was almost certainly true, but it still must have stung Federico's pride.

Far worse was the matter of Philip's chosen hiking partner: Frank Ruggles, the handsome, twenty-year-old West Point cadet whom Philip called "the Soldier" in his journal. Frank's parents owned the Wayside Inn, a restaurant and dance pavilion built on the narrow strip of land between Route 100 and the edge of the lake, right around the corner from the cottage where the Cummingses were staying. The inn was open for business only during the summer months; in the winter, the Ruggles family lived some fifty miles away in Lyndonville, Vermont, where Frank had gone to school. Frank normally helped out his parents at the inn, but he was obviously free to go hiking that Sunday afternoon.

Frank was in excellent physical shape from his training regimen at West Point. A photo of himself that he gave to Philip shows a slim, dark-haired young man standing crisply at attention in his dress uniform, smiling for the camera. Almost sixty years later, Philip casually told Ian Gibson that he and Frank once went skinny-dipping in the lake, recalling with quiet pleasure, "He certainly was a good-looking boy."[19] By all indications, Frank was oblivious to any sexual or romantic interest that Philip may have had in him, but there is no doubt that Philip found him attractive.

The trail up Mount Norris would have been even more challenging than usual after the rain of the day before. Indeed, Philip lost his footing on a wet rock and fell, though he quickly recovered. Having never climbed the trail before, he must have been reassured by the fact that Frank knew it well. If Philip had any doubts about this, Frank offered proof: At the summit, he pointed out the spot where he and his companions had carved their initials into a rock a few summers before, and Philip happily added his own to the list.[20]

Waiting back at the cottage, Federico had multiple reasons to feel distraught. Without Philip there to provide distraction, he may have been even more conscious than usual of all the things he missed from his life in the city: ready access to music, a vibrant social scene where almost everyone spoke Spanish, and the freedom to go out where and when he chose, or retreat into solitude if he preferred. In addition, he had to contend with his hurt feelings at being excluded from the hike, and perhaps some degree of jealousy about Philip's obvious interest in Frank—along with an uncomfortable awareness of his own relatively advanced age. It was almost certainly under these conditions that Federico composed his deeply personal, heartfelt "Double Poem of Lake Eden" (Poema doble del Lago Eden).

Each part of the poem, beginning with the use of the word "double" in the title, helps elucidate Federico's state of mind at the time he wrote it. Taken literally, the title could be a playful nod to the fact that Lake Eden is actually a double lake: two parallel bodies of water joined by a narrow channel. Or, the word "double" might be a straightforward reference to the reflectivity of the lake, which doubles the visual presence of every object beside, on, or above its surface.

Considered more abstractly, Federico may have been alluding to the double life he felt forced to maintain as a homosexual man living in a heterosexual world, or to the disconnect he felt between his past and his present, between his former state of innocence and his current, unwanted state of knowledge. Perhaps all these things are true, and the apparent simplicity of the title belies its multiple layers of meaning.

The poem opens with an epigraph, a short quotation typically intended to suggest the theme of the work that follows: "Our cattle graze, the wind sends forth its breath. — Garcilaso."[21] This may seem almost a throwaway line, a simple nod to the poem's pastoral setting, but it is possible that it signifies a great deal more.

The epigraph is a line of verse from *Égloga II*, a classic composition by the Spanish poet Garcilaso de la Vega, whose work Federico knew well.[22] In Garcilaso's poem, the line is spoken by a shepherd named Salicio to his friend Nemero, who has just told Salicio a sad story about their mutual friend Albanio.

Albanio and his female friend Camila had been boon companions and hunting partners since childhood. But when Albanio confessed to Camila that he had fallen in love with her, she was shocked and fled in alarm, leaving Albanio heartbroken almost to the point of madness. When Nemero pauses in his story, Salicio urges him on, saying, "Tell me more, I implore. Nought interrupts the tale; our flocks are at rest, the fresh soft wind comes whispering from the west," an alternative translation of the phrase Federico chose for his epigraph. In other words, "All is calm and peaceful right now. So please, tell me more about the tragedy that befell Albanio."

Federico may have chosen this epigraph simply to alert knowledgeable readers that, even though things appear tranquil on the surface, there may be pain and turmoil beneath. But this explanation seems insufficient to explain the depth of feeling in his poem, the almost overwhelming sense of pain and injustice expressed by the speaker. Perhaps Federico was making a direct connection between Albanio's experience and his own.

If the rest of the poem is any indication, something had recently happened to Federico that left him bitter and depressed. Perhaps, just as Albanio had finally confessed his love to Camila, Federico had finally revealed his hope for a deeper relationship to Philip, or at least had begun to reveal it. And just as Camila had been taken aback by Albanio's declaration, Philip might have been surprised and dismayed by Federico's. He may have tried to downplay his reaction to spare Federico's feelings, but the damage would have been done. A short time later, when Federico sat down to begin "Double Poem," the sight of his reflection in the lake may have triggered thoughts of Albanio, especially since Albanio had revealed his love to Camila by pointing to his own face reflected in a pool of water.

In the first five stanzas that follow the epigraph of Federico's poem, the speaker looks back on his earlier life with an acute sense of lost innocence and delight:

> It was the voice I had before,
> ignorant of the dense and bitter sap,
> the one that came lapping at my feet
> beneath the moist and fragile ferns.
>
> Ay, my love's voice from before
> ay, voice of my truth,
> ay, voice of my open side,
> when all the roses spilled from my tongue
> and the grass hadn't felt the horse's impossible teeth!
>
> Here you are drinking my blood,
> drinking the humor of the heavy child I was,
> while my eyes are shattered by aluminum
> and drunken voices in the wind.

Let me pass through the arch
where Eve devours ants
and Adam impregnates the dazzling fish.
Little men with horns, let me return
to the grove of easy living
and the somersaults of pure joy.

I know the most secret way
to use an old rusty pin,
and I know the horror of eyes wide-awake
on the concrete surface of a plate.[23]

Perhaps the voice of the first stanza, the voice the speaker "had before," was a younger version of himself that Federico had begun to remember as he worked with Philip on the translation of *Songs*, poems he had written so many years before. He may have normally given little thought to the way he had viewed the world when he was ten years younger, but the process of working through his earlier poems line by line with Philip may have made him acutely aware of the contrast between the happy, carefree person he had been back then, before his devastating episode with Aladrén, and the sadder, more subdued person he had become. Revisiting *Songs* could not help but remind Federico of the simplicity and sweetness of his childhood, when he could still indulge in "somersaults of pure joy," invent secret uses for everyday objects, and shiver at frightening images of the Christian martyr Santa Lucia, who is traditionally depicted carrying her eyes on a plate.[24]

Even though Federico had initiated the *Songs* translation project himself, he may have come to regret it. In these stanzas, the speaker also rages at the person who is "drinking [his] blood," while he himself is blinded by aluminum and assaulted by "drunken voices in the wind"—images that may have been inspired by the glare of the sun on the aluminum boat and the loud voices of revelers in other cottages echoing across the lake. Perhaps, in Federico's mind, Philip had begun to serve as a stand-in for all those who wanted him to allow his poetry, his lifeblood, to be translated into other languages, however much he feared that it could never be done correctly. After a time, their ongoing work on the project may have begun to feel like torture.

Stanzas 6–10 are the heart of the poem. The speaker changes his focus from the past to the present and makes the source of his pain and anguish more explicit. He demands to be allowed to pursue love on his own terms and to have his needs and desires acknowledged and respected by those around him. As he states his demands, he also locates himself very precisely in time and space. He is voicing his lament right here, right now, "on the shore of this lake," Lake Eden. His references to "tin and talc" further link the poem to his Vermont experiences.

But I want neither world nor dream, divine voice,
I want my liberty, my human love
in the darkest corner of the breeze no one wants.
My human love!

Those sea-dogs chase each other
and the wind lies in ambush for careless tree trunks.
Oh, voice of before, let your tongue burn
this voice of tin and talc!

I want to cry because I feel like it—
the way children cry in the last row of seats—
because I'm not a man, not a poet, not a leaf,
only a wounded pulse that probes the things of the other side.

I want to cry saying my name,
rose, child, and fir on the shore of this lake,
to speak truly as a man of blood
killing in myself the mockery and suggestive power of the word.

No, no, I'm not asking, I desire,
my liberated voice lapping at my hands.
In the labyrinth of folding screens my nakedness receives
the punishing moon and the clock covered with ash.[25]

In stanza 9 above, the line after the opening line, "I want to cry saying my name," reflects a significant change Federico later made to his first version of the poem. In his original version, he left no doubt as to the identity of the speaker.

I want to cry saying my name,
Federico García Lorca, on the shore of this lake,
to speak truly as a man of blood
killing in myself the mockery and suggestive power of the word.

Perhaps inspired by Walt Whitman, who often inserted his own name into his poems, Federico originally included his full name in "Double Poem." He gave a copy of the poem with the original wording shown above to Cuban editor Juan Marinello in the spring of 1930.[26] However, his boldness did not last. Not long afterward, he revised the line to read "rose, child, and fir on the shore of this lake," apparently deciding against identifying himself so clearly as the speaker of the poem and instead leaving more room for ambiguity.

In the final stanza of the poem, the speaker steps back and observes himself from a distance, with a detachment that is almost chilling:

I was speaking that way.
I was speaking that way when Saturn stopped the trains
and the fog and the Dream and Death were looking for me.
Looking for me
where cattle with the little feet of a page bellow
and my body floats between contrary equilibriums.[27]

This stanza contains multiple references to objects and events that Federico encountered in Vermont, but the way in which he has woven these images together creates a visceral sense of dread. Now that he has stated his demands so openly, the speaker appears to fear being discovered even more than he longs for freedom. And thus he drifts, alone and unprotected, between conflicting ways of being.

The fourth poem that merits consideration is "Earth and Moon" (Tierra y luna), which Federico dated "28 de August 1929," the day before he left Lake Eden. But since he later chose not to include it with his other Vermont poems in *Poet in New York*, we will explore only a few of its thematic elements and word choices. The poem's speaker first aligns himself with children, who help him feel connected to the fundamental essence of the planet, but he is then distracted by the moon and thoughts of Diana, goddess of the moon, hunting, and fertility. The penultimate stanza seems to convey the core message of the poem: The vital connection the speaker has been seeking is now lost, leaving behind only sadness and injury.

> It's earth. My God! Earth, that I come looking for,
> Muffled horizon, heartbeat, and tomb.
> It's sorrow that runs out, love that consumes itself.
> Charred hands opening a tower of blood.[28]

As with the other poems Federico wrote at Lake Eden, there are references to multiple objects he encountered in Vermont. For example, in all the poems Federico ever wrote, he used the word *talco* in only two: "Double Poem of Lake Eden" and "Earth and Moon." This suggests that his references to talc were a direct result of his discussions with Philip and his exposure to the actual mineral at the talc mine in Moretown.

A final, often overlooked Vermont poem worthy of attention is not really a poem at all but rather an unfinished fragment titled

"Bacchus in New England" (Bacco en New England). Federico may have begun writing this poem on his last morning at the cottage, or perhaps even on the way to the Catskills, only to lose his train of thought or change his mind and abandon it. Fortunately, we know of the fragment's existence because he later turned the same piece of paper over and composed a different poem on the other side, "After a Walk" (Vuelta de paseo). Federico ended the latter poem with the postscript "Bushnell-Ville (ESU), 6 de Septiembre 1929," indicating that he wrote it about a week after arriving in Bushnellsville, a village within the town of Shandaken in the Catskills.[29]

Federico dedicated his poem fragment to "las señoritas de Tyler" (the Misses Tyler), thus connecting it by both title and dedication to his farewell feast with Philip and the Tylers on his last evening at Lake Eden. In addition, Federico's chosen title, "Bacchus in New England," echoes Philip's journal entry about their arrival at the sisters' house that evening: "Ceres and Bacchus celebrated with us the advent of the Autumn. We found the Gods of the harvest at the house of the two Sisters."[30]

That evening is also documented by an iconic photo of Philip and Federico beside the sisters' stone wall, with a sliver of North Road visible behind it.[31] Philip has his arm around Federico's shoulder as the two stand companionably close together, gazing calmly at whichever Tyler sister was holding the camera. Philip is wearing the same casual T-shirt and long pants, but Federico looks quite dapper in his matching jacket and knickers over a crisp white shirt and tie, an outfit he must have packed in anticipation of special occasions. And, just as Philip described in his journal, Federico is carrying a beautiful arrangement of wildflowers that he created for the sisters, making the pair look for all the world like a newly married couple.[32]

Below is my translation of the four lines that appear below Federico's title and dedication on his autograph original of the poem fragment:

Figure 28. Philip Cummings and Federico García Lorca by the stone wall at the Tyler sisters' house, August 1929. Lorca has gathered wildflowers for a centerpiece for the evening meal. Archivo Fundación Federico García Lorca, Centro Federico García Lorca, Granada.

With the dry branches of the drowned moon.
Cape of almonds above the waist
Hedgehog
Deaf hedgehog

None of this makes much sense, but it is an indication of Federico's affection for Elizabeth and Dorothea Tyler that he dedicated his work in progress to them. It is amusing to note that he had clearly picked up on Philip's use of the word "hedgehog" (*erizo* in Spanish) for porcupine. As already mentioned, "hedgehog" is the colloquial Vermont name for the animal, and Philip used it throughout his journal, even though there are no native hedgehogs in Vermont or anywhere else in North America.

Federico's poem fragment, written on a page that belongs half to Lake Eden and half to the Catskills, is a perfect marker for the end of his time in Vermont and the beginning of his three-week stay with Ángel del Río in the Catskills.

PART THREE

Aftermath

CHAPTER NINE

Sleepless in the Catskills

Is there even one other like me—distracted—his friend, his lover, lost to him?

—Walt Whitman, "Hours Continuing Long"

IT WAS ALREADY DUSK on Thursday, 29 August, and Ángel del Río was growing increasingly concerned. Ten days earlier, Ángel had escorted Federico to Grand Central Terminal and helped him board the train to Vermont. At the time, their plan for the weeks ahead had seemed straightforward: Ángel would take his wife and infant son to a summer resort in the Catskill Mountains of New York state, where they could escape the late August heat of the city, and Federico would join them after his visit with Philip Cummings ended. As a result, they could spend the last three weeks of their summer vacation together before the Columbia University term began in late September, a happy prospect all around.

Just as planned, Ángel and his family were happily settled into their lodgings in the town of Shandaken, deep in the Catskills, where a room was waiting for Federico. But the day of reunion had arrived, and there was still no word from the traveler. Ángel had asked Federico to let them know of his arrival time in Kingston, the nearest major railway stop, so they could meet him and take him the rest of the way—but no telegram had come. As Ángel later recalled, they soon learned that Federico's forgetfulness and impetuosity had once again gotten him into trouble:

> Knowing his incapacity for coping with all practical matters, I wrote him detailed instructions. He must wire me the time of arrival in Kingston; in case I were not there, he must take a bus to Shandaken. The day we were waiting for him no telegram came and there was no sign of Lorca. We began to be worried lest he might be lost, when at nightfall we saw a taxi chugging along the dirt road of the farm. The driver wore an expression of resigned ferocity, and Federico, half out of the window, on seeing me began to shout in a mixture of terror and amusement.
>
> What had happened, of course, was that Lorca, finding himself alone in Kingston, had decided to take a taxi without being able to give the right directions to the driver. They had been going around mountain roads until a kindly neighbor had given them our address. The fare was $15. As Lorca had spent all his money, I had to pay the driver and placate his fury. Federico's terror was the outcome of his conviction that he was lost, without money enough to take care of the bill. Immediately he gave the incident a fantastic twist and said that the driver, whom he could not understand, had tried to rob and kill him in a dark corner of the woods.[1]

Federico alluded to this same incident in a letter to his parents a few weeks later, but he expressed significantly more confidence in his navigational abilities and knowledge of local geography than seems warranted under the circumstances: "All these trips have helped me get to know the admirable banks of the Hudson River. I have often sailed up and down it, and know all its villages and towns. And thus the East of the United States, the region least frequently visited by tourists, has become almost familiar to me. You can imagine how many amusing, and sometimes embarrassing, experiences I have had. I have discovered that I have a sense of humor that allows me to get through difficult situations."[2]

Considering the long distances between settled areas in the region, it seems almost miraculous that Federico managed to find Ángel and his family at all. But now that they were finally together, where exactly were they? Ángel, his wife, Amelia, and their three-month-old son, Miguel Ángel, were ensconced in a summer boardinghouse on the far northern edge of Bushnellsville, one of twelve widely dispersed hamlets that together make up the town of Shandaken in Ulster County, New York. (In 1930, the combined population of all twelve hamlets was 2,066.)[3] However, this description of the location of the boardinghouse is not as clear-cut as it sounds. Although it had a Bushnellsville address, it was not actually in Ulster County but rather in neighboring Greene County, on land that technically falls within the town limits of Lexington.[4] But since the area is separated from the rest of Lexington by a narrow mountain pass and is historically an outgrowth of Bushnellsville, the people who live there consider themselves residents of Bushnellsville.

The boardinghouse, known as Rock Terrace House, was on a small farm owned and operated by Roscoe and Phoebe Hogan, a married couple with two young children: Stanton, twelve, and Helen, eight.[5] The building had been constructed by Phoebe's parents, Charles and Helen Whitney, in 1911, during the height of the tourism boom in Bushnellsville, and boasted enough bedrooms, dining areas, and parlors to accommodate up to thirty-five guests. The family also maintained a small dairy herd on the property to provide fresh milk for guests and generate extra income during the off-season.

At 1,647 feet of elevation, the location was one of the coolest in Bushnellsville, a definite asset during the summer months. The building's wide, wraparound front porch was protected by a metal roof, so guests could relax in comfortable rocking chairs and enjoy the view and fresh air in almost any weather. Those who liked to fish could simply stroll down the front walk and across the dirt road to Bushnellsville Creek—a clear, cold brook that offered "the best trout fishing in the state," according to one Rock Terrace House advertisement. Other amenities included "telephone, free baths, farmer's bountiful table, new bowling alleys and all amusements nearby." The latter entertainments were available just a mile and a half down the road at Mountain Brook House, a larger boardinghouse that also offered tennis, swimming, billiards, dancing, and a snack bar, along with two mail deliveries daily.[6]

There is no indication that Federico was ever lured away from Rock Terrace House by any of these attractions. Even though he once again found himself in an isolated rural area full of beautiful scenery but not much else, to others he seemed happy to be there. For one thing, he was once again among Spanish-speaking peers close to his own age: Ángel, twenty-nine, was not only a Spanish intellectual but had also known Federico in Spain, while Amelia, thirty-two, was Puerto Rican and an accomplished poet and scholar in her own right.[7] At thirty-one, Federico fell neatly between them, so he had no reason to feel self-conscious about being older. He even joked about Ángel's premature slide into seniority in a letter to his parents. On the back of a photo of the two of them standing side by side in front of the boardinghouse, Federico wrote: "The difference between getting married and not getting married is this: here you have me, fit and handsome, and there you have Ángelito del Río, who is my age but is a broken-down old man."[8]

In Bushnellsville, Federico was also delighted to find himself coddled and fussed over, especially by Amelia, in a way that he greatly enjoyed. This was in clear contrast to Lake Eden, where both he and Philip had been expected to take care of themselves. He happily reported to his parents, "Ángel's wife mends my clothes, ties my ties, and just about everything else. She's simply charming. She and her South American girlfriends *take care* of me: to them a poet is something fantastic."[9]

He had similar praise for his hosts at Rock Terrace House, telling his parents that "Stanton's family puts us up very well indeed."[10] This level of service may have been due in part to the small number of guests there at the time; Federico and the del Ríos may have been the only ones. (There are no signs of other guests in any of the seven known photos taken at the farm, and no mention of other guests in the writings of either Ángel or Federico.)[11]

Such low occupancy for a boardinghouse designed to hold up to thirty-five people may have been coincidental, but it was more probably a deliberate choice on the part of Phoebe Hogan. Her husband, Roscoe, was battling cancer at the time—and would die from the disease just twenty months later.[12] Even the guests were aware of his illness, suggesting that he was no longer able to handle his usual share of farm and household tasks; he may even have been bedbound and required regular nursing care. With two young children to attend to as well, his wife had many good reasons to limit the number of guests.

Despite his usual outward cheerfulness, Federico arrived at the boardinghouse depressed and anxious, and the illness in the household only compounded his unhappiness. Though Ángel and Amelia were always happy to spend time with Federico, like most new parents they were often caught up in caring for little Miguel Ángel. The unusually warm weather during the first few days of Federico's visit would have added to the challenges; temperatures were in the mid-nineties, and it was hot enough to make everyone, including the baby, cranky and uncomfortable. In photos taken during this period, Federico wears his usual white cricket sweater but is minus a shirt, while Ángel has his long sleeves rolled up and tie undone; only Amelia, in a sleeveless summer dress, looks relaxed. Fortunately, the heat wave abated after a few days, with average daytime highs dropping to a comfortable seventy-five degrees and overnight lows to fifty-five. In photos taken during this cooler period, the whole group is dressed more warmly: Federico wears a collared shirt under his pullover, Ángel sports a vest and jacket, Amelia has added a cardigan sweater, and the baby is bundled up in blankets.

Federico loved little Miguel Ángel and was happy to help with childcare duties as needed. When Amelia developed a mild throat

Figure 29. Lorca with Ángel del Río, his wife Amelia, and their infant son, Miguel Ángel, at Rock Terrace House in the Catskills, September 1929. Archivo Fundación Federico García Lorca, Centro Federico García Lorca, Granada.

infection, Federico helped Ángel care for the baby while she rested. When the doctor suggested that moving the baby's crib into Federico's room for a few nights might speed Amelia's recovery, Federico readily agreed. He took the assignment very seriously and worried incessantly about the child's well-being, so much so that he stayed awake most of the night watching and listening while the baby slept.[13]

Nights at the boardinghouse may have been difficult for Federico, with or without the baby present, especially when he first arrived. On the sleeping porch at Lake Eden, whenever he heard a strange or startling sound in the night, Philip was always beside him to explain what it was and calm his fears. In Bushnellsville, Federico was once again surrounded by unfamiliar sights and sounds, but this time he was on his own. In his distraught emotional state, he was tormented by threats both real and imaginary, which kept him awake and on edge, threats that soon began to emerge in his poems.[14]

During the daylight hours, in addition to their understandable focus on the baby, Ángel and Amelia may both have needed to work on their course materials for the coming academic session.[15] Under other circumstances, their consequent lack of time for Federico might have made him feel a bit abandoned, but after so many days of close contact with Philip, he did not seem to mind being left to his own devices. Their preoccupation not only gave Federico ample time to write; it may have also allowed him to avoid answering questions about his visit to Vermont. It is clear from his later behavior that Ángel knew his friend was homosexual, but it is unclear how much Federico actually told him about his relationship with Philip. Federico may well have held back many details, uncertain how Ángel would react or perhaps embarrassed that he had once again allowed himself to imagine reciprocal feelings in another man that were not really there.

Figure 30. Lorca at his makeshift desk on the porch of Rock Terrace House, September 1929. Archivo Fundación Federico García Lorca, Centro Federico García Lorca, Granada.

Alone in his room or at a makeshift desk on the front porch of the boardinghouse, Federico turned his attention to his immediate surroundings and the unexpected distractions he found on the farm in Bushnellsville. Chief among these were Stanton and Helen Hogan, the owners' children, who were home from school for the summer and delighted to find an adult so willing to spend time with them. According to Ángel del Río, despite their lack of a common spoken language, the three quickly became friends: "How he communicated with the children was a marvel of inventiveness. They were fascinated by Federico, especially when he sang or improvised folk songs on a dilapidated and out-of-tune piano or when he told them stories in an incredible Spanish, often acting the parts of the characters and dramatizing the action."[16]

Stanton and Helen introduced Federico to their favorite animals on the farm, including Stanton's shaggy black dog, their father's blind horse, and the cows grazing peacefully in the pasture—all of which later made appearances in his poems. It is striking, however, that Federico transformed what must have been idyllic interludes with the children and their animals into four very dark poems—"Landscape with Two Graves and an Assyrian Dog," "Little Stanton," "Ruin," and "Cow"—each full of threatening, even terrifying images.

Federico had demonstrated in Vermont that he was quite capable of maintaining a cheerful public demeanor while privately feeling profoundly unhappy, relying on poetry as an outlet for expressing the emotional pain he felt compelled to keep hidden. However, these four poems go beyond personal anguish and unhappiness to something much deeper: the fear of a painful and untimely death. This may have been brought to the forefront of Federico's mind by the presence of cancer in the Hogan household; being in such close proximity to a forty-six-year-old man who was visibly dying from an incurable disease clearly shook Federico to his core.[17]

According to Ángel del Río, Federico was also afraid of Stanton's big black dog, despite its old age and partial blindness, and hated the fact that the animal often slept in the hallway outside his bedroom

Figure 31. Lorca and Ángel del Río with Stanton and Helen Hogan, children of the Rock Terrace House owners, September 1929. Archivo Fundación Federico García Lorca, Centro Federico García Lorca, Granada.

door at night.[18] These fears, combined with a general sense of dread and foreboding, seem to color all his work from this period. For example, the following lines, marked by the hushed urgency of the speaker's warning to his sleeping friend, appear at the beginning of "Landscape with Two Graves and an Assyrian Dog" (Paisaje con dos tumbas y un perro asirio):

> Friend,
> get up and listen
> to the Assyrian dog howl.
> Cancer's three nymphs have been dancing,
> my son.
> They carried mountains of red sealing wax

and stiff bed sheets to the place where cancer slept.
The horse had an eye in its neck
and the moon was in a sky so cold
that she had to tear open her mound of Venus
and drown the ancient graveyards in blood and ashes.[19]

In the final stanzas of this poem, the speaker's alarm when the mountains stop breathing, coupled with his devotion to a small child, seem to echo Federico's anxious worries for little Miguel Ángel. But despite the speaker's tender memories, the threat does not recede; instead, it comes ever closer:

Friend,
wake up, the mountains still aren't breathing
and the grass of my heart is somewhere else.
It doesn't matter if you're full of seawater.
For a long time I loved a child
who had a tiny feather on its tongue,
and we lived inside a knife for a hundred years.
Wake up. Be still. Listen. Sit up in your bed.
The howling
is a long purple tongue that releases
terrifying ants and the liquor of irises.
Here it comes toward the rock. Don't spread out your roots!
It approaches. Moans. Friend, don't sob in your dreams.

Friend!
Get up and listen
to the Assyrian dog howl.[20]

In the first stanza of the next poem in this group, "Little Stanton" (El niño Stanton), the threat has become even more immediate. The sleeping cancer is now fully awake, an active, malevolent force intent on harming the speaker's imagined son, who shares the name of the real patient's son. Again, the poem begins with night terrors, but "in the house where there is cancer," even the light of day offers no protection to the boy, Stanton, who in his simple innocence is "idiotic and beautiful among the little animals":

When I'm by myself
your ten years stay with me.
So do the three blind horses,
your fifteen faces with the face after the stoning
and tiny frozen fevers on leaves of corn.
Stanton, my son, Stanton.
At twelve midnight, cancer wandered through the corridors
and spoke with the documents' empty snails,
cancer springing to life, full of clouds and thermometers,
with an apple's chaste longing to be pecked by nightingales.
In the house where there is cancer,
the white walls shatter in the delirium of astronomy
and the burn glows brightly for many years
in the smallest stables, in forests where paths intersect.
My sorrow bled in the afternoons
when your eyes became two walls,
when your hands became two countries
and my body murmured like grass.
My agony went looking for its clothes,
dusty, bitten by dogs,
and you went with it, without trembling,
to the threshold of dark water.
Oh, Stanton, idiotic and beautiful among the little animals,
your mother hammered to pieces by the village blacksmiths,
one brother under the arches
and the other one eaten by the anthills,
and cancer, free of barbed wire, beating in the rooms like a heart!
There are wet nurses who give children
rivers of moss and bitter feet,

and black women who go upstairs to spread rat potion.
Because it's true, there are people
who want to dump doves in the sewers
and I know what else they want—the people
hanging out in the street who suddenly squeeze our fingertips.[21]

Note that cancer is not the only threat that lurks in the lines of this poem; the speaker also mentions biting dogs. The recurrence of dogs as a potential source of pain and injury in both poems suggests that Federico may have had a generalized fear of dogs, perhaps from an earlier experience with an aggressive animal. We can only hope that he eventually felt more at ease with Stanton's dog. Another danger mentioned in these lines is more subtle, the deceptively benign "threshold of dark water." Federico revisits this theme in another poem, "Little Girl Drowned in the Well (Granada and Newburgh)," which we will discuss later in this chapter.

The dark mood continues in the third poem of this group, "Ruin" (Ruina). This time, the speaker himself is directly under attack, but the threat is not cancer; it is the very grass itself. At first, the speaker and his son are protected from its blades by a window, but their protection gives way: "Hold my hand, my love. The grass! / Through the house's broken windows, / the blood unleashed its waves of hair."[22] In the end, the speaker and his son remain, but the attack has reduced them to skeletons in a sort of living death.

In the final poem of this group, titled simply "Cow" (Vaca), the unfortunate cow has suffered some grievous wound. The speaker is close enough to see blood on the animal's head as she bellows in pain, though he is in no apparent danger himself. The cow's injury is so serious that she cannot survive it, and her fate is even more horrifying than the outcome threatened by cancer or malicious grass:

The wounded cow lay down,
trees and streams climbing over its horns.
Its muzzle bled in the sky.

Its muzzle of bees
under the slow mustache of slobber.
A white cry brought the morning to its feet.

Cows, dead and alive,
blushing light or honey from the stables,
bellowed with half-closed eyes.

Tell the roots
and that child sharpening his knife:
now they can eat the cow.

Above them, lights
and jugulars turn pale.
Four cloven hoofs tremble in the air.

Tell the moon
and that night of yellow rocks:
now the cow of ash has gone.

Now it has gone bellowing
through the wreckage of the rigid skies
where the drunks lunch on death.[23]

There is nothing in Ángel del Río's writings or Federico's letters to indicate that Federico ever witnessed an injured cow being slaughtered on the farm, but this disturbing image was clearly on his mind as he wrote this poem. Did he perhaps identify with the suffering animal at some level, and imagine that a similar fate might befall a person whom others considered damaged beyond repair?

It is possible that the cow of the poem was based on an actual wounded animal that Federico saw with Philip on a farm near Lake Eden, as Philip later told researcher Kessel Schwartz.[24] However, Philip also remembered that the cow was being treated by a veterinarian, an expense no Vermont farmer would incur unless the animal was expected to fully recover. If that cow was indeed Federico's inspiration, he clearly transformed its injury into something far more severe when he composed the poem in Bushnellsville. This ominous shift in both the severity of the wound and its dire consequences suggests the extent to which Federico's anxieties and the somber mood of the household had colored his thinking.

However, a few of the poems he composed in Bushnellsville have a somewhat calmer tone. In "Little Girl Drowned in the Well (Granada and Newburgh)" (Niña ahogada en el pozo [Granada y Newburgh]), for instance, a hapless innocent is once again the victim of a malign force, but here the speaker's voice is more measured. The sense of urgency is still there, but so, too, is a feeling of resignation, even acceptance.[25] Though Federico appended the line "New York 8 de Diciembre 1929" in his final manuscript version of "Little Girl Drowned in the Well," Ángel remembered him reading it aloud in Bushnellsville—and it clearly began there.[26]

The deep well featured in the poem stems directly from one of Federico's adventures with Stanton and Helen Hogan, who not only showed him around the farm, but also took him to their favorite places in the nearby woods. The most unusual of these was a spot where all the trees had been cut down and part of the underlying rock ledge blasted away, leaving behind a barren, rubble-strewn clearing in the middle of the otherwise lush forest. The most striking feature of the clearing was an apparently bottomless pit, some fourteen feet across, in the center.[27] To compound the visual strangeness of the place, anyone brave enough to approach the edge of the pit could hear the unexpected sound of rushing water echoing from far, far below. For Federico, the eerie combination triggered thoughts of a well so deep that anyone who fell into it was beyond the reach of rescuers, lost forever in the darkness and mysterious currents below. Federico had a long-standing fear of drowning, which must have made the experience particularly disturbing.[28]

The distant sound of water made no sense unless the listener understood why the pit had been constructed in the first place. It is unclear how much the children knew about its history and purpose, but Federico would have been unable to understand what they said in any case. Not even Ángel was aware of its true origins, as his description makes clear: "Near the farm, where everything seemed abandoned, there were several great pits that had once been quarries. The place, with its bleeding earth and skeletal rocks, had a desolate grandeur. It was, Federico used to say, like a lunar landscape. The water in the pits could not be seen, but one could hear its murmuring crash at the bottom."[29]

It is possible that Ángel never visited the site himself, relying instead on Federico's description, since he referred to multiple pits when there was only one and assumed that they were former quarries. The mystery would have been quickly resolved if Roscoe Hogan, the children's father, had been well enough to talk with his guests. A civil engineer for New York City, Roscoe had worked on the pit project himself for over two years and could have answered any questions that Ángel or Federico might have had.[30] As it was, they were left to reach their own, faulty conclusions.

The pit was the surface opening of shaft 6, one of eight vertical shafts that had been bored at carefully planned locations across the region, starting in 1918, to facilitate the construction of the Shandaken Tunnel. This tunnel was a huge, concrete-lined aqueduct that carried fresh water from the Schoharie Reservoir high in the Catskills to the Ashokan Reservoir near Kingston, which provided much-needed water to the people of New York City.[31] Completed in only five years, the 18.5-mile aqueduct was a marvel of engineering and the longest tunnel in the world at the time.[32]

When construction was completed, the empty shafts, which now provided ventilation for the tunnel far below, remained in place. Shaft 6, the one near Rock Terrace House, was the deepest of all eight shafts, reaching down a full 647 feet to the aqueduct and its unending torrent of water. Imagine how otherworldly the place must have seemed, especially to someone who had no idea what it was.

In "Little Girl Drowned in the Well," Federico combines the bewildering sound of moving water coming from deep within the pit with his memories of a young girl's accidental drowning in a well in Granada. The result is a tragic tale of loss with a haunting refrain:

Statues suffer the darkness of coffins with their eyes,
but they suffer even more from water that never reaches the sea . . .
that never reaches the sea.

The townspeople ran along the battlements breaking the fishermen's
poles.
Quickly! To the edge! Hurry! And the tender stars sounded like
bullfrogs.
. . . that never reaches the sea.

At peace in my memory, heavenly body, circumference, boundary,
you cry on the shores of a horse's eye,
. . . that never reaches the sea

But no one in the darkness will be able to give you distances,
only sharpened limits: diamond future.
. . . that never reaches the sea.

While the people look for pillowed silences,
you pulsate forever, defined by your ring.
. . . that never reaches the sea.

You'll always be undying at the end of waves that accept
the combat of roots and anticipated solitude.
. . . that never reaches the sea.

They're coming up the ramps! Arise from the water!
Every point of light will toss you a chain!
. . . that never reaches the sea.

But the well pulls you back with small mossy hands,
you, unforeseen nymph of the chaste ignorance.
. . . that never reaches the sea.

No, that never reaches the sea. Water fixed in one place,
breathing with all its unstrung violins
on the musical scale of wounds and deserted buildings.
Water that never reaches the sea![33]

Despite everyone's efforts to rescue the child, she remains caught in the well's mysterious grip, separated forever from all that she knows and loves. For Federico, the girl's inability to escape her fate may have served as a metaphor for his own fear of being trapped in a life of unending despair and loneliness. But he also gives voice to another, less obvious victim of the malevolent well in the poem—the water itself. It, too, is an involuntary captive of the well. The water longs for the sea, but the well provides no pathway, so it can only continue breathing and making its own strange music while it waits to be set free. The water's fate is torturous and difficult, but at least it leaves some room for hope.

This poem, quieter and more focused on helplessness and inescapable loss than on death, seems to mark a turning point in the themes Federico explored in the Catskills. Perhaps, as everything at the boardinghouse became more familiar, he was able to move beyond the sense of panic and dread that dominates the other poems he wrote there. This shift suggests he may have also begun to more directly address his feelings of sadness and abandonment in the aftermath of his failed hopes for a closer bond with Philip.

The poem "Nocturne of Emptied Space" (Nocturno del hueco) reflects this change. Unlike the other poems Federico wrote in Bushnellsville, here there is no threat of bodily harm, only loneliness and despair as the speaker bares his soul to a lover who is leaving him. In the words of critic Paul Binding, "Few of the poems [in *Poet in New York*] are more desolate—or more moving in their desolation." Binding suspected that Federico was thinking of Salvador Dalí when he wrote the poem, but it seems much more likely that the speaker's unnamed lover is Philip.[34]

Some translators have dealt with the sexual content of this poem more directly than others. The Spanish word *hueco*, for example, appears in the poem's Spanish title ("Nocturno del Hueco") and many of its verses. In three different bilingual editions of *Poet in New York*, each translator chose a different but equally neutral English equivalent for hueco: "emptiness," "void," and "emptied space."[35] However, in their translation of the collection, Pablo Medina and Mark Statman deliberately chose a sexually explicit alternative, explaining: "By translating *hueco* as 'hole,' we are being literal and charging the English version with the sexuality Lorca intended in his original."[36]

Though it is not certain that the speaker in this poem is meant to represent Federico himself, his use of the first person—"I," "me," and "mine"—gives it a markedly intimate tone. The poem has two distinct parts, marked by roman numerals. In the first part, the speaker implores his lost love to notice that all traces of their time together are gone, leaving only emptiness behind. He describes the disjointed landscape that now surrounds him and is lost in his almost unbearably sad memories. He makes no attempt to hide or discount his pain, but rather presents it as a simple, immutable fact:

> I.
>
> *If you want to see that nothing is left,*
> *see the emptied spaces and the clothes,*
> *give me your lunar glove,*
> *your other glove of grass,*
> *my love!*
>
> The air can tear dead snails
> from the elephant's lung

and blow the stiff, cold worms
from budding light or apples.

Faces erased of all emotion sail
beneath the faint uproar of the grass
and the frog's little breast is in the corner
with a clouded heart and mandolin.

On the great deserted plaza,
the cow's freshly severed head kept bellowing
and shapes that looked for the serpent's coiling
crystallized completely.

If you want to see that nothing is left,
give me your speechless, emptied space, my love,
grade-school nostalgia and sad sky!
If you want to see that nothing is left![37]

In the next stanzas, the speaker recalls their sexual relationship with startling candor. The speaker cherishes his lover's willingness to share his body but now understands that his lover's heart was always impenetrable and remains unavailable to him. Chastened, the speaker accepts the limits of his own love to generate love in another:

Inside you, my love, in your flesh,
the silence of derailed trains!
So many mummies' arms in bloom!
What a dead-end sky, my love, what a sky!

Stone in water, voice on the breeze—
love's limits burst free from their bleeding trunk.
Feeling the pulse of our love today is enough
to make flowers spring from other children.

If you want to see that nothing is left,
see the emptied spaces of clouds and rivers,
give me your laurel boughs, my love.
If you want to see that nothing is left!

The pure spaces spin through me, through you, at dawn,
preserving the tracks of the bloody branches
and some profile of tranquil plaster that depicts
the punctured moon's instant sorrow.

Look at the concrete shapes in search of their void.
Lost dogs and half-eaten apples.
Look at this sad fossil world, with its anxiety and anguish,
a world that can't find the accent of its very first sob.

When I search the bed for murmuring thread,
I know you've come, my love, to cover my roof
The emptied space of an ant can fill the air,
but you moan with nothing to guide you through my eyes.

No, not through my eyes, because now you show me
four rivers wrapped tightly around your arm,
in the rough lean-to where the imprisoned moon
devours a sailor in front of the children.

If you want to see that nothing is left,
my impenetrable love, now that you have gone,
don't give me your emptied space. No.
Mine is already traveling through the air!
Who will pity you, or me, or the breeze?
If you want to see that nothing is left.[38]

The repeated refrain of the first part captures the full depth of the speaker's despair with incredible grace and clarity. It encompasses even the loss of Federico's ties to Lake Eden, where nothing remains except an empty cottage. Philip and his family are gone, along with the summer, leaving behind only shorter, cooler days that signal the approaching winter.

In the second part of the poem, the speaker is now completely alone. He has survived his lover's departure, but not without damage, and sees only continued struggle ahead:

II.

Me.
With the white emptied space of a horse,
ashen-maned. Pure and folded plaza.

Me.
My emptied space pierced with what remains of my armpits.
Like a neutered grape's shriveled skin and asbestos of dawn.

All the world's light fits inside an eye.
The rooster crows and his song lasts longer than his wings.

Me.
With the white emptied space of a horse,
Ringed by onlookers with their ant-teeming words.

In the circus of cold weather with no mutilated profile,
Among the chipped capitals of cheeks bled white.

Me.
My emptied space without you, city, without your voracious dead.
Rider through my life finally at anchor.

Me.

No new age. No enlightenment.
Only a blue horse and dawn.[39]

The visual starkness of these lines is almost as powerful as the words themselves in conveying the intense grief and utter hopelessness Federico must have been feeling. But the very act of writing the poem may have allowed him to break the grip of his despair. Perhaps he finally realized that, while he could continue seeking a committed, loving relationship with another man, the cost of giving in to wishful thinking about someone who did not share this goal was simply too high to pay.

When their stay in Bushnellsville ended, Ángel and Amelia went back to New York City, while Federico spent a further three days in Newburgh, New York, at the invitation of Federico de Onís, head of the Spanish department at Columbia.[40] He was not the only guest at the professor's summer home during this period. The Spanish poet and translator León Felipe, then immersed in his study of the poems of Walt Whitman, was staying there as well.

León Felipe later claimed that he was the first person to introduce Federico to Whitman's work, telling an interviewer, "We were in Newburgh, and that's when I spoke of Whitman and told [Federico] those things. . . . I think the first things he learned about Whitman were what I told him, and he always spoke that way."[41] He added that, when Federico asked him if it was true that Whitman had been homosexual, he had explained that this was a misunderstanding; in reality, Whitman had loved everyone—men, women, and children—equally. Federico, he said, seemed "wounded" by this answer.[42]

Critics have generally accepted Felipe's claim, but it does not quite add up. If Federico knew nothing at all about Whitman at that time, why would he ask Felipe about the poet's sexual orientation, and then be upset by his reply? The obvious answer is that Federico already knew about Whitman's homosexuality from his discussions with Philip at Lake Eden and felt distressed that Felipe did not acknowledge this aspect of Whitman's identity.

Federico's own way of speaking may explain why Philip's contribution to his knowledge of Whitman was overlooked for so long. Federico always referred to Philip as "Felipe," the Spanish equivalent of Philip, which has exactly the same spelling and pronunciation as León Felipe's last name. Federico himself may have contributed to this misunderstanding. If someone asked who first introduced him to Whitman, and he replied, "Felipe," a listener would naturally conclude that he meant León Felipe.

The most interesting outcome of Federico's discussion with León Felipe is that he apparently decided to ignore the older man's assessment of Whitman's sexuality and instead place his faith in what Philip had told him. If Philip had translated even a few of the "Calamus" poems for Federico, as evidence suggests, Federico would have been well aware of Whitman's praise for romantic and sexual relationships between men.

The impact of his exposure to this aspect of Whitman's work became clear a few months later, when Federico wrote his controversial "Ode to Walt Whitman" (Oda a Walt Whitman).[43] In the poem, the speaker refers to Whitman with great affection and applauds his preference for rugged working men:

> Not for a moment, Walt Whitman, lovely old man,
> have I failed to see your beard full of butterflies,
> nor your corduroy shoulders frayed by the moon,
> nor your thighs as pure as Apollo's,
> nor your voice like a column of ash;
> old man, beautiful as the mist,
> you moaned like a bird
> with its sex pierced by a needle.
> Enemy of the satyr,
> enemy of the vine,
> Lover of bodies beneath rough cloth.[44]

However, the speaker also condemns homosexuals who embrace the debauched, decadent lifestyle of New York's gay demimonde, which Federico saw on public display in his own New York neighborhood. For the speaker, the greatest, most unforgivable sin of these men, whom he labels "urban faggots," is that they dare to claim Walt Whitman as one of their own. The poem presents a surprisingly rigid view of the correct behavior for a homosexual man, suggesting that, at least at the time, Federico was holding himself to the standard of a stereotypically masculine, heterosexual man.

In the weeks that followed his time in the Catskills, Federico seemed to recover his bearings and begin moving on with his life. In at least one instance, he chose to gloss right over the Vermont episode. In a November 1929 letter to his close friend Carlos Morla Lynch, who had provided ongoing emotional support during his most difficult times with Emilio Aladrén in Madrid, Federico wrote, "I spent the summer in Canada [*sic*] with some friends and I'm now in New York, which is a city of unexpected happiness."[45] Whatever his mental state at the time, now that he had actually been to Vermont, it seems unlikely that he could not remember where he had spent the summer.

Whether or not Federico truly wanted to forget his affair with Philip, Philip himself, seemingly unaware of the emotional turmoil he had caused his friend, was intent on maintaining their relationship. In the months ahead, he would devote considerable time and energy to finding a way to return to Spain and reunite with Federico, even as he embarked on his first professional job as a teacher of modern languages.

CHAPTER TEN

Heedless in St. Louis

Wherever I have been,
I have charged myself with contentment and triumph.

—Walt Whitman, "Song at Sunset"

WHEN WE LAST SAW Philip, he had said his final good-byes to Federico at the Burlington train station and headed back to Lake Eden with his father. But circumstances gave him little time to reflect on Federico's visit or his departure. With the cottage rental period about to end, he and his parents had to quickly prepare to vacate the premises. As he packed his things, Philip made sure that his most precious souvenirs from Federico's visit—the journal he kept during their time together, any photos that had already been developed, his English translations of Federico's *Canciones*—were safely tucked into his suitcase along with his clothes and books.

When all was ready, the family loaded their vacation gear and supplies into the Model T and drove back to their apartment in Hardwick. Once there, even with so many other things to think about, Philip found time to write a brief introduction to his translations, clearly hoping to have them published at some future date.[1] He then placed the translations in a box for safekeeping and turned his attention to a much more pressing matter: his upcoming trip to

St. Louis, Missouri, where he would be spending the next nine months.

In St. Louis, Philip was slated to begin his first job as an official college graduate, "a fine position in an educational institution teaching Spanish," according to the local paper.[2] The institution in question was the Principia Upper School, a private, co-ed, Christian Science high school that accommodated both boarding and day students. The upper school was just one part of the Principia system; it also included a lower school for grades 1–8 and a separate junior college. Philip was not a Christian Scientist, but clearly the school did not make official membership in the Church of Christ, Scientist, a condition of employment for its teachers.

On Sunday, 15 September 1929, three days before classes were to begin, Philip was happily ensconced in his rooms at the Principia. That day, he wrote a short foreword for his Lake Eden journal, adding the date and his location as a postscript.[3] It is unclear whether he brought the actual journal with him to St. Louis or composed the foreword without having it in hand. Either way, he eventually mailed whatever pages he had with him back to Hardwick, where the entire journal, along with his translations, remained hidden away in a storage box for almost twenty years.

Meanwhile, Philip carried on with his busy life. His teaching load at the Principia was light enough to leave plenty of time for other activities, a fortunate circumstance for a young man with aspirations that stretched far beyond St. Louis. As soon as he arrived there, he began pursuing two separate but related goals—obtaining a graduate degree in Spanish and finding a way to return to Spain, or at least Europe, in the coming year—both of which would make it easier to stay in contact with Federico.

The graduate degree was the easiest to tackle, especially once Philip learned that the Principia was less than three miles away from the hilltop campus of Washington University at St. Louis, a nationally known institution of higher learning. He applied to the university's graduate school, was approved as a candidate for the master of arts degree in Spanish and history, and enrolled in a two-semester graduate course in early Spanish literature—all before Washington University's first classes began on 26 September.[4]

Philip's campaign to find a way to return to Spain was more complicated, involving efforts on two fronts. The first required winning any sort of academic award that would cover the cost of his continuing graduate studies overseas. He had become familiar with the Institute of International Education (IIE) and its parent organization, the Carnegie Endowment for International Peace (CEIP), while enrolled at Rollins College and kept track of the various programs offered by both groups.[5] Sometime that October, he learned about a CEIP fellowship in international law being offered for the 1930–1931 academic year and immediately wrote to request an application. Though he could list no related coursework or evidence of prior law-related activity, Philip submitted the application anyway, noting on the form that he would prefer to do his fellowship abroad. He may not have realized that most of the other applicants already had a law degree, making his attempt a particularly long shot.[6]

While he waited to hear the results of the fellowship competition, Philip began seeking out people who could potentially exert some influence on his behalf in the United States or Spain. His most successful contact was with maestro Enrique Fernández Arbós, the renowned director of the Madrid Symphony Orchestra, who was serving as guest conductor for the St. Louis Symphony Orchestra for its fall 1929 season. Almost as soon as Fernández Arbós and his wife arrived in the city and settled into their suite in the Coronado Hotel, Philip wrote to him in Spanish. His letter has not survived, but extrapolating from a translation of the maestro's gracious reply (see below), Philip mentioned his past trips to Spain, his fondness for the country, and his friendship with Federico. He must also have asked Fernández Arbós for an autograph, which did not appear to cause any offense:

6 November 1929

My very dear sir,

I received your first letter, so pleasant, which I deeply appreciated, and I didn't reply to it immediately (for which I beg your pardon) because I have had to work a great deal all of these days, and I haven't been able to find a free moment to do so. I thank you for your affectionate sentiments towards me and towards Spain. It gives me the greatest pleasure to send you the enclosed autograph that you requested. If you attend concerts and would care to go to the trouble of coming, after one of them, to my room at the Odeon [Theatre] it would be a great pleasure to make your acquaintance personally. In the meanwhile, please receive this testimony of my sympathy and believe me your affectionate friend.

Sincerely, E. Fernández Arbós

P.S. I don't know whether you know that the poet García Lorca has been in New York for the past 3 months.[7]

Philip loved classical music and would have probably attended all the orchestra's concerts anyway, but the prospect of getting to meet Fernández Arbós in person afterward would have made going irresistible. Whenever their first meeting occurred, Philip clearly made a good impression on the maestro and his wife, Paquita. In journal entries written a few years later, Philip reminisced about his frequent late-afternoon visits with the couple in their hotel suite, where they would converse about music, Spain, and various people they knew in common.[8] Fernández Arbós may have also facilitated Philip's meeting with the famed French pianist Alfred Cortot in mid-November, when Cortot was the orchestra's featured performer.[9]

Philip's strategy for approaching Cortot mirrored his first contact with Federico, suggesting a possible pattern: "I dedicated a short poem to [Cortot] and took it out to him after the symphony concert at which he was soloist."[10] Cortot was rumored to be homosexual; perhaps this speculation had reached Philip's ears and motivated his gesture.[11] In any case, Philip provided no further details about their encounter except to note that "two months afterward, I had a charming letter from him from his Paris studio."[12]

Cortot was well known for his artful interpretation of the piano music of French composer Claude Debussy, so it is possible that Philip's soulful "To One Who Loves Debussy," published by the *Tampa Tribune* in March 1930, was the same poem he had given to Cortot in St. Louis:

> I sit beside the mahogany heart
> as it breathes and beats.
> I would touch its vibrant arteries
> but I must only watch
> and pick each throb from twilight dusk
> She who taught you first to breathe
> has you singing to her fame.
> Oh that I could teach
> your ivory scores of mouths
> to sing for me;
> and refine twilights to such gold
> that I might with it gild
> trees in the rain
> which sing so faunishly.
> There are ten keys
> to your soul-sealed lips
> and I watch them fly
> from lock to lock;
> and loose the ringing voices
> so eagered by their silence.
> Oh give me keys![13]

It may seem odd that a poem Philip wrote in St. Louis was published by a Florida newspaper, but while a student at Rollins College he had gained a loyal fan in Phil Barney, associate editor of the *Tampa Tribune*.[14] Though Philip left Florida for good in March 1929, Barney continued to feature his work for five more years, publishing eighteen of Philip's poems between September 1929 and June 1930 alone.

Philip was remarkably productive, from a poetic perspective, during his nine months at the Principia. In addition to his *Tampa Tribune* poems, during that same period he had four poems published in *Driftwind from the North Hills*, a Vermont literary journal; one poem in the *Christian Science Monitor*; and one poem in each of three major literary anthologies.[15] There are no surviving letters or other evidence that Philip sent copies of any of these published pieces to Federico; however, considering the effort Philip typically expended to stay in touch with people whose acquaintance he valued, it is hard to imagine that he did not share at least some of them with his friend, whether or not Federico wanted to see them. After all, what better way to demonstrate his continued commitment to both poetry and their relationship?

There are other indications that Federico was still on Philip's mind, at least occasionally. During the Principia's two-week winter break, from 20 December to 4 January, Philip traveled by train from St. Louis to Mexico City. He was fascinated by the city's vibrancy and rich historical traditions and greatly enjoyed his time there.[16] He also took the opportunity to send a postcard of the US embassy in Mexico City to Federico:

Sr. Federico García Lorca Acera del Casino 31 Granada, España	Mr. Federico García Lorca Acera del Casino 31 Granada, Spain
Mis recuerdos a usted y a su familia en la fiesta de la Navidad. Me encanta México. Su siempre amigo, Felipe Cummings	*My regards to you and your family at Christmas time. I love Mexico.* *Your friend always,* Felipe Cummings[17]

It is unclear why Philip addressed the postcard to Federico at his family home in Granada rather than to his dormitory room at Columbia; perhaps he incorrectly assumed that Federico would have returned to Granada for Christmas. Philip knew that, once his postcard reached Granada, there was a good chance that others would read it before it reached Federico. He once again used the formal *usted* to refer to Federico, rather than the informal *tú* that is typical among good friends. As with his first letter to Federico, this may have been a deliberate choice on Philip's part to downplay the intimacy of their friendship to Federico's family.

When the Christmas vacation ended and Philip returned to the Principia, he may have been disappointed to find that he still had not received any word about the CEIP fellowship competition. If so, his disappointment would have been short-lived. With perfect timing, an article in the February 1930 newsletter of the IIE announced a whole new possible avenue for returning to Spain.[18] The piece described a newly created Spanish-American student exchange program, funded by a decree of the king of Spain, that would cover participants' tuition, board, and lodging for one academic year. However, the article mentioned only half of the exchange—Spanish students coming to the United States in the fall of 1930—and said nothing about American students going to Spain. The stated rationale for this omission, given in a report written a few months later, was that "arrangements will not be completed to make it advisable for American students to undertake their studies in Spain before the academic year 1931–32."[19]

The delay was undoubtedly due to the fraught political situation in Spain, particularly at Spanish universities. Beginning in May 1928, universities across Spain periodically closed and then reopened in response to various political actions. The government of General Primo de Rivera, with the tacit approval of the king, would institute measures designed to control university appointments, degree requirements, course offerings, and even course content. Students and faculty would speak out or go on strike against the repressive measures, leading to further government decrees, which closed the universities for weeks or sometimes months at a time. The situation would begin to calm down and the universities would be allowed to reopen, then the government would issue new restrictions, and the whole cycle would begin again.[20] Considering the unpredictability and volatility of the situation, it would have been difficult for IIE program administrators to ensure that American students could complete a full year of study in Spain—and do so safely.

The announcement of the new program must have given Philip hope nonetheless, as he immediately started trying to figure out the best way to approach the IIE about becoming one of the first Americans to participate. We can imagine how he might have made his case, explaining with his usual flair that, since he was already fluent in Spanish, enrolled in a Spanish graduate program, and familiar with Madrid and its universities from his previous visits there, he would need far less on-the-ground support and guidance from the organization than would other Americans. He would have surely found a way to mention his friendships with maestro Fernández Arbós and his wife, various faculty members at the Residencia de Estudiantes, Dr. Hamilton Holt of Rollins College, and of course the renowned Spanish poet Federico García Lorca.

Whatever methods Philip used to convince the IIE program administrators that he was the perfect candidate to initiate the American side of the exchange, they were resoundingly successful—even if the IIE waited until the very last minute to decide. Fortunately for Philip, following Primo de Rivera's resignation in January 1930, all of the general's university-related decrees were revoked, and by June the political situation in Spain appeared to be stabilizing.[21] Sometime in early September 1930, Philip was officially informed that he had been awarded an IIE fellowship to spend the 1930–1931 academic year in Spain, the sole American student to receive this honor. Philip must have alerted both of the daily newspapers in Burlington, Vermont, about his award, since both printed articles about it on 9 September.[22] Both papers also noted that Philip would be sailing for Europe on the *Britannic* on 14 September, just five days later, so he must have learned that he was the winning candidate sometime earlier and already booked his passage.[23]

It is unclear whether Philip paid for his voyage using his own savings or funds provided by benefactors, but the money definitely did not come from his parents. Tragically, his father's mental health had deteriorated to the point where he was admitted to the Vermont State Hospital for the Insane in May 1930, where he remained until his death in February 1934. Though it is almost certain that neither Philip nor his mother knew that Harry's condition was the result of tertiary syphilis, Philip's willingness to be away from home for nine months at such a difficult time for his family may indicate a desire to escape the stigma of his father's mental illness. The situation could have also increased his fear that, without additional academic credentials, he might not be able to support himself, and potentially his mother, through his teaching.[24] Since there was no way to pursue an advanced degree in Hardwick, he might as well continue his graduate work in Spain—where he could also see Federico again.

By the time Philip reached Madrid in late September 1930, Federico was back at his family's home in Granada and preparing to leave for Madrid himself. Federico had returned to Granada on 1 July after being away almost thirteen months: eight months in the United States, three months in Cuba, and travel time in between. Federico's activities in New York and Cuba from October 1929 through June 1930 have been well documented by other biographers, so they will not be discussed at length here.[25] Suffice it to say that, once back in New York after his time in Vermont and the Catskills, he gave up any pretense of attending classes and soon fell into a regular routine of reading novels, writing poems, and socializing with friends, while giving occasional paid lectures to supplement his monthly stipend from his parents. In Cuba, where everything was new to him, his days were more varied; he presented a series of lectures as planned but also took every opportunity to explore all the island had to offer—including its vibrant and welcoming gay community.[26]

As he began the long ocean voyage back to Spain in June 1930,

Federico's thoughts had returned in part to "Two Lovers Murdered by a Partridge," the unusual prose poem discussed in chapter 2. He had written the original version of the poem during the fall of 1928, after his liaison with Philip at the Residencia ended but well before he traveled to the United States.[27] However, on board the ship, Federico described "Two Lovers" to his traveling companion, Adolfo Salazar, as a new composition, so perhaps he had begun revising it in Cuba.[28]

Interestingly, one detail in the final version of the poem mirrors the makeup of the household at Lake Eden. The beginning lines of the poem make it clear that both the mother and cousin of one of the two lovers were well aware of their affair. However, the gendered nature of Spanish nouns reveals a little more: The cousin in question was female. As already discussed, Philip and Federico shared the Lake Eden cottage with Philip's parents, his aunt, and his cousin Edna, but perhaps this is just a coincidence.

According to Salazar, Federico repeatedly read the poem aloud to him and their fellow shipmates in a tone of great seriousness and was delighted when his listeners laughed in confusion at the end of his recitation.[29] He had apparently begun to think of "Two Lovers" as connected to his more recent work, despite the fact that it dated from an earlier time in his life. Early Lorca scholars who encountered "Two Lovers" were puzzled by the poem's form, content, and date of composition. They were convinced that it did not belong in *Poet in New York*, a collection supposedly devoted exclusively to poems written during Federico's time in the United States and Cuba. Accordingly, "Two Lovers" was simply left out of English-language editions of the work until 1955, then did not appear again until 1998.[30]

However, in 2003, the original manuscript that Federico had left for his editor, José Bergamín, in Madrid in July 1936 finally resurfaced and was made available to scholars. Among the recovered pages was the list of poems that Federico wanted Bergamín to include in *Poet in New York*, confirming earlier evidence that

Federico intended "Two Lovers" to be part of the collection.[31] A few scholars continued to question whether the poem really belonged there, but they appeared to be in the minority.[32] Most significantly, Federico not only included "Two Lovers" in his list of poems for *Poet in New York*, but also specified its placement in one of the two sections of the book linked to Vermont.[33]

CHAPTER ELEVEN

The End of the Affair

> Of the uncertainty after all, that we may be deluded,
> That maybe reliance and hope are but speculations after all.
>
> —Walt Whitman, "Of the Terrible Doubt of Appearances"

BY LATE SEPTEMBER 1930, both Philip and Federico were preparing for their respective returns to Madrid. It is unclear exactly when Philip arrived in the city. His official University of Madrid student identification card is dated 15 October 1930, but since classes started on 1 October, he was almost certainly settled into his dormitory and ready to begin by then. The identification card was actually more like a passport: a small, bound booklet with multiple pages for recording the names of courses and instructors. According to Philip's pages, that fall he took courses in Spanish literature, philosophy, and art, as well as the Arabic language.

The front section of Philip's identification document reveals a great deal about his situation when he first arrived in Madrid. The photo affixed to the inside cover shows a handsome young man with wavy auburn hair and an intense, solemn gaze; he is wearing a thick wool coat over his shirt and tie and a scarf around his neck, suggesting that the weather in Madrid had already turned cooler. The document also shows that he was living at the Fundación del

Núm. 17.986

Y LETRAS

Firma del interesado.

Madrid 15 de Octubre de 1930

El Secretario General,

V.º B.º
El Rector,

Carta de identidad del Alumno de la Facultad de Filosofía y Letras

D. Philip Harry Cummings

que nació el día 19 de noviembre de 1906 en Hardwick (Vermont) provincia de Estados Unidos domiciliado en esta Corte, en la calle de Fundación del Amo Ciudad Universitaria Moncloa

Domicilio del padre o encargado

D. Dr. el Vizconde de la Casa Aguilar
Pueblo Madrid provincia Madrid calle Fernando VI
n.º 4 piso —

Madrid 15 de octubre de 1930

El interesado.

— 1 —

Figure 32. Philip Cummings's University of Madrid student identification card, October 1930. Private collection.

Amo in the University City area of Madrid and that his local sponsor was Dr. Florestán Aguilar, viscount of the House of Aguilar.

Aguilar was a highly respected intellectual and doctor of dentistry who was attached to the royal court as both King Alfonso XIII's dentist and his educational advisor.[1] Originally from Cuba, he had earned his medical degree in the United States, where he also formed deep connections with the Rockefeller Foundation, an important patron of the IIE. With ties to both the palace, which funded Philip's fellowship, and the IIE, which granted it, Aguilar was the logical person to serve as Philip's official sponsor at the university.

Philip's residence at the Fundación del Amo was partly due to Aguilar as well. In his role as educational advisor, Aguilar was a key participant in the king's ambitious project to replace the existing University of Madrid, with its aging, widely scattered buildings, with a completely new university complex modeled on the campuses of the most prestigious universities in the United States. The king had embarked on this enterprise to mark the twenty-fifth year of his monarchy, intending that the totally redesigned University of Madrid would serve as his legacy to the Spanish people. He was also well aware that he had lost considerable popular support since allowing Primo de Rivera to take over the government in 1923 and must have hoped that the project would convince his restless subjects that he was fully committed to both intellectual freedom and the modernization of Spain's antiquated educational system.

The University City project had attracted the attention of Dr. Gregorio del Amo, a wealthy Spaniard who had married an American woman and moved to Los Angeles. Eager to show his support for strong connections between the United States and Spain, del Amo donated the princely sum of 30,000 Spanish pesetas (equivalent to almost US$500,000 today) to the project through his charitable foundation. The funds were specifically targeted for the construction of a modern dormitory for young American men who came to study at the university. The resulting building, known as the Fundación del Amo or Casa del Amo, was one of the first to be completed in the planned University City complex on the west side of the city. It opened just in time for Philip to become one of its first residents.[2]

Though the 150-room dormitory was intended for Americans, only ten such students, including Philip, were studying in Madrid that term, so the remaining 140 rooms were assigned to Spanish students.[3] One resident called the four-story building "a masterpiece of modernistic architecture [with] every comfort, . . . [that] would make our best American universities envious."[4] Another guest was equally impressed: "The students who live in it are very fortunate. They are domiciled in what is practically a fine hotel, yet at ridiculously small expense."[5]

Circumstances were finally in place for Philip and Federico to see each other again after more than a year apart. The exact date of their reunion is unknown, but considering the project that brought them together, it was probably in early November. Upon his return to Madrid, Federico had begun working with his friend Margarita Xirgu, the principal actress and producer for the Teatro Español, on the company's production of *La Calle*—a Spanish-language adaptation of the Elmer Rice play *Street Scene*.[6] Federico enlisted Philip's help with the staging of the play, particularly the design of the large, double-hung windows that are an essential part of the set.[7] Since the windows are regularly opened and closed as part of the action during the play, it seems likely that they would have been designed, constructed, and put into place well before the 14 November premiere to allow adequate time for rehearsal.

Philip recalled the experience in a journal entry he wrote in Wyoming a few years later: "My acquaintance with the great Xirgu and her whole company was very thrilling, especially when I was able to help them give the Elmer Rice play called 'Street Scene' in English and 'La Calle' in Spanish. I owed my acquaintance with her to her friend and my chum, Don Federico García Lorca, the Granadan poet who has acquired national fame and has visited America and spent ten days up in remote Vermont with me."[8]

Elsewhere in his Wyoming journal, Philip wrote, "During my

Figure 33. Philip Cummings in a bullfighter's traditional suit of lights, Madrid, 1930. Private collection.

year of 1930–1931 in Spain, I saw [Federico] often and learned again to appreciate his poetry."[9] Unfortunately, there is little evidence to support this contention. In 1986, Philip showed Spanish poet Dionisio Cañas a studio portrait of himself taken in Madrid that fall, adding that it had been Federico's favorite.[10] It is easy to understand why: Philip is wearing a bullfighter's traditional, tight-fitting suit of lights, complete with an elaborately embroidered cape tossed over his shoulder. The costume suits him; he looks handsome and dashing as he gazes calmly into the camera and might even be thought to be Spanish were it not for his auburn hair. But other than the photograph and Philip's comment about it years later, there is no indication that the men spent much time together. It seems far more likely that they saw little of each other, and that when they were together, Federico, wary of further entanglement, was careful to keep his distance.

This was a new side of Federico, one of several changes his friends had noticed since his return to Spain. He appeared more confident and relaxed and, most importantly, more comfortable with his sexuality—even writing to a friend that he had recently completed a play with a frankly homosexual theme, perhaps his best work ever.[11] And he was somehow tougher, less trusting, and more inclined to question the motives of those who sought his company.[12] Besides, Federico was too busy with his own projects to have much time for Philip. After helping Margarita Xirgu launch *La Calle*, he became deeply involved in preparations for the staging of her next production, *The Shoemaker's Prodigious Wife*, a play he had written, which premiered in late December.[13] At the same time, he kept up his usual busy social life and, of course, his writing.

In addition, Federico again began spending time with Emilio Aladrén, the young sculptor who had broken his heart two years earlier.[14] Aladrén had written to Federico at his family's home in Granada in late August, welcoming him back to Spain and suggesting that they get together when he returned to Madrid. It is unclear how often they saw each other in the city, but Aladrén did accompany Federico to

San Sebastián when he gave a lecture there in early December.[15] Whatever happened between them, it did not last long. Federico moved on with no apparent regret, and Aladrén married a young Englishwoman less than a year later.

Philip must have missed Federico's company, but he had always been very good at keeping himself busy. In addition to his classes, he attended various cultural events in Madrid and traveled to other parts of the country whenever he got the chance. He also periodically sent short letters about his experiences to the editor of the *Hardwick Gazette*, who was always happy to publish his work. In his letters, he reported that he had attended a bullfight in Madrid, toured several small villages in the region west of the city, and spent time in Morocco. He also happened to be at the Fundación del Amo when King Alfonso XIII stopped by with his retinue to show off the place to some visiting royals. The king took the time to shake the hands of all present then drove himself back to the palace in a shiny Ford coupe.[16]

King Alfonso's visit was also witnessed by John Steven McGroarty, a journalist with the *Los Angeles Times*. McGroarty had spent two weeks living at the Fundación del Amo as a guest of the king while he worked on a profile of the monarch for his paper. In the resulting article, he included many details about the facility, its comfortable accommodations, and the multicultural makeup of the student population. In one intriguing anecdote, he mentioned getting to know two of the American students, one of whom was from Vermont; given his birthplace and sociable nature, this was almost certainly Philip. The two students were very proud of having saved money on their travels by hitchhiking whenever possible, demonstrating a level of resourcefulness that McGroarty applauded.[17] This detail makes it even more likely that the Vermonter in question was Philip, as he was perennially short of funds.

But despite everything going on in his life, Philip could not ignore the growing political tensions in Spain, especially since universities were so often at the center of the turmoil. In November, he witnessed Madrid's "little revolution," a disturbance triggered by attempts to block the funeral procession for four workers killed by falling debris at a construction site, the probable result of poor materials and corrupt dealings by the project's managers. The resulting riot led to a crackdown by police, which in turn led to a citywide strike that closed all schools, businesses, and transit systems. Everything returned to normal two days later, but people were shaken by how quickly the situation had escalated into violence.[18]

Over the Christmas holidays, Philip visited the city of Granada and its surrounding mountains with a fellow student, though he apparently had no contact with Federico or his family while he was there.[19] When he returned to Madrid, he found that the political situation had continued to decline, with ongoing strikes and intense speculation about the potential fall of the monarchy and the long-awaited return to a republican form of government. As he told his readers in Hardwick: "Things have been happening fast in Madrid lately. One week ago the University closed for the third time and then they tried to open it up again on last Monday. After a forenoon of battle within the walls of the University it has been closed again, several arrests made and this time the closing is more permanent."[20]

Fearing that the university might never reopen, Philip ultimately decided that the prospect of being able to complete his planned year of study there was simply too tenuous to merit the risk and expense of staying put. He wrote his last published letter from Spain in late January, but this time from on board a train that was taking him from Spain to France—and eventually Scotland, where he spent the next eight weeks before returning to the United States.[21] It is unclear whether Philip told Federico about his decision to leave Spain a full six months before his fellowship ended or whether, at that point, Federico would have paid much attention.

Philip wrote several letters to Federico over the next few months, until Federico finally asked him to stop, saying that he feared his mail was being read so it would be better if they ceased contact.[22] Even if these fears were well founded, Philip was still hurt and confused by Federico's decision to end their communication so abruptly. His feelings of loss and disbelief are revealed in three poems published by the *Tampa Tribune* later in 1931, all of which appear to be directly linked to their estrangement.[23] Perhaps, like Federico, Philip had learned to use poetry to express difficult emotions that were too painful to hold inside, yet impossible to state openly.

HAVE YOU FORGOTTEN?

Oh, have you forgotten
The pool, the rock, the sun,
The path in the wilderness,
The birches by the lake,
The slippery mossy edge?
Oh, have you forgotten
A hushed hour spun
On moonlight's holiness,
A brook, an opening brake,
A stormcloud's opal edge?
Oh, have you forgotten
The dawn just begun;
That love can bless,
That no wine can slake
The thirst of a heart awake?
No! As in the jade
Of the icy midmountain pool
We saw the bottom laid
Granitely, by a slavic rule,
And then inversely from that depth
Imperfectly we view a leopard sky,
So, opaquently in unguarded ways
You must be aware of those April days!

THE POET (TO FEDERICO LORCA.)

The youth of the crimson passion
Sat on a square of cold blue,
The night and the sky raced around him
And he grasped the stars he wished,
Fastened them to his dark cape,
Then threw it to the deep waters.
He of the crimson passion
Picked up a cold reflection.

TAKE ADIEU

What? Not leave the lake,
The shore with its single pine?
That is not wise; you must not hold
Forever the afternoon, the skies
Crackled with the hanging of the years.
No? Then linger, friend,
And be ye not surprised to find
The vesper songs are filled with tears.

For his part, Federico simply wrote Philip out of the story of his time in the United States, which was perhaps the only way he knew then to deal with his bittersweet memories of their days together in Vermont. In March 1932, Federico gave his first public lecture about his trip to the United States and shared several of the poems he had written there. During his talk, he explained that in August 1929 he had gone to the countryside to escape the heat of the city, but he did not mention exactly where he had been. He spoke at length about the Tyler sisters, their charming eccentricities, and the beautiful lake and woods near their home, adding that, in such surroundings, his poetry naturally "took on the tone of the forest." He read his "Double Poem of Lake Eden" to the attentive audience, presenting it as the last work of his "summer vacation." But he did not mention Philip at all or even allude to his presence.[24]

Four years later, Federico appeared to have achieved enough distance to look at things differently. In July 1936, as he was finalizing the list of poems he wanted José Bergamín to include in *Poet in New York*, Federico added his prose poem "Two Lovers Murdered by a Partridge" to the list, placing it at the end of the section he titled "Introduction to Death (Poems of Solitude in Vermont)." He made this choice even though he had composed the poem many months before he traveled to the United States, and it had no apparent connection to either New York or Vermont. Perhaps Federico had simply decided that the collection needed one more poem and chose "Two Lovers" to fill the gap. But if the poem does indeed describe, however obliquely, his brief affair with Philip at the Residencia in July 1928, his decision to include it may indicate that he had come to terms with his complicated feelings about Philip at last.

Epilogue

HOW DID IT HAPPEN that the full story of Lorca's visit to Vermont and his relationship with Philip Cummings remained unknown for so many years? The primary culprit was the conscious and unconscious homophobia that was pervasive in Spain and the United States during Federico's lifetime and still continues in some quarters to this day.

After Federico's sudden and unexpected death in Spain in 1936, his family and friends determined that protecting his literary legacy also required concealing his homosexuality. As part of this effort, those who were aware of his trip to Vermont deliberately chose not to disclose what they knew about it—a conspiracy of silence that lasted almost twenty years. But secrets rarely remain secret; beginning in the mid-1950s, a new generation of scholars, biographers, and journalists began to wonder exactly where and how Federico had spent the last two weeks of August 1929. As they started digging deeper, their curiosity and persistence led to the progressive unveiling of a great deal of new information about Federico, Philip, and their time together at Lake Eden, which served as the foundation for my own research. However, of this group, only Daniel Eisenberg was aware that Federico and Philip had any sexual contact, and even he never considered that they might have been more deeply involved. Fortunately, when I began my own investigation, new evidence of their affair had become available, inspiring me to seek a better understanding of their relationship and its role in Federico's poems of the period.

The simple fact that Federico had set foot in Vermont, let alone spent ten days with a young American friend there, went unacknowledged by Professor Ángel del Río and others in the Spanish department at Columbia University until 1955. Since del Río, in particular, was fully aware of Federico's trip to Vermont and his friendship with Philip, it is hard not to view his silence as a deliberate act of concealment.

It is impossible to know exactly how much del Río knew, but consider this: On or about 30 August 1929, Federico went directly from Lake Eden to Bushnellsville, New York, where he spent twenty days with del Río, his wife, and their infant son. Federico and del Río had been friends for many years, so it seems highly unlikely that they did not discuss Federico's experiences in Vermont in some detail over the course of almost three weeks together. Before he even arrived in Bushnellsville, Federico had written to del Río from Lake Eden to express, among other things, his eagerness to tell his friend "all about it."[1]

Del Río's failure to reveal what he knew about the Vermont trip may have been in part a reflection of the continuing shock and confusion felt by Federico's friends and family in the aftermath of his arrest and execution by Franco's forces in Granada in August 1936.[2] Federico's surviving relatives in Spain did all they could to ensure that the poet's papers were secured in safe places, even as they feared for their own lives. But as the war raged on with no sign of resolution, del Río and his colleagues at Columbia took on the daunting task of preserving and promoting Federico's literary legacy from afar on behalf of his embattled family.

This new responsibility would have only heightened del Río's instinct to try to protect his friend from any social disapproval that might have compromised the appeal of his work to a wide audience. He was well aware that if any hint of Federico's homosexuality became public, it would almost certainly destroy the poet's personal and literary reputation, and perhaps del Río's own reputation as well. Since there was no easy way for del Río and his colleagues to talk publicly about Federico's visit to Vermont without naming his host, whom del Río must have known or suspected was also his lover, they chose to say nothing at all.

If their silence on the subject confused critics who read *Poet in New York* when it was first published in 1940, there is no evidence of it. Perhaps the word "Vermont" in the title of one section of the book and the place names "Lake Eden" and "Lake Eden Mills" were simply taken as allegorical. In the absence of any known link between the poet and the actual state of Vermont, this may have seemed like the only reasonable explanation.

In 1941, del Río ignored at least two opportunities to clarify the situation in his influential monograph on Federico's life and work. The biographical section contained not a single mention of Vermont. Regarding the poet's whereabouts in the late summer of 1929, del Río wrote only, "Al fin del verano Federico pasó una temporada en el campo, en las Catskill Mountains" (At the end of the summer, Federico spent some time in the countryside, in the Catskill Mountains).[3]

Del Río did include a typed transcription of the handwritten letter Federico sent to him from Lake Eden, in which the poet referred to Eden Mills and a person named Cummings (see chapter 8).[4] However, del Río did not explain that Eden Mills is a place in Vermont or provide any further details about the mysterious Cummings.

To compound the problem, del Río placed the transcribed letter in the "Obras Inéditas" (Unedited Works) section of his monograph. The irony of this placement did not become apparent until 2013, when a new transcription of the original letter was published by Christopher Maurer and Andrew A. Anderson.[5] The original version revealed that del Río had actually edited the letter, deliberately leaving two sentences out of his transcription in an obvious act of censorship. The first excised sentence reads: "My young friend Cummings translates my songs and looks at me with the tenderness of a wounded cow." Del Río apparently decided that any mention of tender glances, particularly in connection with Philip and Vermont, was simply too hazardous to include. The second deleted sentence had nothing to do with Philip but instead concerned a request from Federico for financial assistance. It reads: "Did you ask Fernando de los Ríos for the silver [money]?" Taken together, the two omitted sentences illustrate del Río's inclination to simply leave out anything that he feared might cast an unflattering light on Federico.

Del Río's silence about the Vermont interlude continued until 1954, when he began working on the introduction for a new edition of *Poet in New York* being planned by Grove Press. In a carefully worded letter to poet Ben Belitt, the translator for the new edition, he expressed his concern about just how much to reveal:

> As to content, I am not entirely sure, for instance, whether some parts could be greatly shortened or eliminated, especially the account of Federico's life in New York. Do you think that the details about his friends or about his trips to Vermont and the Catskills have any interest for an American reader of poetry for whom the book was intended? . . .
>
> I am worried also about the allusion to problems into which it might be advisable not to delve. You know, of course, to what I am referring. I feel that a discreet allusion should be made but by being too discreet I do not want to imply too much and, above all, I do not want to remove [*sic*] a delicate matter which I know troubles Federico's family and friends a great deal.[6]

In the end, del Río chose to say only the following about Vermont and Philip:

> At the end of the Summer Session [at Columbia University] the group dispersed, and Federico, as we always called him, went to Vermont to visit an American friend. This was a fellow-poet, according to him, a Mr. Cummings, whom he had met a few

months before in the Residencia at Madrid. This friend, I regret to say, I have never been able to identify; and if he was indeed a poet he would have been Federico's only contact with an American creative writer during his stay in this country.[7]

The 1955 Grove Press edition of *Poet in New York* attracted the attention of many interested readers, including Philip Cummings. Dismayed to find himself described in such vague terms, Philip wrote to del Río in an attempt to jog his memory:

> I have before me your introduction to the comparatively new book, Federico García Lorca with the translation by Ben Belitt. On page xiv you state "This was a fellow-poet according to him, a Mr. Cummings, whom he had met a few months before in the Residencia in Madrid. This friend, I regret to say, I have never been able to identify; and if he was indeed a poet he would have been Lorca's only contact with an American creative writer during his stay in this country." Perhaps I can help you out.
>
> [Federico] came to us in Vermont and stayed for ten days at Eden Lake, Eden Mills, Vermont, with my father, my mother, and myself. . . . He was with us in August, 1929. I hope this identification and clarification may be of interest to you. While there may be doubt as to my being a full flowering poet, there is none about our pursuing this subject hour after hour in the cool dusk of a northern Vermont lake shore. . . .
>
> Sometime when I am in New York we might have lunch together and I can add to my few details in this letter. How well I recall his clutching your letter of details when my father and I put him on the train in Burlington with destination of Shandaken.[8]

Philip's letter prompted an almost immediate response from del Río. In his conciliatory reply, del Río did his best to soothe any hurt feelings and portray his omissions as regretful but unavoidable:

> Your letter came to me as a most pleasant surprise and I was, indeed, glad to finally identify the person whose existence especially interested me, but who was, much against my own desires, fast becoming a fantasmal one. I do now clearly recall that Federico spoke frequently of Philip.
>
> I trust that my brief reference to you and subsequent dismissal of the matter in that one paragraph of the Introduction did not appear unduly hasty. I had, of course, never had the pleasure of meeting you personally nor was I ever able to glean an iota of concrete evidence that "Mr. Cummings" was a real live person. . . . Do contact me when you are in New York and we shall make arrangements to get together.[9]

The two men never met in New York or elsewhere. However, in 1958, a Spanish translation of del Río's introduction to the 1955 edition of *Poet in New York* was published as a stand-alone monograph in Spain. In this version, del Río added a note stating that Cummings was indeed a real person who still lived in Vermont. However, he was careful to leave himself blameless by asserting that he had learned of Philip's existence only after the 1955 edition was published.[10]

The exchange of letters with Philip spurred del Río to take one other important step toward disclosure. Sometime in 1955 or 1956, he shared a crucial piece of information about the elusive Vermonter with a newly minted professor of Spanish named Kessel Schwartz.

After Kessel Schwartz completed his PhD at Columbia under Ángel del Río in 1953, he accepted a teaching position at the University of Vermont. He and del Río stayed in touch after Schwartz moved to Vermont to begin his new job, which paid very poorly but came with an unexpected benefit. Not long after del Río received Philip's letter, he casually suggested to Schwartz that, since he was now living in Vermont, he should take the opportunity to look up a fellow resident who had once known Federico. Del Río gave Schwartz Philip's name and address and left it to him to follow up if he wished.[11]

Fortunately, Schwartz greatly admired Federico's work and was curious about his connection to Vermont. After some preliminary investigations, he wrote to Philip in April 1957. The timing was perfect: Philip was fifty-one at the time and eager to share his memories of Federico and Lake Eden with an interested scholar, especially in the wake of his near-invisibility in del Río's introduction. He readily agreed to talk with Schwartz, who traveled to the family home in central Vermont and interviewed Philip at length. Schwartz later summarized his findings and impressions in an article for the journal *Hispania*, the first published work to document the links between Federico, Philip, and the Vermont poems in *Poet in New York*.[12]

Over the next two decades, a few other researchers followed in Schwartz's footsteps. In July 1967, journalist Mildred Adams was working on a biography of Federico, whom she had known in Spain and New York, when she first heard about Philip. Unaware of Schwartz's earlier paper, Adams felt sure that she had stumbled on a scoop.[13] She began corresponding with Philip, visited him and his wife at their home, and accompanied them on a day trip to Lake Eden. But due to multiple delays, Adams's book was not published until 1977. To her great disappointment, by that time Daniel Eisenberg had already published the same information—and more—about Federico, Philip, and Vermont.

Eisenberg, then an up-and-coming professor of Hispanic studies at Florida State University, Tallahassee, was familiar with Schwartz's paper and corresponded with Schwartz before contacting Philip in 1974. After meeting with Philip and studying his cherished journal, translations, and photos from Lake Eden, Eisenberg took on the daunting task of getting them published. With Philip's permission to do whatever he wished with the material, Eisenberg poured his prodigious energies into the project. The resulting book, called simply *Songs*, includes an introduction by Eisenberg, the translations of Federico's *Canciones* that Philip and Federico worked on together at Lake Eden, and Philip's August 1929 journal.

Eisenberg's introduction to *Songs* is primarily a profile of Philip, with special emphasis on his early contacts with Spain and Federico. In light of his subject's unreliable memory and tendency toward self-aggrandizement, Eisenberg did extensive research to try to verify the chronology and details that Philip provided. But despite Eisenberg's best efforts, due to the unavailability of certain key sources at the time, he inadvertently included multiple incorrect statements about Philip's life.

Unfortunately, Eisenberg later came to believe that Philip had deliberately lied to him about at least one important matter. Philip told Eisenberg that in 1961 he had discovered a forgotten sealed envelope of papers that Federico had left with him in 1929. Philip said he had opened the envelope and skimmed the pages, but the contents were so full of vitriol about the poet's perceived enemies that it seemed clear he should follow Federico's instructions to burn them if he never asked to have them back. Philip told Eisenberg he had done just that, but then would say nothing more about them.[14] The idea that someone would destroy anything Federico had written infuriated Eisenberg, who in an article published during the year of Philip's death referred to him as a liar and expressed doubt that the papers in question had ever existed.[15] It is unclear how much impact Eisenberg's assessment had at the time, but his claims were repeated in one scholarly publication as recently as 2021.[16]

One additional researcher who met with Philip in the 1970s was a Vermont college student named William Sackett. Sackett loved Federico's work and was especially drawn to *Poet in New York*. In the fall of 1972, two years before Eisenberg appeared on the scene, Sackett managed to locate both Philip and poet-translator Ben Belitt and interview them in their respective homes for his senior thesis project. Sackett's videotapes of his unpublished interviews are lost, but his audiotapes and personal memories provided many unexpected insights.[17]

Interest in Philip reached its peak in the 1980s, especially in the years leading up to the fiftieth anniversary of Lorca's death in 1986.

During that period, Philip was approached by a series of scholars, biographers, journalists, and filmmakers who wanted to talk with one of the last surviving people who had known Federico personally. Philip usually enjoyed these encounters, but he had long ago said all that he wanted to say and ended up repeating the same stories and catchphrases to each visitor.

Writer Leslie Stainton was an MFA graduate student in Amherst, Massachusetts, when she became interested in Federico's life and work. At the time, Stainton was just beginning the research for what would become her biography of Federico.[18] She contacted Philip at his home in Vermont and made her first visit there in July 1984. The two got along famously and conversed for hours.[19]

Stainton received a Fulbright fellowship to continue her research in Spain and traveled there in late 1984. In Madrid, she arranged to meet with Irish historian Ian Gibson, a well-known Lorca expert. Gibson had just completed the first volume of his comprehensive

Figure 34. Philip Cummings with Leslie Stainton at Cummings's home in Vermont, 1984. Private collection.

Spanish-language biography of Federico, which ended with Federico's arrival in New York in June 1929.[20] Stainton gave Gibson Philip's address and phone number, launching a collegial relationship between the two men that continued for several years.

Gibson was hard at work on volume 2 of his biography when he began corresponding with Philip in July 1985.[21] He was also planning a trip to the United States and decided to include a stop in Vermont to finalize his research for the Lake Eden section of his book.[22]

When Gibson told Mike Dibb, the director of a BBC documentary about Federico then in production, about his upcoming trip, Dibb suggested that they include Philip in the film. As a result, when Gibson and Philip finally met in Vermont in April 1986, their conversations about Federico, Spain, and Lake Eden were captured on camera. The completed documentary, titled *The Spirit of Lorca*, was released later that year.[23]

Figure 35. *Left to right*: Author Ian Gibson, BBC director Mike Dibb, and Philip Cummings at Cummings's home in Vermont, 1986. Private collection.

In an August 1985 letter to Gibson, Philip had hinted that he had something private to share when they met in person: "There are admittedly some things I cannot talk to Leslie Stainton about which I might discuss with you I believe."[24] But Gibson arrived just a little too late. In November 1985, Dionisio Cañas, a gay Spanish poet who was then teaching Spanish literature at Baruch College in New York, landed on Philip's doorstep. During a school break, Cañas and two friends had decided to visit the same places Federico once visited in Vermont and the Catskills. When they got to Lake Eden, Cañas was amazed to find Philip's name in the local telephone book. He called Philip on the spot and received reluctant permission to stop by at his home, almost one hundred miles away.[25]

Philip and Cañas connected immediately. Flattered by the Spaniard's rapt attention and charmed by his dark eyes and quick smile, Philip relaxed and let down his guard. When they had a chance to be alone, he spoke to Cañas in fluent Spanish and with complete candor about his private life as a gay man and his sexual relationship with Federico. When Cañas asked for permission to publish a summary of their conversation in a Spanish literary journal, he was surprised when Philip agreed. Perhaps, with his wife no longer alive and his own health precarious, Philip had finally decided he had nothing to lose from these disclosures—especially in a publication that his neighbors were never likely to see.[26]

All of these writers helped tell the story of Federico García Lorca's time in Vermont and his relationship with Philip Cummings, but their descriptions of the Lake Eden episode shared one common weakness: They relied almost exclusively on Philip himself as the primary source. Fortunately, new sources of information began to surface in the late 1980s, thanks in large part to Lorca scholar Christopher Maurer, editor of a definitive edition of *Poet in New York* published in 1988. This edition of the work offered the first new English translations of the collected poems in thirty-three years, along with numerous supporting materials. It quickly supplanted previous editions and introduced a whole new generation of readers to Lorca's poetry.

Figure 36. Dionisio Cañas and Philip Cummings at Cummings's home in Vermont, 1985. Private collection.

Among its other contributions, the book also included the first English translations of fourteen letters Federico wrote to his family between June 1929 and April 1930.[27] The letters are both informative and entertaining and provide a fascinating window on the poet's experiences, impressions, and state of mind during this critical period in his life. The set includes only one communication from Vermont: a short letter (originally on birch bark) that Federico wrote to his younger sisters in late August 1929. However, some of the earlier letters the poet wrote in New York corroborated parts of Philip's story. For example, in a letter written a few days after he arrived in the city, Federico told his parents about his plans to visit Vermont (which he initially confused with Canada) and the young man who had invited him there: "Do you remember my telling you about a young American poet who wrote a poem to me in the Residencia after hearing me play the piano? I met him again on the train from Madrid to Paris, and he invited me to spend the month of August (the hottest month here) in his house in Canada. . . . I've accepted and, God willing, if all goes as planned, I'll spend the month of August in Canada."[28]

Federico may have misunderstood exactly where Philip lived, but his description of their initial meeting in Madrid matched Philip's.

There was more to come. In late 1989, an additional eighty-three pieces of correspondence from Federico to his friends and family were discovered at a relative's home in Granada, Spain. To the delight of scholars interested in the poet's 1929–1930 travels, the collection contained eleven items sent from the United States and Cuba during that time, including a letter and a postcard from Vermont.

To celebrate the discovery, ten representative letters from the collection were published in a literary supplement to the Spanish newspaper *ABC* in February 1990. Among those chosen for publication was the letter from Vermont dated 22 August 1929—the day after Federico arrived at Lake Eden.[29] In it, the poet described his long train ride to Vermont and the people and places he encountered there, confirming many additional details in Philip's August 1929 journal and his later recollections.[30] Sadly, Philip died from complications of Alzheimer's disease and pneumonia in June 1991, at the age of eighty-four, unaware that additional documentation of his halcyon days with Federico had come to light.

Today, Federico's letters and postcard to his family stand with Philip's journal as the only contemporaneous accounts of the Lake Eden episode. Together with the few surviving photographs from the period, they provided the starting point for my research.[31]

Fortunately, new information continues to emerge. In 2020, scholar Andrew Samuel Walsh began trying to determine the identity of the unknown translator of the first two of Federico's poems ever published in English, as discussed in chapter 6. The poems in question had appeared in the August 1929 issue of the New York literary journal *Alhambra*, and the two most likely translators were Ángel Flores, the journal's editor, and Philip Cummings. After a detailed textual analysis of the two translated poems, as well as other Spanish-to-English translations done by both men, Walsh concluded that the unknown translator was almost certainly Philip.[32] Ironically, not only was Philip's role as Federico's first translator into English not discovered until twenty years after his death, but it also appears that Federico never told Philip that his translations had been published.

In his article, Walsh acknowledged Philip's frustration at being denied recognition for his influence on Federico's life and work, and Walsh did not fault him for that. However, many other scholars have chosen to simply follow the lead of those who downplayed whatever Philip had to say, never questioning the assumption that Philip was interested only in gaining unwarranted attention for himself. It is my hope that the material presented in this book will encourage the research community to reconsider this conclusion and take a closer look at the relationship between these two young men—and what it might have meant to them both.

Acknowledgments

This book has been in the making in one way or another for almost two decades, and I have a great many people to thank for helping it finally come to fruition. My apologies in advance to anyone I have forgotten to mention.

In Vermont, historians Allen Davis and Charles Morrissey and researcher Lorraine Hussey shared their knowledge, enthusiasm, and friendship from the very beginning. Other Vermont friends and colleagues include Elizabeth Dow, El Towle, Bonnie Britz, Isla Awen, Donna Whitcomb, and Susan Holmes. Special thanks to playwright Noah Mease for helping me see the story of Federico and Philip through his eyes.

I received invaluable support and assistance from a wide range of Lorca scholars, biographers, and translators along the way, including Andrew A. Anderson, Dionisio Cañas, Daniel Eisenberg, David Gershator, Ian Gibson, Jonathan Mayhew, Christopher Maurer, Pablo Medina, William Sackett, Kessel Schwartz, Leslie Stainton, Roger Tinnell, D. Gareth Walters, and Andrew Samuel Walsh, several of whom were kind enough to share research materials they had never shown anyone else. In addition, professor Santiago López-Ríos Moreno of Universidad Complutense de Madrid and local historian Maria A. García Valdecasas of Granada provided many helpful insights and graciously invited me to their home cities to discuss my findings.

I would also like to thank the dedicated and resourceful archivists at Florida State University, Tallahassee, Stetson University, Rollins College, Middlebury College, Harvard University, and Radcliffe

College who assisted me with my research. Special thanks to Inma Hernández Baena at the Centro de Estudios Lorquianos in Fuente Vaqueros, Spain, and to Rosa Illán and her colleagues at the Centro Federico García Lorca in Madrid and Granada, for their thoughtful help and guidance. My thanks as well to Laura García Lorca, president of the Fundacíon Federico García Lorca, for her interest in this project.

I am indebted to the many readers who reviewed my draft materials and shared their informed and perceptive feedback, including Erica Verillo, Lisa Sheehy, Selena Kerr, Kris Reichart-Anderson, Jill Ross, Jane Leung Larson, Jeff Keith, Daniel Bullen, Gloria Black, Sara Henry, Velma García-Gorena, Laura Tilsley García, Elizabeth Maxey, Allen Young, Dennis Helmus, and Madelaine Zadik. I am especially grateful to my fellow members of the literary biographers' roundtable group of Biographers International Organization, whose generosity and wise advice made all the difference.

Special thanks to my agent Roseanne Wells, formerly of Lucinda Literary, for her endless patience, enthusiasm, and expertise in guiding my book forward, and to my astute editor Elise McHugh at University of New Mexico Press, along with James Ayers and his stellar editorial and design team, for making it real at last.

Finally, none of this would have been possible without the unwavering support and encouragement of my late husband John Merritt and our children, Michael, Anna, and Daniel. My love and gratitude always.

Notes

Prologue

1. Andrew A. Anderson, "The Evolution of García Lorca's Poetic Projects 1929–36 and the Textual Status of *Poeta en Nueva York*," *Bulletin of Hispanic Studies* 60:3 (1983): 221–46.
2. Christopher Maurer, "Notes on the Poems," in García Lorca, *Poet in New York* (1998), 270.

Chapter One

1. Cummings, "A Glimpse of a Man," in García Lorca, *Songs*, 171–72.
2. Cummings, "A Glimpse of a Man," in García Lorca, *Songs*, 171–72.
3. Cano, *García Lorca*, 36. A *tonadilla* is a type of short, satirical song featured in Spanish musical comedies of an earlier era.
4. Moreno Villa, *Vida en Claro*, 108.
5. Moreno Villa, *Vida en Claro*, 107.
6. Cummings's original passport, issued in February 1926, shows that he entered Spain for the first time at Irún on 5 July 1928, and that his passport was *visé* (examined and endorsed) at a government office in Madrid on 7 July, two days before classes began.
7. "Curso de vacaciones para extranjeros," *ABC* (Madrid), 10 July 1928, 23.
8. Sáenz de la Calzada, *Residencia de Estudiantes*, 52–53.
9. Miguel Allué Salvador, "Las Residencias de Estudiantes de España," *Universidad: Revista de Cultura y Vida Universitaria* 2:1 (Jan.–Mar. 1925): 3–24.
10. Trend, *Picture of Modern Spain*, 34.
11. For Dalí's and Lorca's influences on each other's work, see Dalí and García Lorca, *Sebastian's Arrows*.
12. Pérez-Villanueva Tovar, *La Residencia de Estudiantes*, 340, 344.
13. "Cursos de Lengua y Literatura Española para Extranjeros en Madrid," *Hispania* 3:6 (Dec. 1920): 331–34.
14. "Cursos de Lengua y Literatura Española."
15. Cesar M. Arconada, "En la Residencia de Estudiantes," *La Gaceta Literaria* (Madrid), 15 Aug. 1928, 2.

16. The 1928 summer program began the week of 9–13 July, but Lorca was away from Madrid most of that week in the city of Zamora. Gibson, *Federico García Lorca*, 1:550.
17. Arconada, "En la Residencia de Estudiantes," 2.
18. Salinas, *Presagios*, inscribed by the poet, private collection.
19. Philip Cummings, unpublished interview by William Sackett, 8 Nov. 1972. The other poets staying at the Residencia in July 1928 are noted in Arconada, "En la Residencia de Estudiantes," 2.
20. Lorca to his parents, 8 Aug. 1929, in García Lorca, *Poet in New York* (2013), 215.
21. Cummings's passport and letters to his parents indicate that he spent the spring and early summer of 1928 visiting Scotland, England, Germany, Switzerland, France, and Algeria before entering Spain on 5 July.
22. Cummings, "Algeria," in Cummings, *Mother-Tongue*, 34.
23. Undergraduate transcript of Philip Cummings, Stetson University Archives, duPont-Ball Library, DeLand, FL. Cummings's enrollment at a college in Florida, when there were so many other choices closer to home, was a result of his father's involvement in the Florida real estate market in the 1920s. Patricia A. Billingsley, "How Highland Lodge Got Its Name," *Hazen Road Dispatch* 36 (Summer 2011): 18–25.
24. "Hamilton Holt Scores Old College Systems, Tells of New Scheme He Has Installed at Rollins, Replacing Lecture Methods," *New York Times*, 4 May 1928, 15.
25. Cummings's high school and Stetson University transcripts show that he first studied Spanish in his junior year at Stetson (1927–1928) and received top marks in his classes. One of Cummings's daughters (name withheld on request) described her father's unusual facility with languages in a phone conversation with me on 23 October 2006.
26. See, for example, Guy Forshey, "A St. Louis School Teacher, a Live Arab, and a Dead Language," *St. Louis Post-Dispatch*, 9 Feb. 1930, 82, 85. The deep tan Cummings developed during his sojourn in North Africa is evident in the official photo attached to his passport.
27. Cummings, unpublished interview by Dionisio Cañas, 15 Feb. 1986. Summary and notes provided to me by Dr. Cañas. Cañas also shared this information with Jaime Manrique, as recounted in Manrique's *Eminent Maricones*, 81–83.
28. Cummings, "Youth," in Cummings, *Mother-Tongue*, 48.
29. Cummings interview by Sackett, 8 Nov. 1972.
30. Cummings, "A Glimpse of a Man," in García Lorca, *Songs*, 172.
31. Cummings described various instances of being bullied in an unpublished memoir, ca. 1935, private collection. Among other forms of teasing, Lorca's

classmates mocked his way of walking and called him "Federica." Stainton, *Lorca*, 22–23.

32. Cummings, unpublished memoir, ca. 1935.
33. Cummings, unpublished memoir, ca. 1935.
34. Harrison, *View from Vermont*, 50–56.
35. Billingsley, "How Highland Lodge Got Its Name," 18–25.
36. García Lorca to Sebastian Gasch, late summer 1927, in García Lorca, *Selected Letters*, 121. The family purchased the Huerta de San Vicente (Orchard of St. Vincent) outside Granada in 1927. See Ortega, *Álbum*.
37. For excerpts from reviews of *Canciones* by critics Estéban Salazar y Chapela and Ricardo Baeza, published in *El Sol* (Madrid) on 20 and 31 July 1927, see Gibson, *Federico García Lorca: A Life*, 188, 190.
38. For example, Federico had worked closely with composer Manuel de Falla to organize Granada's first festival celebrating Romani *cante jondo* (deep song) in 1922. Gibson, *Federico García Lorca: A Life*, 108–16.
39. Lorca to Sebastian Gasch, mid-Jan. 1928, in García Lorca, *Epistolario Completo*, 543.
40. López Campillo, *Revista de Occidente*, 268.
41. Miguel Allué Salvador, "Las Residencias de Estudiantes de España," *Universidad: Revista de Cultura y Vida Universitaria* 2:1 (Jan.–Mar. 1925): 6.
42. Lorca to his parents, 3 Apr. 1926, in García Lorca, *Epistolario Completo*, 340.
43. Arconada, "En la Residencia de Estudiantes," 2.
44. Gibson, *Federico García Lorca: A Life*, 210.
45. Stainton, *Lorca*, 179–84.
46. Emilio Aladrén Perojo and Eleanor Dove were married in Northumberland, England, in December 1931. The couple had one son, Jaime, born in 1932. See Dove family records, Ancestry.com.
47. Lorca to José Antonio Rubio Sacristán, Aug. 1928, in García Lorca, *Epistolario Completo*, 573, translated by Leslie Stainton in *Lorca*, 183.
48. Cummings, interview by Sackett, 8 Nov. 1972.
49. Cummings, "A Glimpse of a Man," in García Lorca, *Songs*, 172.
50. López Campillo, *Revista de Occidente*, 268.
51. Julio Forniés, "Postales Ibéricas, Andalucía. Del diario de un lector de García Lorca," *Gaceta Literaria* (Madrid), 15 Aug. 1928, 6.
52. Lorca to his parents, 26 July 1928, in García Lorca, *Epistolario Completo*, 569–70.
53. "García Lorca," *El Defensor de Granada*, 2 Aug. 1928, 3.
54. New York Passenger Lists, 1820–1957, Ancestry.com.
55. Crockett and Crockett, *Satchel Guide to Spain and Portugal*, 5, 9; *Handbook to Paris and Its Environs*, 19.

Chapter Two

1. Cummings's original letter to Lorca is in the archives of the Fundación Federico García Lorca, Granada, Spain. My translation.
2. "Last year, as an exercise in his Spanish class, he translated two of the *Gypsy Ballads* into English." Lorca to his parents, 28 June 1929, in García Lorca, *Poet in New York* (2013), 201.
3. "Two Walden School House Fires Within a Month," *Hardwick (VT) Gazette*, 27 Jan. 1927, 1.
4. Archie M. Palmer, "International Ambassadors of Good Will," *Rollins College Alumni Quarterly* (Dec. 1928): 2, 15–16.
5. Rollins College Archives, Winter Park, FL.
6. Cesar M. Arconada, "En la Residencia de Estudiantes," *La Gaceta Literaria* (Madrid), 15 Aug. 1928, 2.
7. Stella Weston, telephone interview with Daniel Eisenberg, 1974, Journal of Hispanic Philology Collection, Special Collections, Florida State University Libraries, Tallahassee.
8. See, for example, "To Stella" and "After the Dance," in Cummings, *Mother-Tongue*, 61, 67.
9. "At one time I didn't know whether you were going to marry Stella Weston or Greta Garbo." Hamilton Holt to Cummings, 16 Jan. 1940, Archives and Special Collections, Olin Library, Rollins College, Winter Park, FL. For more about the Cummings family's financial problems circa 1928, see chapter 3.
10. "Miss Stella Weston to Wed Mr. Harry Tuttle," *Orlando Sentinel*, 3 May 1931, 9. See also Claire C. Mager, "The Mother of Miami: Julia Tuttle's Orange Blossom Diplomacy Paid Off," *Miami News*, 27 July 1979, 11–12.
11. "Chase Hall," *Rollins Sandspur*, 26 Oct. 1928, 3.
12. WDBO Collection, Archives and Special Collections, Olin Library, Rollins College, Winter Park, FL. See also "Hardwick," *Burlington Free Press*, 13 Feb. 1929, 19.
13. Jessie B. Rittenhouse, "Foreword," in Rittenhouse, *Rollins Book of Verse*, viii. This collection of poems by students in Rittenhouse's winter seminar included five written by Cummings.
14. "Jessie Rittenhouse Becomes Member of Rollins Faculty," *Orlando Sentinel*, 1 June 1927, 12.
15. E. D. Lambright, "Rollins Senior Uses 'Mother-Tongue,'" *Tampa Tribune*, 6 Jan. 1929, 35.
16. To view the book's catalogue listing, enter "Cummings" in the search field on this page: https://realbiblioteca.patrimonionacional.es/.
17. Rollins News, "For Release," late Jan. or early Feb. 1929, Archives and Special Collections, Olin Library, Rollins College, Winter Park, FL.

18. "Rollins Student Gets Letter from Monarch," *Orlando Sentinel*, 3 Feb. 1929, 24.
19. Richard L. Kagan, "The Old World in the New: Florida's Discovery of the Arts of Spain," in Díaz Balsera and May, *La Florida*, 192–208.
20. Kagan, "The Old World in the New."
21. "Study of Spanish Making Big Gains: Now Leads All Other Languages in New York High Schools," *New York Times*, 6 Oct. 1918, 75.
22. Cummings's official Rollins College transcript lists every course for which he received credit from high school onward.
23. In 1932, Cummings was hired to teach Spanish, French, and German at the Valley Ranch School for Boys outside Cody, Wyoming, primarily on the basis of his familiarity with all three languages.
24. "Rollins Student Gets Letter from Monarch," 24.
25. The full inscription reads: "A su majestad Don Alfonso El Rey de España, 1 Enero 1929, Philip H. Cummings, Versos escritos en España Páginas 27, 29, 30, 32, 35" (To his majesty Don Alfonso, King of Spain, 1 January 1929, Philip H. Cummings, Poems written in Spain [on] pages 27, 29, 30, 32, 35).
26. García Lorca to Sebastian Gasch, Sept. 1928, in García Lorca, *Selected Letters*, 134.
27. Andrew A. Anderson, "García Lorca's *Poemas en Prosa* and *Poeta en Nueva York*: Dalí, Gasch, Surrealism, and the Avant-Garde," in Havard, *Companion to Spanish Surrealism*, 163–27. For a discussion of the time period in which the poems must have been composed, see 168.
28. García Lorca to Gasch, Sept. 1928, in García Lorca, *Selected Letters*, 135.
29. The Guadiana River was historically used to transport invading soldiers to inland regions of the Iberian Peninsula. https://algarvedailynews.com/nautical/6284-a-history-of-the-guadiana-river.
30. García Lorca, "Two Lovers Murdered by a Partridge" (Amantes asesinados por una perdiz), in García Lorca, *Poet in New York* (2013), 115, 117.
31. García Lorca, *Poeta en Nueva York y Otras Hojas y Poemas*, 124–45.
32. García Lorca, "Amantes asesinados por una perdiz (Hommage à Guy Maupassant)," *DDOOSS: Revista de Poesía* (Valladolid) 3 (Mar. 1931): 13–16.
33. García Lorca to Jorge Zalamea, autumn 1928, in García Lorca, *Selected Letters*, 143.
34. Dalí to García Lorca, early Sept. 1928, in Gibson, *Federico García Lorca: A Life*, 216–17. For more about the personal and artistic relationship between García Lorca and Dalí, see Dalí and García Lorca, *Sebastian's Arrows*.
35. García Lorca to Sebastian Gasch, 8 Sept. 1928, in García Lorca, *Selected Letters*, 136. *Putrefactos* (putrid ones) was a derogatory term used by Lorca, Dalí, and their friends to refer to critics they perceived as overly conventional and thus incapable of understanding and appreciating their work.
36. García Lorca to Jorge Zalamea, 1928, in García Lorca, *Selected Letters*, 145.

37. García Lorca to Jorge Guillen, Jan. 1927, in García Lorca, *Selected Letters*, 94.
38. Gibson, *Federico García Lorca: A Life*, 228–29.
39. Stainton, *Lorca*, 205.
40. Martínez Nadal, *Federico García Lorca*, 32–33.
41. Gibson, *Federico García Lorca: A Life*, 247–48.
42. Martínez Nadal, *Federico García Lorca*, 33.
43. García Lorca to Carlos Morla Lynch, early June 1929, in García Lorca, *Selected Letters*, 146.
44. Crockett and Crockett, *Satchel Guide to Spain and Portugal*, 5, 9.
45. "Rivera Will Await New Constitution. Spain Quiet and Orderly After the University Troubles—Reopening of Madrid School Likely," *New York Times*, 3 Apr. 1929, 8.
46. A. J. Hanna to Philip Cummings, 16 May 1929, Rollins College Archives, Winter Park, FL.
47. Philip Cummings to A. J. Hanna, 7 June 1929, Rollins College Archives, Winter Park, FL.
48. New York Passenger Lists, 1820–1957, Ancestry.com.
49. Guy Forshey, "A St. Louis School Teacher, a Live Arab, and a Dead Language," *St. Louis Post-Dispatch*, 9 Feb. 1930, 82, 85.
50. In a series of unpublished essays currently in a private collection, Cummings wrote about the Alpine sites he visited in the spring of 1929. He invariably used the pronoun "we."
51. "Personal Mention," *Orlando Sentinel*, 21 Apr. 1929, 24.
52. Lorca to his parents, 28 June 1929, in García Lorca, *Poet in New York* (2013), 201.
53. Philip Cummings, "August in Eden," in García Lorca, *Songs*, 178–79.
54. Philip Cummings, interview by Dionisio Cañas, 15 Feb. 1986. Notes provided to me by Dr. Cañas.
55. Even though same-sex intercourse had been legal under Spain's penal code since 1822, new legislation enacted under General Primo de Rivera in 1928 reintroduced punishment for male-male sexual activity. In addition to the threat of criminal prosecution, queer Spanish men continued to face repression and social stigmatization in the late 1920s. Richard Cleminson, "Male Homosexuality in Contemporary Spain: Signposts for a Cultural Analysis," *Paragraph* 22:1 (Mar. 1999): 35–54.
56. Gibson, *Federico García Lorca: A Life*, 238.

Chapter Three

1. For more details about Lorca's activities in Paris and England, see Gibson, *Federico García Lorca: A Life*, 239–41; C. Brian Morris, "Brief Encounter:

Federico García Lorca and Edouard Roditi in Paris (June 1929)," *Bulletin of Spanish Studies* 86:3 (2009): 331–43.

2. García Lorca, *Selected Letters*, 148.
3. New York Passenger Lists, 1820–1957, Ancestry.com.
4. Gibson, *Federico García Lorca: A Life*, 247–48.
5. Christopher Maurer, "The Poet Writes to His Family from New York and Havana," in García Lorca, *Poet in New York* (2013), 195–259.
6. Lorca to his parents, 28 June 1929, in García Lorca, *Poet in New York* (2013), 201.
7. Lorca to his parents, 28 June 1929, in García Lorca, *Poet in New York* (2013), 201–2.
8. Boston Passenger Lists, 1820–1943, Ancestry.com. On 4 July 1929, the *Hardwick Gazette* reported that "Philip Cummings arrived in town a few days since from a several months' tour of Europe."
9. For more information about Columbia's 1929 summer program, see "Summer School at Columbia to Open on July 8," *New York Herald Tribune*, 3 Mar. 1929, A9.
10. The original manuscript of this letter is held by the Hispanic Society of America in New York. For a transcription, see García Lorca, *Songs*, 6–7. This English translation is from García Lorca, *Selected Letters*, 149.
11. *World Almanac and Book of Facts for 1930*, 577, 710. The almanac gives the population of Madrid (813,991) and Granada (103,783) as measured in the 1923 Spanish census.
12. James D. Fernandez, "The Discovery of Spain in New York, Circa 1930," in Sullivan, *Nueva York*, 216–33.
13. Philip's original letter in Spanish is in the archives of the Fundación Federico García Lorca in Granada, Spain. My translation.
14. Two of the statements here about his upcoming trip were wildly off base, even for someone as prone to exaggeration as Federico was. The distance from Granada, Spain, to the neighboring town of Loja is only 39 miles, compared to the 300 miles from New York City to Burlington, Vermont. Also, it took only nine (rather than twenty) hours to make the trip by train. *Official Guide of the Railways and Steam Navigation Lines*, 146.
15. Lorca to his parents, 8 Aug. 1929, in García Lorca, *Poet in New York* (2013), 218–19. Regarding the cost of the trip, at that time train tickets were priced individually based on the number of miles to be traveled. In 1933, for example, the charge for a reserved seat was $0.0275 per mile, so Federico's 300-mile trip to Burlington would have cost $8.25 one-way. He would have paid an extra fee for a sleeping berth on the trip north but would have also received a discount for buying a round-trip ticket back to New York. All told, the final cost of Federico's train ticket would been very close to the $20 Philip sent him. US Coordinator of Transportation, *Passenger Traffic Report*, 67, 255–56.

16. While there is no known record that specifies exactly which train Federico took to Vermont, at the time the *Mount Royal* was the only overnight train from New York to Burlington that traveled along the Hudson River and also offered Pullman service—two aspects of the trip Federico later described in a letter (see chapter 4). *Official Guide of the Railways and Steam Navigation Lines*, 122, 140, 146.
17. Daniel Eisenberg, "A Chronology of Lorca's Visit to New York and Cuba," *Kentucky Romance Quarterly* 24:3 (1977): 233–50, http://www.cervantesvirtual.com/obra-visor/a-chronology-of-lorcas-visit-to-new-york-and-cuba-0/html/000be1e8-82b2-11df-acc7-002185ce6064_2.html.
18. The dinner was hosted by Federico de Onís and described by Spanish writer Concha Espina, who noted the presence of García Lorca and Fernando de los Ríos in her account of the evening. See Maurer and Anderson, *Federico García Lorca en Nueva York y La Habana*, 224–25.
19. Scholars Christopher Maurer and Andrew A. Anderson contend that Lorca must have left New York on the evening of 21 August and arrived in Vermont on 22 August, but this is not consistent with my analysis. See Maurer and Anderson, *Federico García Lorca en Nueva York y La Habana*, 43n1, 224n1.
20. In 1930, Hardwick's population was 2,720. *Vermont in 1930*, https://vermonthistory.org/client_media/files/Learn/Census%20Records/1930-Census.pdf.
21. *Walton's Vermont Register Business and Legal Directory*, 113–15.
22. Brayley, *History of the Granite Industry*, 102–13.
23. Dow, "Hardwick on the Map," 104–5.
24. For a fascinating study of granite workers and multiculturalism in nearby Barre, Vermont, in that era, see Tomasi and Richmond, *Men Against Granite.*
25. Adams, *García Lorca*, 99.
26. Philip Cummings described his experiences growing up in Hardwick, including his difficult relationships with his peers and his father, in an unpublished, unfinished memoir written ca. 1935, now in a private collection.
27. Cummings, unpublished memoir, ca. 1935.
28. Philip Cummings, "A Poet in the Sagebrush," unpublished 1932–1933 journal, private collection.
29. *Hardwickian*, June 1924, 20–21.
30. *Hardwickian*, June 1924, 20–21.
31. "Local Lumps," *Hardwick (VT) Gazette*, 20 Mar. 1919, 8, and 23 July 1923, 8.
32. For more about Harry Cummings's land development projects in Florida and Vermont, see Patricia A. Billingsley, "How Highland Lodge Got Its Name," *Hazen Road Dispatch* 36 (Summer 2011): 18–25.
33. "Local Lumps," *Hardwick (VT) Gazette*, 12 May 1928, 8, and 29 Sept. 1928, 8.

34. The ad was published in the "Shore and Mountain—For Sale" section of the *Burlington Free Press* real estate pages on multiple dates in July and August 1926.
35. Adams, *García Lorca*, 100.

Chapter Four

1. Lorca to his parents, 22 Aug. 1929, in García Lorca, *Poet in New York* (2013), 223. The date of this letter in the 2013 edition is shown as [August 23?, 1929], but translator Christopher Maurer later reverted to his original estimated date of 22 August. See Maurer and Anderson, *Federico García Lorca en Nueva York y La Habana*, 43.
2. Ángel del Río, "Introduction," in García Lorca, *Poet in New York* (1955), xv.
3. Del Río, "Introduction," in García Lorca, *Poet in New York* (1955), xiv–xv.
4. "Train de Luxe: Rutland Railroad to Provide Extra Service between Montreal and New York," *Burlington Free Press*, 17 June 1924, 8.
5. The many special features of the Pullman cars were described in promotional brochures distributed by various railroad companies at the time. See, for example, *Real Beds for Night Travel Comfort Between New York and Baltimore* (Baltimore & Ohio Railroad, Feb. 1929).
6. *Official Guide of the Railways and Steam Navigation Lines*, 122, 140, 146.
7. Lorca to his parents, 22 Aug. 1929, in García Lorca, *Poet in New York* (2013), 223. The full moon was on 20 August that month, so there would have been plentiful moonlight even after midnight.
8. Jesús Ortega, cultural director of the Huerta de San Vicente Casa-Museo Federico García Lorca, Granada, Spain, pers. comm., 13 Oct. 2014.
9. Gibson, *Federico García Lorca: A Life*, 240. Gibson does not specifically mention the iconic cricket sweater, but it was almost certainly among the items of clothing Lorca purchased during his shopping trip in Oxford.
10. Chauncey. *Gay New York*, 50–57, 182.
11. *Official Guide of the Railways and Steam Navigation Lines*, 122.
12. "Burlington's Union Railroad Station—New $150,000 Structure Will Be Opened for Business Sunday Morning," *Burlington Daily News*, 21 Jan. 1916, 5. See also https://en.wikipedia.org/wiki/Alfred_T._Fellheimer.
13. Cummings to Ángel del Río, 24 Nov. 1955, Journal of Hispanic Philology Collection, Special Collections and Archives, Florida State University Libraries, Tallahassee.
14. Cummings to Mildred Adams, 29 Aug. 1967, Journal of Hispanic Philology Collection, Special Collections and Archives, Florida State University Libraries, Tallahassee.
15. Cummings to Daniel Eisenberg, 30 Sept. 1974, Journal of Hispanic Philology Collection, Special Collections and Archives, Florida State University

Libraries, Tallahassee; Cummings to Ian Gibson, 15 Mar. 1986, Ian Gibson Collection, Centro de Estudios Lorquianos, Fuente Vaqueros, Spain.

16. Central Vermont Railway timetable, in *Official Guide of the Railways and Steam Navigation Lines*, 1246.
17. Lorca to his parents, 8 Aug. 1929, in García Lorca, *Poet in New York* (2013), 219.
18. Patricia A. Billingsley, "How Highland Lodge Got Its Name," *Hazen Road Dispatch* 36 (Summer 2011): 18–25.
19. See, for example, Ravogli, *Syphilis*.
20. García Lorca, *Gypsy Ballads*, 72–81.
21. McKay, *Walk Through the Garden of Eden*, 49, 59.
22. Lorca to his parents, 22 Aug. 1929, in García Lorca, *Poet in New York* (2013), 223–24.
23. McKay, *Walk Through the Garden of Eden*, 50–56.
24. Wallace Stegner captured this clash of cultures in his novel *Second Growth*, which is based on his experiences as a visitor to the small agricultural village of Greensboro, Vermont, in the 1930s. Greensboro, only forty miles from Eden Mills, had its own beautiful lake and summer colony of city dwellers.
25. Cummings, "August in Eden," in García Lorca, *Songs*, 155.
26. McKay, *Walk Through the Garden of Eden*, 53.
27. *Effect of Tuberculosis Institutions*, 51.
28. Death notice for Frank Southwick, *Boston Globe*, 12 Jan. 1928, 22.
29. García Lorca, *Poet in New York* (2013), 241.
30. Maurer, *Federico García Lorca Escribe a Su Familia*, 23.
31. García Lorca, *Poet in New York* (2013), 242.
32. Lorca to his parents, 22 Aug. 1929, in García Lorca, *Poet in New York* (2013), 224.
33. Descriptions of the Lake Eden cottage are based on my own observations during several extended stays there. Over the years, the owners have added electricity, phone service, indoor plumbing, and a two-story addition, but they have otherwise gone to great lengths to preserve the cottage just as it was when Lorca and Cummings were there.
34. Lorca to his parents, 22 Aug. 1929, in García Lorca, *Poet in New York* (2013), 224.
35. For more about New England cottage architecture, see Clifford, "Retreat to Vermont."
36. "Vermont's Energy Use: Past, Present, and Future," in *Fueling Vermont's Future*, 3–16. Electrical service did not reach Eden Mills until 1939. "Vermont's First Rural Electrification Project Is Completed," *Burlington Free Press*, 8 May 1939, 2.
37. In his 22 August letter to his parents, Lorca wrote, "At night we see and

speak to one another by the light of oil lamps." García Lorca, *Poet in New York* (2013), 224.

38. Lorca to his parents, 24 July 1929, in García Lorca, *Poet in New York* (2013), 213–14.
39. Kessel Schwartz, "García Lorca and Vermont," *Hispania* 42 (Mar. 1959): 51.
40. E. Towle, pers. comm., 21 May 2011.

Chapter Five

1. Only three of the thirty-five poems in *Poet in New York* can be definitively dated to the period between Federico's arrival in New York City in late June 1929 and his trip to Vermont in mid-August, though the composition dates of at least three other poems in the collection are unknown. Andrew A. Anderson, "The Evolution of García Lorca's Poetic Projects 1929–36 and the Textual Status of *Poeta en Nueva York*," *Bulletin of Hispanic Studies* 60:3 (1983): 221–25; Christopher Maurer, "Notes on the Poems," in García Lorca, *Poet in New York* (2013), 267–78.
2. Cummings, "August in Eden," in García Lorca, *Songs*, 129.
3. McKay, *Walk Through the Garden of Eden*, 57–59, 137.
4. Philip Cummings, interview with Ian Gibson, Eden Mills, VT, 4 Apr. 1986, Ian Gibson Collection, Centro de Estudios Lorquianos, Fuente Vaqueros, Spain.
5. John Frank Ruggles, West Point class of 1931, had attained the rank of major general by the time he retired from the US Army in 1966. Cullum Files, West Point Association of Graduates, West Point, NY.
6. Lorca to his parents, 22 Aug. 1929, in García Lorca, *Poet in New York* (2013), 224.
7. In August 1928, the fact that the sisters climbed to the top of Belvidere Mountain, a 3,376-foot peak near Eden Mills, was noteworthy enough to be mentioned in the local paper. *Morrisville News Citizen*, 22 Aug. 1928, 6. In his August 1929 journal, Cummings also reported that the sisters routinely walked from Eden Mills to the next town and back, a twenty-mile round trip. Cummings, "August in Eden," in García Lorca, *Songs*, 155.
8. Lorca to his parents, 22 Aug. 1929, in García Lorca, *Poet in New York* (2013), 225.
9. Cummings, "August in Eden," in García Lorca, *Songs*, 155.
10. Brown, *Back to the Land*.
11. Brown, *Back to the Land*, 10–11.
12. Brown, *Back to the Land*, 98.
13. The school was the legacy of wealthy Philadelphia philanthropist Robert Carson, who left virtually his entire estate, including the land on which the school was built, for the creation of a homelike boarding school that would

prepare destitute, orphaned girls to lead happy, productive lives. The school opened in 1918 under the direction of Elsa Ueland, a former settlement house worker who had studied with John Dewey and Maria Montessori, leading progressive educators of the day. For a full history of this remarkable school, see Contosta, *Philadelphia's Progressive Orphanage*.

14. Staff minutes, book 1, Carson Valley School (Flourtown, PA) Records, Urban Archives Collection, acc. 510, Special Collections Research Center, Temple University Libraries, Philadelphia, PA.
15. Management Committee reports, Carson Valley School (Flourtown, PA) Records.
16. Pennsylvania Death Certificates, 1906–1963, Ancestry.com.
17. *Burlington Free Press*, 11 July 1927, 9.
18. Harrison, *View from Vermont*, 56–74.
19. *Morrisville News Citizen*, 11 July 1928, 9. Although the article refers to the sisters' plan to use the house only in the summer, later events indicate that they hoped to live there year-round once it was in better repair and they were better established. Note that the deed for the property was not officially transferred to the sisters until October 1928.
20. Cummings, interview with Ian Gibson, 4 Apr. 1986.
21. Lorca to his parents, 22 Aug. 1929, in García Lorca, *Poet in New York* (2013), 225.
22. Jenny Bourne Wahl, "New Results on the Decline in Household Fertility in the United States from 1750 to 1900," in Engerman and Gallman, *Long-Term Factors in American Economic Growth*, 391–439.
23. Lorca to his parents, 22 Aug. 1929, in García Lorca, *Poet in New York* (2013), 225.
24. Lorca had been surprised to discover that French-speaking Americans could understand his French, even though he was out of practice and knew very few words. Lorca to his parents, 14 July 1929, in García Lorca, *Poet in New York* (2013), 208.
25. García Lorca, "Lecture: A Poet in New York," in García Lorca, *Poet in New York* (2013), 189.
26. See data for Burlington, Vermont, http://www.world-timedate.com/astronomy/.
27. Lorca to his parents, 8 Aug. 1929, in García Lorca, *Poet in New York* (2013), 219.
28. The composition of this theoretical dinner reflects the meats, produce, and dairy products that were both in season and available for purchase from local farmers at the time. See, for example, McKay, *Walk Through the Garden of Eden*, 7, 61.
29. García Lorca to Ángel del Río, Aug. 1929, in García Lorca, *Selected Letters*, 150; Lorca to his parents, 8 Aug. 1929, in García Lorca, *Poet in New York* (2013), 216.

30. See https://en.wikipedia.org/wiki/Congregationalism_in_the_United_States.
31. 1930 US Census, Ancestry.com.
32. Correspondence between Daniel Eisenberg and Edna Southwick Stimpson, 22 Oct. and 4 Nov. 1975, Journal of Hispanic Philology Collection, Special Collections, Florida State University Libraries, Tallahassee.
33. Lorca to his parents, 22 Aug. 1929, in García Lorca, *Poet in New York* (2013), 222–26.
34. Kessel Schwartz to Daniel Eisenberg, 13 Nov. 1974, Journal of Hispanic Philology Collection, Special Collections, Florida State University Libraries, Tallahassee.
35. Lorca to his parents, 22 Aug. 1929, in García Lorca, *Poet in New York* (2013), 224.
36. Record of climatological observations for Garfield Station, Hyde Park, VT, Aug. 1929, NOAA National Centers for Environmental Information, https://www.ncdc.noaa.gov/cdo-web/datasets/GHCND/stations/GHCND:USC00433240/detail.
37. Cummings, "August in Eden," in García Lorca, *Songs*, 144.
38. Cummings, interview with Gibson, 4 Apr. 1986.
39. Cummings, interview with Gibson, 4 Apr. 1986. In a 1932 lecture about his time in the United States, Lorca explained how hearing a cuckoo (an obvious misremembrance of the loon) by a silent lake made him restless and helped inspire his "Double Poem of Lake Eden." García Lorca, "Lecture: A Poet in New York," in García Lorca, *Poet in New York* (2013), 191.
40. Cummings to Ángel del Río, 24 Nov. 1955, Journal of Hispanic Philology Collection, Special Collections, Florida State University Libraries, Tallahassee.

Chapter Six

1. Henry Toledano, "The Modern Library," talk given at Book Club of California, San Francisco, 23 Sept. 2002, http://www.modernlib.com/General/ToleHistroySpeech.html.
2. Stella Weston Tuttle Chapman, telephone interview by Daniel Eisenberg, 1974. She recalled Cummings sending a copy of his own collection, *Mother-Tongue*, to Carl Sandburg as a token of his esteem soon after it was published by Rollins Press in December 1928. Journal of Hispanic Philology Collection, Special Collections, Florida State University Libraries, Tallahassee.
3. See, for example, Erkkila, *Walt Whitman's Songs of Male Intimacy and Love*; Martin, "Walt Whitman," in his *Homosexual Tradition in American Poetry*, 3–89.

4. Sedgwick, *Between Men*, 206.
5. Whitman, "From Pent-Up Aching Rivers," in *Leaves of Grass* (1921), 79.
6. "Kalamos," https://en.wikipedia.org/wiki/Kalamos.
7. Whitman, "These I Singing in Spring," in *Leaves of Grass* (1921), 101.
8. Whitman, "Recorders Ages Hence," in *Leaves of Grass* (1921), 104.
9. Russell, *Jeb and Dash*, 65, 178, 188.
10. Whitman, "When I Heard at the Close of the Day," in *Leaves of Grass* (1921), 104–5.
11. Cummings, "August in Eden," in García Lorca, *Songs*, 128.
12. Whitman, "This Moment Yearning and Thoughtful," in *Leaves of Grass* (1921), 108.
13. The first partial translation of Whitman's *Leaves of Grass* into Spanish was Álvaro Armando Vasseur's *Walt Whitman: Poemas* (1912). The first full translation was Concha Zardoya's *Obras Escogidas* (1946). Rachel Price and Matt Cohen, "Introduction to Walt Whitman, *Poemas*, by Álvaro Armando Vasseur," *Publications of the Modern Language Association* 123:2 (2008), https://whitmanarchive.org/item/anc.00158.
14. In their 2008 article, "Introduction to Walt Whitman," Price and Cohen note: "The problematic features of what [Álvaro Armando] Vasseur termed his 'adaptation' include but are not limited to outright errors; the completion of sentences Whitman had deliberately rendered opaque; the omission of Whitmanesque gerunds; and, perhaps most glaringly, a tendency to cover over Whitman's homosexuality with, in the most benign cases, a vague rhetoric of brotherly love. In the most radical instances of Vasseur's censoring, the translator changes originally homoerotic or at least ambiguous phrases into expressions of clearly heterosexual desire." https://whitmanarchive.org/item/anc.00158.
15. Lorca to his parents, 22 Aug. 1929, in García Lorca, *Poet in New York* (2013), 225.
16. Adams, *García Lorca*, 106.
17. Lorca to his parents, 8 Aug. 1929, in García Lorca, *Poet in New York* (2013), 215.
18. Cummings, *Mother-Tongue*.
19. García Lorca, "Ballads," *Alhambra* 1:3 (Aug. 1929): 24–25. The two translated poems were "Preciosa y el aire" (Ballad of Preciosa and the Wind) and "Romance de la pena negra" (Ballad of the Black Sorrow).
20. Andrew Samuel Walsh, "Who Translated Lorca into English First? An Analysis of the 1929 New York Translations and Their Possible Authorship," *Bulletin of Hispanic Studies* 28:7 (2021): 661–77.
21. Gibson, *Federico García Lorca: A Life*, 249, 252.
22. Cummings, "The Poems," in García Lorca, *Songs*, 183.

23. This choice may have been driven in part by the aversion Lorca felt toward *Gypsy Ballads* at the time, which arose from his fear of being typecast as a "gypsy poet." Eisenberg, "Introduction," in García Lorca, *Songs*, 13.
24. The first edition of *Canciones* was published by Imprenta Sur in Málaga in 1927, but only 115 copies were printed, and they quickly sold out. The second edition was published on 27 June 1929, just days after Lorca's departure for the United States. See López Campillo, *Revista de Occidente*, 268.
25. Lorca to his parents, second week of August 1929, in García Lorca, *Poet in New York* (2013), 220.
26. Cummings's inscribed copy of the book is held in the archives of the Hispanic Society of America in New York.
27. García Lorca to Ángel del Río, late Aug. 1929, in Maurer and Anderson, *Federico García Lorca en Nueva York y La Habana*, 49–50.
28. Cummings to Daniel Eisenberg, 8 July 1974, Journal of Hispanic Philology Collection, Special Collections, Florida State University Libraries, Tallahassee.
29. The two photos are grainy and overexposed, which may explain why they were mislabeled as showing Lorca with Ángel del Río in the Catskill Mountains when I first found them in the archives of the Fundación Federico García Lorca in Madrid in 2011.
30. Cummings, "The Poems," in García Lorca, *Songs*, 183.
31. Cummings, "Introduction," in García Lorca, *Songs*, 23.
32. C. Brian Morris, "Brief Encounter: Federico García Lorca and Edouard Roditi in Paris (June 1929)," *Bulletin of Spanish Studies* 86:3 (2009): 341.
33. Cummings to Daniel Eisenberg, 5 July 1974, Journal of Hispanic Philology Collection, Special Collections, Florida State University Libraries, Tallahassee.
34. See, for example, D. R. Harris, "García Lorca, Federico, '*Songs*,' trans. Philip Cummings, ed. Daniel Eisenberg (Book Review)," *Bulletin of Hispanic Studies* 55:1 (1978): 76; Allen Josephs, "García Lorca, Federico. *Songs* (Book Review)," *Hispania* 61:2 (1978): 381–82.
35. One particularly harsh critic referred to Cummings's translations as "utterly incompetent." Edmund L. King, "Lorca, Guillén, Salinas, and Aleixandre (Book Review)," *Hudson Review* 31:4 (Winter 1978–1979): 693–703.
36. Jonathan Mayhew, author of *Apocryphal Lorca* (2009), pers. comm., 28 Apr 2011.
37. D. Gareth Walters, author of *Canciones and the Early Poetry of Lorca* (2002), pers. comm., 4 July 2011.
38. For Lorca's original version of the poem and a translation by Alan S. Trueblood, see García Lorca, *Collected Poems*, 466–67. For Cummings's translation, see García Lorca, *Songs*, 49.

39. Walters, *Canciones*, 221.
40. Eisenberg, "Introduction," in García Lorca, *Songs*, 14–16.
41. Mayhew, pers. comm., 28 Apr. 2011.

Chapter Seven

1. Based on rainfall data for August 1929 collected at the Garfield weather station near Hyde Park, Vermont, eight miles south of Lake Eden. Historical weather data obtained from the NOAA (National Oceanic and Atmospheric Administration), National Centers for Environmental Information, https://www.ncei.noaa.gov/cdo-web/.
2. Chamberlain, *On the Trail*, 66–70.
3. Harrison, *View from Vermont*, 111–23.
4. Cummings, "August in Eden," in García Lorca, *Songs*, 125–66. The original typescript of the journal, held by the Hispanic Society of America in New York, consists of thirty-one typed entries across thirty-eight pages.
5. In a September 1974 letter to Eisenberg, Cummings stated that he wrote the entire journal during the ten days of Lorca's visit. Eisenberg, "Cummings' Diary," in García Lorca, *Songs*, 17.
6. *Fifth Biennial Report of the State Highway Board*. The highway map in the front of this report shows that Route 100 from Waterbury to Newport, including the stretch through Eden Mills, was surfaced with treated gravel.
7. Cummings, "August in Eden," in García Lorca, *Songs*, 135.
8. Journalist Mildred Adams, who spent time with Lorca in both Spain and New York, mentioned "the limp that always signaled fatigue." According to his brother Francisco, this limp was due to a slight difference in the length of Federico's legs and helped explain "his reluctance to participate in games that required great physical agility" as a child. Adams, *García Lorca*, 126; García Lorca, *In the Green Morning: Memories of Federico*, 45–46.
9. Philip Cummings, interview with Ian Gibson, Eden Mills, VT, 4 Apr. 1986, Ian Gibson Collection, Centro de Estudios Lorquianos, Fuente Vaqueros, Spain.
10. Lorca to his parents, 22 Aug. 1929, in García Lorca, *Poet in New York* (2013), 224.
11. O'Kane, *Trails and Summits*, 276–87. A comparable 2015 hiking guide describes the same route that Philip and Federico took as "a gorgeous but challenging hike." Green Mountain Club, *Explorer's Guide*, 235–37.
12. O'Kane, *Trails and Summits*, 282; Cummings, "August in Eden," in García Lorca, *Songs*, 134.
13. Cummings, "August in Eden," in García Lorca, *Songs*, 131. See Graff, *Looking Back at Vermont*. For a history of asbestos mining in Eden, see McKay, *Walk Through the Garden of Eden*, 39–48.
14. Cummings, "August in Eden," in García Lorca, *Songs*, 138.

15. Cummings, "August in Eden," in García Lorca, *Songs*, 139.
16. Cummings, "August in Eden," in García Lorca, *Songs*, 135; Act No. 200 in *Acts and Resolves Passed by the General Assembly*, 211.
17. Cummings, "August in Eden," in García Lorca, *Songs*, 138–39.
18. Cummings's summer job on a steamboat "sailing between the various ports on Lake Memphremagog" was reported in the *Hardwick (VT) Gazette*, 24 Aug. 1924, 8.
19. Cummings to Ian Gibson, 15 Mar. 1986, Ian Gibson Collection, Centro de Estudios Lorquianos, Fuente Vaqueros, Spain.
20. García Lorca to his family, late Aug. 1929. This translation of Federico's message is by Christopher Maurer in García Lorca, *Poet in New York* (2013), 229. The photo on the postcard was taken from Shattuck Hill in Newport. For a more recent view of the same scene, see "The Road to Lake Memphremagog," *Vermont Life* 39:1 (Autumn 1984): 9–16.
21. Both quotes are from Cummings, "August in Eden," in García Lorca, *Songs*, 140.
22. Cummings, "August in Eden," in García Lorca, *Songs*, 142.
23. García Lorca, *Poeta en Nueva York y Otras Hojas y Poemas*, 124–25.
24. Cummings, "August in Eden," in García Lorca, *Songs*, 154–55; "Eden," *Burlington (VT) Free Press*, 3 Aug. 1929, 6.
25. The trail to the top of Mount Norris rises 1,482 feet over 1.8 miles and is rated "difficult" by the Green Mountain Club. "Outings," *Long Trail News: Quarterly of the Green Mountain Club* 80:1 (Spring 2020): 29.
26. Cummings, "August in Eden," in García Lorca, *Songs*, 149.
27. Cummings did not give the name of the mine or its location in his journal, but the Moretown mine was the correct distance away and was the only mine in the region with talc deposits hard enough to produce pencils for marking marble and steel. Ladoo, *Talc and Soapstone*, 95–98.
28. Cummings, "August in Eden," in García Lorca, *Songs*, 151–52.
29. Cummings, "August in Eden," in García Lorca, *Songs*, 153. Then, as now, each segment of the Long Trail was monitored and maintained by Green Mountain Club staff members and volunteers. Green Mountain Club, *Explorer's Guide*, 24.
30. Cummings, "August in Eden," in García Lorca, *Songs*, 153.
31. García Lorca, *Poeta en Nueva York y Otras Hojas y Poemas*, 216–17. Both misspellings are per the original.
32. Cummings, "August in Eden," in García Lorca, *Songs*, 159.
33. Cummings, "August in Eden," in García Lorca, *Songs*, 164.
34. Cummings, "August in Eden," in García Lorca, *Songs*, 158.
35. Daniel Eisenberg, pers. comm., 25 Mar. 2014.
36. Cummings, "August in Eden," in García Lorca, *Songs*, 160.
37. Cummings, "August in Eden," in García Lorca, *Songs*, 160.

38. Cummings, "August in Eden," in García Lorca, *Songs*, 160.
39. Cummings to Ángel del Río, 24 Nov. 1955, Journal of Hispanic Philology Collection, Special Collections, Florida State University Libraries, Tallahassee.

Chapter Eight

1. Gibson, *Federico García Lorca: A Life*, 216–17.
2. Cummings, "August in Eden," in García Lorca, *Songs*, 160, 163.
3. Lorca to his parents, 22 Aug. 1929, in García Lorca, *Poet in New York* (2013), 226.
4. García Lorca, *Selected Letters*, 150. Note that the two sentences that begin "My young friend Cummings" and "Did you ask Fernando de los Ríos" were translated by me. These sentences were deleted by Ángel del Río prior to the letter's first publication in 1941 and rediscovered circa 2011 in photocopies of the original. Maurer and Anderson, *Federico García Lorca en Nueva York y La Habana*, 49–50. The date of this letter is unknown, but it reached del Río in time for him to send a reply to Eden Mills, possibly by telegraph. Cummings mentioned this fact in a 1955 letter to del Río: "How well I recall his clutching your letter of details when my father and I put him on the train in Burlington with destination of Shandaken." Cummings to del Río, 24 Nov. 1955, Journal of Hispanic Philology Collection, Special Collections, Florida State University Libraries, Tallahassee.
5. In his journal, Cummings wrote about attending a community dance in Eden Mills during Lorca's visit, and wondering afterward whether his future grandchildren would ever learn the same old-fashioned square dances. Cummings, "August in Eden," in García Lorca, *Songs*, 155.
6. "Cornelia Weston Becomes a Bride," *New York Times*, 24 June 1938, 16.
7. This statement is based on my private conversations with several members of Philip's family and others with direct knowledge of his ongoing secret relationships with men.
8. It is unclear why Lorca chose to add place and date information to several of the poems he composed in Vermont and the Catskills. Perhaps the practice helped him stay oriented in an unfamiliar setting, or he knew the information might later prove helpful as a memory aid.
9. García Lorca, *Poet in New York* (2013), 79, 81.
10. C. Brian Morris, pers. comm., 30 Mar. 2014.
11. Andrew A. Anderson, "Lorca's 'Cielo Vivo,' the Other Lake Eden Poem," *Symposium* 71 (2017): 28–47.
12. Kessel Schwartz, "García Lorca and Vermont," *Hispania* 42 (Mar. 1959): 50.
13. "The Drought," *Burlington (VT) Free Press*, 28 Aug. 1929, 6.
14. "Ayrshires in Vermont," *Ayrshire Digest* 7:4 (15 June 1921): 11. I learned

about the breed's relatively small, dainty feet from Ralmon Black, a retired Massachusetts dairy inspector, in July 2012. See also "Breed History," http://www.usayrshire.com/about-us.

15. Cummings, "August in Eden," in García Lorca, *Songs*, 134.
16. In his planned organization for the poems to be included in *Poet in New York*, Lorca placed the eight poems he associated with Vermont into two sections: "Poems of Lake Eden Mills" and "Introduction to Death (Poems of Solitude in Vermont)." He chose not to include another poem, "Tierra y luna" (Earth and Moon), that was also written at Lake Eden. García Lorca, *Poeta en Nueva York* (2013), 49–58.
17. García Lorca, *Poet in New York* (2013), 101.
18. "Seraph," https://en.wikipedia.org/wiki/Seraph.
19. Philip Cummings, interview with Ian Gibson, Eden Mills, VT, 4 Apr. 1986, Ian Gibson Collection, Centro de Estudios Lorquianos, Fuente Vaqueros, Spain.
20. Cummings, "August in Eden," in García Lorca, *Songs*, 146–49.
21. García Lorca, *Poet in New York* (2013), 79, 81. This translation by Greg Simon and Steven F. White is used throughout this discussion.
22. Garcilaso de la Vega, *The Works of Garcilaso de la Vega*.
23. García Lorca, *Poet in New York* (2013), 79.
24. "Saint Lucy," https://en.wikipedia.org/wiki/Saint_Lucy.
25. García Lorca, *Poet in New York* (2013), 81.
26. Marinello, *Contemporáneos*, 218–25.
27. García Lorca, *Poet in New York* (2013), 81.
28. García Lorca, *Collected Poems*, 758–63. For the autograph original, see García Lorca, *Poeta en Nueva York y Otras Hojas y Poemas*, 212–17.
29. Photographs of the page in question show distinctive brown stains, possibly from a glass of water, in corresponding locations on each side. See García Lorca, *Poeta en Nueva York y Otras Hojas y Poemas*, 28, 204. Despite its postscript, Lorca later placed "Vuelta de paseo" in the section of *Poeta en Nueva York* he titled "Poems of Solitude in Columbia University."
30. Cummings, "August in Eden," in García Lorca, *Songs*, 164.
31. This photo is one of twelve taken by the Tyler sisters that they later pasted into a handmade album covered with medallion-printed wallpaper and sent to Lorca as a memento of his visit. The album is in the archives of the Fundación Federico García Lorca in Granada, Spain.
32. Regarding the photo, Jaime Manrique commented, "Federico looks like a beautiful *señorita*. It's impossible to look at that photo and not notice how delicate, how feminine, Lorca could be at times." Manrique, *Eminent Maricones*, 81.

Chapter Nine

1. Ángel del Río, "Introduction to *Poet in New York*: Twenty-Five Years After," in García Lorca, *Poet in New York* (1955), xv–xvi.
2. Lorca to his parents, 21 Sept. 1929, in García Lorca, *Poet in New York* (2013), 226.
3. 1930 US Census, https://en.wikipedia.org/wiki/1930_United_States_census.
4. People in that area pay their property taxes to Lexington and are counted as Lexington residents in the US Census, complicating the search for relevant historical records.
5. Charles W. Whitney and Helen E. Hammond were the parents of Phoebe Whitney, who married Roscoe S. Hogan in September 1916. Roscoe and Phoebe had two children: Stanton and Helen. US Census records and New York state marriage and death records on Ancestry.com.
6. Classified ads for Rock Terrace House appeared periodically in the *Brooklyn Daily Eagle* from 1911 through 1929. Ads for Mountain Brook House began running in the 1890s and continued into the 1960s.
7. Ángel del Río was born in 1900 in Soria, Spain; emigrated to the United States in 1926; and began teaching in the Spanish department at Columbia University in the spring of 1929. His wife, Amelia Agostini de del Río, was born in 1896 in Yauco, Puerto Rico; moved to New York in 1918; and became the first Latina graduate of Vassar College in 1922. At Barnard College, the sister institution of Columbia University, she taught Spanish language and literature and headed the Spanish department from 1929 to 1962.
8. Lorca to his parents, 23 Sept. 1929, in García Lorca, *Poet in New York* (2013), 235–36.
9. Lorca to his parents, 21 Sept. 1929, in García Lorca, *Poet in New York* (2013), 229.
10. Lorca to his parents, 23 Sept. 1929, in García Lorca, *Poet in New York* (2013), 233.
11. Maurer, *Federico García Lorca Escribe a Su Familia*, 26–29.
12. Del Río mentions Roscoe Hogan's cancer and the air of sadness it created in the household in his introduction to García Lorca, *Poet in New York* (1955), xxxvii.
13. Stainton, *Lorca*, 228; Maurer and Anderson, *Federico García Lorca en Nueva York y La Habana*, 234.
14. Ángel del Río alluded to Lorca's nighttime restlessness, citing the "nocturnal character and inspiration" of many of his poems. Del Río, "Introduction," in García Lorca, *Poet in New York* (1955), xvii.
15. Ángel and Amelia were scheduled to teach several classes at Columbia and Barnard, respectively, during the 1929–1930 winter session, which began on 25 September 1929. Columbia University, *Catalogue Number for the Sessions of 1929–30*, 286–87.

16. Del Río, "Introduction," in García Lorca, *Poet in New York* (1955), xv–xvi.
17. Del Río, "Introduction," in García Lorca, *Poet in New York* (1955), xxxvii–xxxviii.
18. Del Río, "Introduction," in García Lorca, *Poet in New York* (1955), xxxvii.
19. García Lorca, *Poet in New York* (2013), 109.
20. García Lorca, *Poet in New York* (2013), 109.
21. García Lorca, *Poet in New York* (2013), 89, 91.
22. García Lorca, *Poet in New York* (2013), 111, 113. "Ruin" is undated, but del Río recalled Lorca working on the poem in Shandaken. Del Río, "Introduction," in García Lorca, *Poet in New York* (1955), xvii.
23. García Lorca, *Poet in New York* (2013), 93.
24. Kessel Schwartz, "García Lorca and Vermont," *Hispania* 42:1 (Mar. 1959): 50–55.
25. For the full text of the poem, see García Lorca, *Poet in New York* (2013), 95, 97.
26. Del Río, "Introduction," in García Lorca, *Poet in New York* (1955), xxxvii. See also García Lorca, *Poeta en Nueva York y Otras Hojas y Poemas*, 138.
27. The forest has reclaimed the area around the shaft except for an access road and path, and the shaft opening is fully covered and capped by a tubular steel air vent. The original width of the shaft is specified in *Shandaken Tunnel*, 11. For a photo of the shaft clearing as it appeared in 1922, see New York City Department of Environmental Protection Archives, image ID: p015252, 20 May 1922.
28. C. Brian Morris, "Agua que no Desemboca," in Morris, *"Cuando Yo Me Muera,"* 163–64, 170.
29. Del Río, "Introduction," in García Lorca, *Poet in New York* (1955), xxxvii.
30. The 1910 US Census shows Roscoe Hogan living in Ulster County and working as an inspector for New York City. In the 1920 Census, Roscoe and Phoebe Hogan are living on the farm in Greene County, with Roscoe's profession listed as salaried civil engineer. The census data also show nineteen water works laborers boarding nearby.
31. In 1975, Daniel Eisenberg was able to find and interview Stanton Hogan, then fifty-eight, from whom he learned about the underground aqueduct near the farm. Unfortunately, Stanton did not remember Lorca or the del Río family, but he shared what he knew about the design, construction, and location of shaft 6. See Eisenberg, "Cuatro Pesquisas Lorquianas," *Thesaurus* 30:3 (1975): 530–31.
32. For a complete contemporaneous description of the tunnel project, see *Shandaken Tunnel*.
33. García Lorca, *Poet in New York* (2013), 95, 97.
34. Binding, *Lorca*, 74, 78.
35. The three editions are, respectively, García Lorca, *The Poet in New York*

(1940), García Lorca, *Poet in New York* (1955), and García Lorca, *Poet in New York* (2013).

36. García Lorca, *Poet in New York (Poeta en Nueva York)* (2008), 103, 105, 107, 180.
37. García Lorca, *Poet in New York* (2013), 103, 105, 107.
38. García Lorca, *Poet in New York* (2013), 103, 105, 107.
39. García Lorca, *Poet in New York* (2013), 103, 105, 107.
40. Lorca to his parents, 21 Sept. 1929, in García Lorca, *Poet in New York* (2013), 229–30.
41. Ruis, *León Felipe*, 161.
42. Ruis, *León Felipe*, 72.
43. García Lorca, *Poet in New York* (2013), 153, 155, 157, 159, 161.
44. García Lorca, *Poet in New York* (2013), 155.
45. Lorca to Carlos Morla Lynch, Nov. 1929, in García Lorca, *Selected Letters*, 152.

Chapter Ten

1. Cummings, "Introduction," in García Lorca, *Songs*, 23.
2. "Hardwick," *Burlington (VT) Free Press*, 19 Sept. 1929, 5.
3. Cummings, "Foreword," in García Lorca, *Songs*, 127.
4. Sue Hosack, Office of Student Records, Washington University at St. Louis, pers. comm., 13 Apr. 2010.
5. Rollins College president Hamilton Holt was a strong advocate for international peace through student exchanges and had forged strong bonds between the college and the IIE. "Holt Secures Foreign Fellowship for Rollins," *Rollins Sandspur*, 9 Nov. 1928, 1.
6. Archives of the Carnegie Endowment for International Peace, ser. IV, Division of International Law, Fellowships, Academic Year 1930–1931, Rare Book and Manuscript Library, Columbia University, New York.
7. Enrique Fernández Arbós to Philip Cummings, 4 Nov. 1929, private collection. Translation by Lisa Sheehy.
8. Cummings, foreword written in 1984 for "A Poet in the Sagebrush," unpublished 1932–1933 journal, private collection.
9. "Alfred Cortot to Be Piano Soloist with Symphony," *St. Louis (MO) Star and Times*, 9 Nov. 1929, 13.
10. Cummings, entry dated 20 Feb. 1933 in "A Poet in the Sagebrush," unpublished 1932–1933 journal, private collection.
11. Alfred Cortot, though "reputedly homosexual, entered into what was universally taken to be a marriage of convenience with an older, socially connected woman from a wealthy family to advance his career." Terry Teachout, "The Pianist Who Sold His Soul," *Commentary Magazine* 149:5 (May 2020): 55–58.

12. Cummings, entry dated 20 Feb. 1933 in "A Poet in the Sagebrush," unpublished 1932–1933 journal, private collection.
13. Philip H. Cummings, "To One Who Loves Debussy," *Tampa (FL) Tribune*, 15 Mar. 1930, 10.
14. Philip Elmer Barney moved to Florida with his parents when he was a boy, but he was born in Barre, Vermont. In fact, his mother came from Cabot, Vermont, the same small village where Addie Cummings grew up. It is unclear whether the two Philips were aware of this coincidence or ever met each other in person. However, Addie facilitated the connection between her son and at least one other person who helped advance his poetic career, so she may have done the same in this case.
15. The three poems published in anthologies during Cummings's time at the Principia were "Whether," in Davis, *Davis Anthology of Newspaper Verse for 1929*, 112; "The Path to the Ozarks," in Harrison, *Grub Street Book of Verse*, 27; and "Whip-poor-will," in Scollard and Rittenhouse, *Bird-Lovers' Anthology*, 199.
16. Cummings, entries dated 14 Oct. 1932, 17 Dec. 1932, and 28 Feb. 1933, in "A Poet in the Sagebrush," unpublished 1932–1933 journal, private collection.
17. The original Spanish text is reprinted in Roger Tinnell, "Correspondencia y Documentos Inéditos en la Fundación Federico García Lorca," *Cuadernos Hispanoamericanos* 739 (Jan. 2012): 53–75. My translation. The year in the postcard's stamped postmark must be smudged, because Tinnell hypothesized that it had been sent in late December 1928. However, based on the dates of Cummings's trip to Mexico City and on the fully legible postmark on a similar postcard he sent to a friend in Vermont (in a private collection), the correct year is 1929.
18. "The Creation of a Spanish American Student Exchange," *News Bulletin of the Institute of International Education, Latin American Number* 5:5 (Feb. 1930): 3.
19. Hewlett, *Decade of International Fellowships*, 10.
20. Consuelo Flecha García, "Education in Spain: Close-Up of Its History in the 20th Century," *Analytical Reports in International Education* 4:1 (Oct. 2011): 17–42.
21. For detailed reports of university-related political events in Spain during the 1929–1930 academic year, see "Spain Week by Week," *Bulletin of Spanish Studies* 7:26–28 (Apr.–Oct. 1930).
22. "Hardwick Man Receives Valuable Spanish Fellowship," *Burlington (VT) Free Press*, 9 Sept. 1930, 2; "Vermonter Wins Honor from Spanish Crown," *Burlington (VT) Daily News*, 9 Sept. 1930, 3.
23. Both papers also misspelled the name of the "motor vessel" Cummings would be taking to Europe as *Britania*, suggesting that Cummings himself had misspelled it when he notified them. He boarded the MV

Britannic in Boston on 14 September 1930, arriving in Liverpool on 22 September. On 26 September, he took the *Hakusan Mari* from London to Gibraltar, arriving there on 28 September. See Boston Passenger Lists, 1820–1943, and UK Outward Passenger Lists, 1890–1960, both at Ancestry.com.

24. Cummings's concern about his future employability was well founded. As the economic effects of the Great Depression spread across all segments of society, competition for teaching jobs increased sharply, and schools at all levels began to demand that candidates hold advanced degrees. R. H. Eliassen and Earl W. Anderson, "Investigations of Teacher Supply and Demand Reported Since November 1930," *Educational Research Bulletin* 10:18 (9 Dec. 1931): 479–83.
25. For a full timeline of Lorca's 1929–1930 visit to the Americas, see Daniel Eisenberg, "A Chronology of Lorca's Visit to New York and Cuba," *Kentucky Romance Quarterly* 24:3 (1977): 233–50.
26. Gibson, *Federico García Lorca: A Life*, 267–302; Stainton, *Lorca*, 229–51.
27. García Lorca, "Two Lovers Murdered by a Partridge," in García Lorca, *Poet in New York* (2013), 115, 117, 119. The date of the poem's composition is identified in Andrew A. Anderson, "García Lorca's *Poemas en Prosa* and *Poeta en Nueva York*: Dalí, Gasch, Surrealism, and the Avant-Garde," in Havard, *Companion to Spanish Surrealism*, 163–82.
28. Eisenberg, *"Poeta en Nueva York,"* 202–3.
29. Adolfo Salazar, "La Casa de Bernarda Alba," *Carteles, Carteles, Carteles* (10 Apr. 1938): 30.
30. The first English translation of the poem was published without comment or explanation in an appendix to the 1955 Grove Press edition of *Poet in New York*, but it was left out of the first (1988) Farrar, Straus and Giroux bilingual edition of the work. It finally secured a place in the second (1998) Farrar, Straus and Giroux edition, in which editor Christopher Maurer noted on page 276 that a manuscript held by the Lorca foundation provided "unassailable proof" that "Two Lovers" belonged in the collection.
31. See Christopher Maurer, "Notes on the Poems," in García Lorca, *Poet in New York* (1998), 301.
32. In 2014, poet and translator Mark Statman reminded an interviewer that the poem had been written before Federico's 1929 trip to New York, which was the apparent justification for omitting it from the 2008 Grove Press edition of *Poet in New York* that he cotranslated with Pablo Medina. Regina Galasso, "An Interview with Mark Statman," *Translation Review* 90:1 (2014): 3.
33. García Lorca, *Poeta en Nueva York* (2013), 103, pl. 11.

Chapter Eleven

1. Pablo Campos Calvo-Sotelo, "European University—American Campus: Bridges Between Cultures," in Cooke, *Frontiers in Higher Education*, 31–63.
2. "Dormitory in Madrid Open for Students," *News Bulletin of the IIE* 4:4 (Jan. 1931): 13.
3. "Institute Activities: Exchange Fellowships," in *Eleventh Annual Report of the Director* (New York: Institute of International Studies, 1930), 7–8.
4. The building's striking interior design is documented in a series of photographs in the Del Amo Foundation Collection at California State University, Dominguez Hills. Sadly, photos in that collection also document the complete destruction of the building by bombs dropped during the Spanish Civil War.
5. John Steven McGroarty, "Seen from the Wander Trail," *Los Angeles Times*, 30 Nov. 1930, 118.
6. Rice's *Street Scene* opened on Broadway in January 1929. After 601 performances, it toured the United States and ran for six months in London. The play received the 1929 Pulitzer Prize for Drama and was adapted as a motion picture in 1931. https://en.wikipedia.org/wiki/Street_Scene.
7. Gil Fombellida, *Rivas Cherif, Margarita Xirgu y el Teatro de la II República*, 192.
8. Cummings, entry dated 1 Nov. 1932 in "A Poet in the Sagebrush," unpublished 1932–1933 journal, private collection.
9. Cummings, entry dated 16 Feb. 1933 in "A Poet in the Sagebrush," unpublished 1932–1933 journal, private collection.
10. Dionisio Cañas, pers. comm., 12 June 2010.
11. Lorca to Rafael Martínez Nadal, late summer 1930, in García Lorca, *Obra Completa*, 7:1104. The play was *The Audience*, unproduced during Lorca's lifetime. See Stainton, *Lorca*, 255–57.
12. Stainton, *Lorca*, 254.
13. Gibson, *Federico García Lorca: A Life*, 306–7.
14. Stainton, *Lorca*, 260.
15. Stainton, *Lorca*, 260.
16. "Local Boy's Description of a Bullfight," *Hardwick (VT) Gazette*, 30 Oct. 1930, 5; "Sees and Enjoys Visit to Old Spanish Towns," *Hardwick Gazette*, 1 Jan. 1931, 9; "Cummings Visits Morocco," *Hardwick Gazette*, 8 Jan. 1931, 3; "King Drives a Ford," *Hardwick Gazette*, 29 Jan. 1931, 8.
17. John Steven McGroarty, "Seen from the Wander Trail," *Los Angeles Times*, 30 Nov 1930, 118.
18. "Hardwick Boy on Spain's Little Revolution," *Hardwick (VT) Gazette*, 4 Dec. 1930, 5.
19. Philip Cummings, entry dated 28 Oct. 1932 in "A Poet in the Sagebrush," unpublished 1932–1933 journal, private collection.

20. "University Closes and Cummings Leaves Spain," *Hardwick (VT) Gazette*, 12 Feb. 1931, 5.

21. "University Closes and Cummings Leaves Spain," 5.

22. Cummings to Ian Gibson, 15 Mar. 1986, Ian Gibson Collection, Centro de Estudios Lorquianos, Fuente Vaqueros, Spain.

23. The three poems were published on 14 July 1931, 17 Sept. 1931, and 18 Nov. 1931, respectively.

24. García Lorca, "A Poet in New York," lecture given in Madrid, Mar. 1932, in García Lorca, *Poet in New York* (2013), 179–94.

Epilogue

1. García Lorca, *Selected Letters*, 150.

2. What seems to be the first report in an American newspaper dates from 12 September 1936, almost a month after Lorca's death on 18 August: "Consternation was caused here by the news that the well-known poet Federico García Lorca had been killed. Apparently he was assassinated behind the insurgent lines." "Bayonets Are Used in Sietamo Battle," *New York Times*, 12 Sept. 1936, 6.

3. Del Río and García Lorca, *Federico García Lorca, 1899–1936*, 19.

4. Del Río and García Lorca, *Federico García Lorca, 1899–1936*, 19.

5. Maurer and Anderson, *Federico García Lorca en Nueva York y La Habana*, 49–50.

6. Ángel del Río to Ben Belitt, 6 Dec. 1954, Ben Belitt Literary Collection, Howard Gotlieb Archival Research Center, Boston University. Although he wrote the letter in English, del Río appears to have mistakenly used a form of the Spanish verb *remover*—which can mean "stir," as in stir coffee, or "stir up," as in stir up controversy—in the last sentence. My thanks to C. Brian Morris for suggesting this possibility.

7. Del Río, "Introduction to *Poet in New York*: Twenty-Five Years After," in García Lorca, *Poet in New York* (1955), xiv–xv.

8. Cummings to del Río, 24 Nov. 1955, Journal of Hispanic Philology Collection, Special Collections, Florida State University Libraries, Tallahassee.

9. Del Río to Cummings, 1 Dec. 1955, Journal of Hispanic Philology Collection, Special Collections, Florida State University Libraries, Tallahassee.

10. Del Río, *Poeta en Nueva York*, 16.

11. Kessel Schwartz, pers. comm., 5 May 2007.

12. Kessel Schwartz, "García Lorca and Vermont," *Hispania* 42:1 (Mar. 1959): 50–55.

13. Mildred Adams, July 1967 diary, Mildred Adams Papers, Schlesinger Library, Radcliffe Institute, Harvard University, Cambridge, MA.

14. Cummings to Eisenberg, 21 Oct. 1974, Journal of Hispanic Philology

Collection, Special Collections, Florida State University Libraries, Tallahassee.

15. Daniel Eisenberg, "Lorca and Censorship: The Gay Artist Made Heterosexual," *Angélica* (Lucena, Spain) 2 (1991): 121–45.
16. Andrew Samuel Walsh, "Who Translated Lorca into English First? An Analysis of the 1929 New York Translations and Their Possible Authorship," *Bulletin of Hispanic Studies* 28:7 (2021): 661–77.
17. William Sackett, pers. comms., Mar. 2010–Apr. 2011. My thanks to Christopher Maurer for facilitating my initial contact with Sackett and arranging for the digitization of his audio files.
18. Stainton, *Lorca*.
19. Leslie Stainton, pers. comm., Mar. 2011.
20. Gibson, *Federico García Lorca*, vol. 1.
21. Gibson, correspondence with Cummings, 1985–1988, Ian Gibson Collection, Centro de Estudios Lorquianos, Fuente Vaqueros, Spain.
22. Gibson, *Federico García Lorca*, vol. 2. For an English version of the Vermont section, see Gibson, *Federico García Lorca: A Life*, 259–64.
23. *The Spirit of Lorca*, dir. Mike Dibb (Film Media Group, 1986), https://www.youtube.com/watch?v=3NkOJwX8FlA&t=3294s.
24. Cummings to Ian Gibson, 4 Aug. 1985, Ian Gibson Collection, Centro de Estudios Lorquianos, Fuente Vaqueros, Spain.
25. Dionisio Cañas, pers. comm., Nov. 2010.
26. Dionisio Cañas, "El amigo no identificado de Lorca en América," *El País*, 22 Dec. 1985. Cañas has written several additional articles about Federico and Philip for Spanish literary journals and newspapers, including "Aquella relación olvidada de Lorca con su novio americano," *El Mundo*, 13 Aug. 2011, UVE suppl., 1–2.
27. Christopher Maurer, "The Poet Writes to His Family from New York and Havana," in García Lorca, *Poet in New York* (1988), 199–256.
28. Lorca to his parents, 28 June 1929, in García Lorca, *Poet in New York* (1988), 206.
29. "Cartas inéditas de García Lorca," *ABC* (Madrid), 17 Feb. 1990, 63–67. Five letters were included in this article, joining five others published two weeks earlier: "Lorca, Cartas inéditas (1916–1925)," *ABC* (Madrid), 3 Feb. 1990, 63–67.
30. Cummings, "August in Eden," in García Lorca, *Songs*, 125–66.
31. Maurer's translations of the newly discovered correspondence were included in the second and third Farrar, Straus and Giroux editions of *Poet in New York* (1998, 2013).
32. Andrew Samuel Walsh, "Who Translated Lorca into English First? An Analysis of the 1929 New York Translations and Their Possible Authorship," *Bulletin of Hispanic Studies* 28:7 (2021): 661–77.

Bibliography

Acts and Resolves Passed by the General Assembly of the State of Vermont at the Twenty-First Biennial Session, 1910. Tuttle, 1911.

Adams, Mildred. *García Lorca: Playwright and Poet*. George Braziller, 1977.

Binding, Paul. *Lorca: The Gay Imagination*. GMP Publishers, 1985.

Brayley, Arthur W. *History of the Granite Industry of New England*. E. L. Grimes, 1913.

Brown, Dona. *Back to the Land: The Enduring Dream of Self-Sufficiency in Modern America*. University of Wisconsin Press, 2011.

Cano, José Luis. *García Lorca: Biografia Ilustrada*. Ediciones Destino, 1962.

Chamberlain, Silas. *On the Trail: A History of American Hiking*. Yale University Press, 2016.

Chauncey, George. *Gay New York: Gender, Urban Culture, and the Making of the Gay Male World, 1890–1940*. Basic Books, 1994.

Clifford, Susannah. "Retreat to Vermont: An Architectural and Social History of a Vermont Summer Community." Master's thesis, Columbia University, May 1987.

Columbia University. *Catalogue Number for the Sessions of 1929–30*. Columbia University, 1929.

Contosta, David R. *Philadelphia's Progressive Orphanage: The Carson Valley School*. Penn State University Press, 1997.

Cooke, Linda W., ed. *Frontiers in Higher Education*. Nova Science Publishers, 2007.

Crockett, William Day, and Sarah Gates Crockett. *A Satchel Guide to Spain and Portugal*. Houghton Mifflin, 1930.

Cummings, Philip. *Mother-Tongue*. Rollins Press, 1928.

Dalí, Salvador, and Federico García Lorca. *Sebastian's Arrows: Letters and Mementos of Salvador Dalí and Federico García Lorca*. Edited and translated by Christopher Maurer. Swan Isle Press, 2004.

Davis, Franklin Pierre, ed. *Davis Anthology of Newspaper Verse for 1929*. Frank P. Davis, Publisher, 1930.

Del Río, Ángel. *Poeta en Nueva York*. Taurus Ediciones, 1958.

Del Río, Ángel, and Federico García Lorca. *Federico García Lorca, 1899–1936: Vida y Obra: Bibliografía, Antología, Obras Inéditas, Música Popular*. Hispanic Institute in the United States, 1941.

Díaz Balsera, Viviana, and Rachel A. May, eds. *La Florida: Five Hundred Years of Spanish Presence*. University of Florida Press, 2014.

Dow, Elizabeth H. "Hardwick on the Map, 1895–1915." Master's thesis, University of Vermont, 1985.

The Effect of Tuberculosis Institutions on the Value and Desirability of Surrounding Property. National Association for the Study and Prevention of Tuberculosis, 1914.

Eisenberg, Daniel. *"Poeta en Nueva York": Historia y problemas de un texto de Lorca*. Editorial Ariel, 1976.

Engerman, Stanley L., and Robert E. Gallman, eds. *Long-Term Factors in American Economic Growth*. University of Chicago Press, 2007.

Erkkila, Betsy, ed. *Walt Whitman's Songs of Male Intimacy and Love: "Live Oak, with Moss" and "Calamus."* University of Iowa Press, 2011.

Fifth Biennial Report of the State Highway Board of the State of Vermont for the Two Years Ending June 30, 1930. Marble City Press, 1930.

Fueling Vermont's Future: Comprehensive Energy Plan and Greenhouse Gas Action Plan. Vol. 2. Vermont Department of Public Service, July 1998.

García Lorca, Federico. *Canciones, 1921–1924*. Imprenta Sur, 1927.

García Lorca, Federico. *Collected Poems: Revised Bilingual Edition*. Edited by Christopher Maurer. Translated by Catherine Brown et al. Farrar, Straus and Giroux, 2002.

García Lorca, Federico. *Epistolario Completo*. Edited by Andrew A. Anderson and Christopher Maurer. Catédra, 1997.

García Lorca, Federico. *Gypsy Ballads*. Translated by Jane Duran and Gloria García Lorca. Enitharmon Press, 2011.

García Lorca, Federico. *Obra Completa*, vol. 7: *Prosa*, vol. 2: *Epistolario*. AKAL/ Básica de Bolsillo, 2008.

García Lorca, Federico. *The Poet in New York and Other Poems*. Translated by Rolfe Humphries. Norton, 1940.

García Lorca, Federico. *Poet in New York*. Translated by Ben Belitt. Grove Press, 1955.

García Lorca, Federico. *Poet in New York*. Edited by Christopher Maurer. Translated by Greg Simon and Steven F. White. Farrar, Straus and Giroux, 1988.

García Lorca, Federico. *Poet in New York*. 2nd ed. Edited by Christopher Maurer. Translated by Greg Simon and Steven F. White. Farrar, Straus and Giroux, 1998.

García Lorca, Federico. *Poet in New York (Poeta en Nueva York)*. Translated by Pablo Medina and Mark Statman. Grove Press, 2008.

García Lorca, Federico. *Poet in New York*. 3rd ed. Edited by Christopher Maurer. Translated by Greg Simon and Steven F. White. Farrar, Straus and Giroux, 2013.

García Lorca, Federico. *Poeta en Nueva York*. Edited by Andrew A. Anderson. Galaxia Gutenberg, 2013.

García Lorca, Federico. *Poeta en Nueva York y Otras Hojas y Poemas: Manuscritos Neoyorquinos*. Edited by Mario Hernandez. Tabapress/Fundación García Lorca, 1990.

García Lorca, Federico. *Romancero Gitano*. Revista de Occidente, 1928.

García Lorca, Federico. *Selected Letters*. Edited and translated by David Gershator. New Directions, 1983.

García Lorca, Federico. *Songs*. Edited by Daniel Eisenberg. Translated by Philip Cummings. Duquesne University Press, 1976.

García Lorca, Francisco. *In the Green Morning: Memories of Federico*. Translated by Christopher Maurer. New Directions, 1986.

Garcilaso de la Vega. *The Works of Garcilaso de la Vega*. Translated by J. H. Wiffen. Hurst, Robinson, 1823.

Gibson, Ian. *Federico García Lorca. Vol. 1: De Fuente Vaqueros a Nueva York (1898–1929)*. Crítica, 1985.

Gibson, Ian. *Federico García Lorca. Vol. 2: De Nueva York a Fuente Grande (1929–1936)*. Ediciones Grijalbo, 1987.

Gibson, Ian. *Federico García Lorca: A Life*. Pantheon Books, 1989.

Gil Fombellida, María Carmen. *Rivas Cherif, Margarita Xirgu y el Teatro de la II República*. Editorial Fundamentos, 2003.

Gracián, Baltasar. *The Art of Worldly Wisdom*. Translated by Joseph Jacobs. Dover Publications, 2012.

Graff, Nancy Price. Looking Back at Vermont: Farm Security Administration Photographs, 1936–1942. Middlebury College Museum of Art, 2002.

Green Mountain Club. *Explorer's Guide: 50 Hikes in Vermont*, 17th ed. Countryman Press, 2015.

Handbook to Paris and Its Environs. Robert M. McBride, 1929.

Harrison, Blake. *The View from Vermont: Tourism and the Making of an American Rural Landscape*. University of Vermont Press, 2006.

Harrison, Henry, ed. *The Grub Street Book of Verse*. Henry Harrison, 1930.

Havard, Robert, ed. *A Companion to Spanish Surrealism*. Tamesis, 2004.

Hewlett, Theodosia. *A Decade of International Fellowships: A Survey of the Impressions of American and Foreign Ex-Fellows*. Institute of International Education, 1930.

Ladoo, Raymond B. *Talc and Soapstone: Their Mining, Milling, Products and Uses*. US Government Printing Office, 1923.

López Campillo, Evelyne. *La Revista de Occidente y la Formación de Minorías (1923–1936)*. Taurus Ediciones, 1972.

Manrique, Jaime. *Eminent Maricones: Arenas, Lorca, Puig, and Me.* University of Wisconsin Press, 1999.

Marinello, Juan. *Contemporáneos: Noticia y Memoria.* Editora del Consejo Nacional de Universidades/Universidad Central de las Villas, 1964.

Martin, Robert K. *The Homosexual Tradition in American Poetry.* University of Texas Press, 1979.

Martínez Nadal, Rafael. *Federico García Lorca: Mi Penúltimo Libro Sobre el Hombre y el Poeta.* Editorial Casariego, 1992.

Marval-McNair, Nora de, ed. *Selected Proceedings of the Singularidad y Trascendencia Conference.* Society of Spanish and Spanish-American Studies, 1990.

Maurer, Christopher, ed. *Federico García Lorca Escribe a Su Familia desde Nueva York y La Habana (1929–1930).* Ministerio de Cultura, 1985.

Maurer, Christopher, and Andrew A. Anderson. *Federico García Lorca en Nueva York y La Habana: Cartas y Recuerdos.* Galaxia Gutenberg, 2013.

Mayhew, Jonathan. *Apocryphal Lorca: Translation, Parody, Kitsch.* University of Chicago Press, 2009.

McKay, Alice, ed. *A Walk Through the Garden of Eden: A History of Eden, Vermont.* Eden Historical Society, 1996.

Moreno Villa, José. *Vida en Claro.* El Colegio de México, 1944.

Morris, C. Brian, ed. *"Cuando Yo Me Muera": Essays in Memory of Federico García Lorca.* University Press of America, 1988.

The Official Guide of the Railways and Steam Navigation Lines of the United States, Puerto Rico, Canada, Mexico and Cuba. Facsimile ed. National Railway Publication, 1930.

O'Kane, Walter Collins. *Trails and Summits of the Green Mountains.* Houghton Mifflin, 1926.

Ortega, Jesús, ed. *Álbum: Huerta de San Vicente, Junio 2014–Julio 2015.* Delegación de Cultura del Ayuntamiento de Granada, 2015.

Pérez-Villanueva Tovar, Isabel. *La Residencia de Estudiantes, 1910–1936: Grupo Universitario y Residencia de Señoritas.* Consejo Superior de Investigaciones Científicas, 2011.

Ravogli, Augustus. *Syphilis in Its Medical, Medico-Legal and Sociological Aspects.* Grafton Press, 1907.

Rittenhouse, Jessie B., ed. *The Rollins Book of Verse.* Angel Alley Press, 1929.

Ruis, Luis. *León Felipe, Poeta del Barrio.* Colección Málaga, 1968.

Russell, Ina, ed. *Jeb and Dash: A Diary of Gay Life, 1918–1945.* Faber and Faber, 1993.

Sáenz de la Calzada, Margarita. *La Residencia de Estudiantes, 1910–1936.* Consejo Superior de Investigaciones Científicas, 1986.

Salinas, Pedro. *Presagios.* Índice, 1923.

Scollard, Clinton, and Jessie B. Rittenhouse, eds. *The Bird-Lovers' Anthology.* Houghton Mifflin, 1930.

Sedgwick, Eve Kosofsky. *Between Men: English Literature and Male Homosocial Desire*. Columbia University Press, 1985.

The Shandaken Tunnel. Ulen, 1923.

Stainton, Leslie. *Lorca: A Dream of Life*. Farrar, Straus and Giroux, 1999.

Stegner, Wallace. *Second Growth*. Houghton Mifflin, 1947.

Sullivan, Edward J., ed. *Nueva York: 1613–1945*. New York Historical Society, 2010.

Tomasi, Mari, and Roaldus Richmond. *Men Against Granite*. Edited by Alfred Rosa and Mark Wanner. New England Press, 2004.

Trend, J. B. *A Picture of Modern Spain: Men and Music*. Houghton Mifflin, 1921.

US Coordinator of Transportation. *Passenger Traffic Report*. Section of Transportation Service, 1935.

Walters, D. Gareth. *Canciones and the Early Poetry of Lorca*. University of Wales Press, 2002.

Walton's Vermont Register Business and Legal Directory for 1906. Walton Register, 1905.

Whitman, Walt. *Leaves of Grass*. Thayer and Eldridge, 1860.

Whitman, Walt. *Leaves of Grass*. James R. Osgood, 1881–1882.

Whitman, Walt. *Leaves of Grass*. Modern Library, 1921.

Whitman, Walt. *Obras Escogidas*. Edited and translated by Concha Zardoya. M. Aguilar, 1946.

Whitman, Walt. *Walt Whitman: Poemas*. Edited and translated by Álvaro Armando Vasseur. Claudio Garcia, 1912.

The World Almanac and Book of Facts for 1930. Press Publishing, 1930.

Index